THE COMMON GOOD

THE COMMON GOOD

Citizenship, Morality and Self-Interest

Bill Jordan

Basil Blackwell

Copyright © Bill Jordan 1989

First published 1989

Basil Blackwell Ltd
108 Cowley Road, Oxford, OX4 1JF, UK

Basil Blackwell Inc.
432 Park Avenue South, Suite 1503
New York, NY 10016, USA

British Library Cataloguing in Publication Data

Jordan, Bill, *1941-*
  The common good : citizenship, morality and
  self-interest
  1. Politics. Moral values
  I. Title
  172
  ISBN 0-631-16486-3
  ISBN 0-631-16487-1 Pbk

Library of Congress Cataloging in Publication Data

Jordan, Bill, 1941-
  The common good : citizenship, morality and self-interest / Bill Jordan.
    p. cm.
  Includes index.
  ISBN 0-631-16486-3   ISBN 0-631-16487-1 (pbk.)
  1. Social ethics. 2. Self-interest. I. Title.
  HM216.J64 1989
  170—dc19

Typeset in 10 on 11½pt Plantin
by Downdell Limited, Abingdon, Oxon
Printed in Great Britain

Contents

Acknowledgements

This book is more my own work than I would have chosen it to be; it would have been better with a little more help from my friends. This is no criticism of them. Alas, I finally exhausted the energies of some of my most faithful advisers and critics, who declared themselves too busy to look at yet another draft of my muddled thoughts.

Even so, I did get a great deal of helpful criticism, comment and encouragement from Iain Hampsher-Monk, David Donnison, Michael Hill, Albert Weale, Bill Forsythe and Jean Packman, to whom I am extremely grateful. I also benefited considerably from correspondence with Philippe Van Parijs and Mark Philp, and from conversations with Paul Spicker and David Crosbie.

Many thanks are also due to Gill Watson, who typed several drafts of the book with great patience and accuracy, and made some helpful suggestions about improvements; and to Sue Ashton for her sympathetic and careful copy-editing.

Prologue: a Modern Utopia

The common good is an attractive idea, but a notoriously difficult one. In Utopia, everyone gladly does what is good for all. But even in the best-organized society, things sometimes go wrong.

After the shipwreck, several swimmers converge on a small inflatable life-raft. All are exhausted, and none will survive in the chilly water, but there is room for only one inside it. Desperate, panicky, they fight and struggle. Eventually all go under, destroyed by their instincts for self-preservation.

In another part of the sea, a lifeboat is picking up survivors. With their grappling hooks, two seamen drag them in from each side. Suddenly, the water is lapping over the gunwales. The bos'n shouts that one person must get back into the water. To his horror, all the rescued immediately hurl themselves in and are lost from view. By chance, they have taken on board an entire boatload of altruists, whose highest goal is to serve the good of others. Each one's self-sacrifice has frustrated the others' intentions, and together they have ensured that all perished, as surely as did the egoism of the first group.

Problems like this arise as soon as we grant individuals choices about their goals. Rational individuals will always choose what gives them the best result (whether their aims are egoistic or altruistic). They cannot *prefer* second best, but someone else may be able to give them a reason for promoting it to best. Not all decisions are all-or-nothing, sink-or-swim, like the shipwreck. Given a chance, there may be room for a compromise which allows all the egoists to gain a bit of the cake and all the altruists to give up a bit.

To reach a compromise, there may have to be a great deal of bargaining between individuals. Setting up an agricultural commune takes a lot of time and energy, and in the end each communard may get less than if they had all stayed home and cultivated their own gardens. Alternatively, a few may end up doing most of the work, or one might abscond with all the produce. Knowing this, we can see that the common good depends on finding reliable systems of bargaining. Barring accidents, Utopia can depend on three of these.

The first is ideally suited for large numbers of bargain-hunters[1] in a hurry. It doesn't require any haggling, or any concern about others' preferences or projects, because it is quite impersonal. But it does allow millions of individuals to coordinate all their preferences with each other's and reach the best deal available. The price mechanism is a supremely efficient way of allocating certain resources between competing uses in a quick and relatively peaceful way.

But in their rush to get to market, the egoistic bargain-hunters cause another kind of problem of coordination. They all drive large cars, which block the access roads; they sit in traffic jams, their engines idling, their exhausts belching foul smoke, which pollutes the air. The market square becomes engulfed in smog, so that the shoppers can no longer properly inspect the fruit and vegetables. If they could see, they would notice that it is scabbed and pitted by the acid rain that falls whenever the smog blows over the distant farmland.

So there has to be another kind of bargaining. No one car owner will sacrifice the convenience of driving his vehicle all the way to market, and loading up the boot, so long as all the others can still do it. Yet by all driving there, those that can get into the market cannot get out, and those that block their way cannot get in. They need a way of agreeing that half of them will bring their cars to market one day and half the next, but the market itself cannot provide a way of making this kind of agreement.

What is more, they would all enjoy their shopping better, and be able to buy nicer fruit, if they used lead-free petrol. But this is more expensive than leaded petrol, so it is not worth any individual paying the extra, so long as all the others will go on buying cheap, and causing pollution. The market itself cannot find a way of supplying the more socially desirable product at a cheaper price.

The answer is to set up an authority to make sure that everyone keeps their side of the bargain that it is only worth one person's while to keep if all the rest keep it. The state has the power to make cars with red number plates stay at home on Mondays, and cars with blue on Tuesdays. It also has the power to tax leaded petrol and subsidize unleaded.

Every individual can now go bargain-hunting in an orderly and hygienic environment, and it seems as if Utopia has almost achieved the common good. But this admirable system provides no way of reproducing the species, or looking after those who can no longer get to market. Individuals must bargain with each other over these more intimate matters in an atmosphere in which their vulnerabilities are respected. They must be able to share, to give and take and trust. In the last resort, they may be required to sacrifice their interests for long periods, for the good of others.

The bargains on which such transactions can rely must be rather long term and enduring. They must be backed up by something more than laws or commercial contracts. The ideal forum for this kind of bargaining links several generations in a system of mutual obligations, but allows members of the system to live in small households, adapted to the needs of the market, and those of reproduction and care.

Optimists in our modern Utopia believe that this combination provides all the ingredients for the common good, because it allows for egoistic and altruistic preferences roughly in proportion to their incidence within the population. Most of us are rather selfish and hedonistic for a large part of our youth and middle age, but capable of short bursts of concern for others in emergencies (such as shipwrecks). But the optimists conclude that, by a happy coincidence, nature gave more than her fair share of altruism to womankind, so that it is a form of benevolence for the male of the species to allow her to rear as well as bear children, and to care for elderly kin in their declining years.

Meanwhile, back in the market, mankind can be busy making the most efficient and productive possible bargains with his commercial fellow-egoists. With the minimum of state regulation, the maximum output can automatically be distributed in the optimum way. Any surplus egoism from the womenfolk can be dissipated in a little part-time job and the regular shopping spree, while the residual altruism of the male world can soon be absorbed by churchgoing and charitable good works.

This popular and fashionable version of the common good is reassuring because it suggests that the interests of all of us are best served if each of us looks after ourselves and those we love. We need feel no pressing concern for those about whom we are indifferent, because they are almost certain to be looking after themselves too. As for those whom we distrust and fear (such as the poor, the mentally ill and the criminal), they have even less need of our compassion. Either somebody else loves them (in which case they are *their* responsibility) or nobody loves them (in which case it is probably their own fault). Anyway, the state will take appropriate measures to deal with them - training (compulsory if necessary) for the poor, treatment for the maladjusted and punishment for the deviant - in much the same spirit as it clears traffic jams and cleans up pollution.

Trouble in Utopia

So far, we have only looked at rural Utopia (where they grow the crops), suburban Utopia (where the good folks live) and downtown Utopia (where they trade together). But there is also the industrial estate, where they make the cars, the household appliances and the television sets. Or rather, where they used to.

Until recently, there were two sizeable factories on the industrial estate. The larger of the two had acquired a technological edge over the other, and was gaining competitive advantage; wages and profits were both higher. A new young accountant arrived at the smaller firm and took stock. He realized that, by selling off the plant and machinery, consolidating the proceeds with the staff pension fund and investing the whole sum overseas, in a newly industrializing country, he could produce a better weekly income for every member of the company. What was more, Utopians could import the same volume of products more cheaply from precisely that overseas enterprise in which he proposed investing. The Board of Directors greeted his plan rapturously, and redundancy terms were quickly reached with the staff, facilitated by the existence of the one-union agreement.

Unfortunately, there were a number of employees who were not on the permanent staff who were also made redundant, but without a share in the deal (they did not have a vote in the decision). These were mainly older unskilled workers, young workers, black workers and a few part-time office and sales staff, mostly married women. The latter were quickly absorbed into other jobs in town, but all the others settled into a life of long-term unemployment, their basic needs for food and rent being met by the state through public assistance. Meanwhile, the redundant staff were living comfortably on their company pensions, fitting neo-Georgian doors to their homes, playing the stock market and setting up in small businesses.

After a while, the workers in the first factory, whose real standards of living did not seem to be rising as rapidly as their money wages, began to realize what was happening. The redundant unskilled workers from next door were being kept on public assistance paid for by taxes on their earnings. Naturally enough, they kicked up a hell of a fuss. As it was just coming up to an election, the ruling party in Utopia (the Christian Conservative Republicans), which had been swept to power on the votes of these same industrial workers, took notice.

In its election manifesto, the Christian Conservative Republican Party announced that benefit rates would be cut by 10 per cent, and that henceforth all claimants would be forced to do repair work on the city's sewers as a condition for receiving assistance. When challenged on the morality of this measure by the opposition (the Socially-conscious Democrats), its leader replied that exactly the same obligations fell on all citizens. If they could not maintain themselves in any other way, they must work; no more was being asked of the claimants than of the factory workers who paid the taxes that maintained them. There were the same two rules for all: look after yourself, and he who pays the piper calls the tune.

As time went by, various small firms making components followed the first into liquidation, the manufacturing giant made some of its unskilled workers redundant, and unemployment grew. The sewer repair scheme was not an outstanding success, public health standards fell and outside contractors were called in. As crime was rising, claimants were put to work on building a new prison, working side by side with convicts from the now overcrowded old one.

·Meanwhile, other changes were taking place in the Utopian economy and society. As productivity improved at the factory, and imported manufactures grew cheaper too, households in suburbia had more to spend, and there were more things to buy. The market area of the city had become congested, so huge new shopping and leisure complexes were built on the outskirts to accommodate the cornucopias of commerce. These employed part-time workers, mainly the wives of better-off industrial workers, who now divided their time almost equally between working in these emporia and spending the household incomes in them. Of course, there were no jobs for members of poor households here. For the men, the part-time wages were not enough to support a family, and for the women, the benefit authorities would have confiscated their wages.

On the domestic front, too, tensions were rising. In suburbia, the ever-improving standard of living meant that old people were living longer, but the falling birthrate and rising employment opportunities meant that there were fewer altruistic daughters to look after them. More and more entered residential care at the state's expense; also there was a sharp increase in admissions to mental hospital of caring daughters who had experienced a severe breakdown in altruism. Experiments in using first claimants and then convicts to look after both old folk and mental patients (in order to defray rising public expenditure) were rather disastrous and had to be abandoned.

Suddenly, Utopian society seems to have lost the dynamism that made it the envy of the advanced world. The retailing boom has ground to a halt; there aren't enough married women left to fill the shelves *and* do the shopping *and* look after the old folks (at home or in a home). And the state is saddled with a large and increasingly expensive scheme for making work for the poor, which seems to do nothing to equip them for the commercial labour market. Indeed, the government's unkindest critics have pointed out that this sector of the economy is very like the Evil Empire, where everyone used to work for the state, compulsorily, for low wages, very inefficiently. This is doubly ironic, since the leader of the Evil Empire appears to have taken heed of the Utopian leader's wise words (imparted most emphatically in many a fireside diplomatic chat), and largely dismantled his country's bureaucratic system of state employment (much to his subjects' disgust as they are now having to work much harder).

More seriously, there is growing unrest among the poor, who skulk around their housing estates and gather menacingly on street corners in the city, more visible and threatening because so many of them are black. Suburban Utopians are frightened. Once more the streets are clogged with cars and petrol fumes because the once-merry pedestrian walkways with their jostling consumers have become a jungle of muggers, junkies and hustlers. Even in the leisure complexes people seem wary and guarded. At home, they keep guns and instal electronic safety devices.

One night there is a riot in the city centre, homes and shops are burnt, and looters roam the streets. For a while the police lose control, and suburban Utopians are shocked by television pictures of unrestrained vandalism and destruction. Surprisingly, there is an apparently spontaneous uprising of sympathetic action by convicts, mental patients and even the residents of some old folks' homes.

In the morning, Utopians count up the cost and decide that something has gone wrong. The bargains that once delivered the goods are instead creating a divided, lawless society, expensive and increasingly impossible to police. Pressed for action to put things right, the government turns to moral philosophers for guidance. Fortunately, they have been for some time concerned about the direction taken by Utopian society, and are ready to suggest a change.

A new direction

What has gone wrong, the philosophers suggest, is that Utopians have mis-understood their interests. This must seem paradoxical, since the whole of Utopian society is a carefully constructed system for allowing people to pursue their interests as freely as possible, and to get the best possible bargains. Above all, it is based on the market, which allows every individual to do all others the most possible good, while actually intending only to help themselves.

But (say the philosophers) this confuses interests with preferences. Although (as Hume pointed out) it takes an emotion or a desire to move a person to action, to be rational is to be capable of overriding our preferences with reasons. As Kant showed, we can persuade ourselves that it is not in our interests to act on our immediate wishes. Were this not so, everyone would be as much a slave to their cravings as the most pathetic junkie.

This has important implications for Utopian society. Its whole construction rests on the idea of coordinated market preferences, with the state providing motives for those preferences which depend on others choosing likewise. Only in the household are individuals required to concern themselves directly with the needs of others, and then only because of their desires for affection, security, offspring and a quiet conscience.

According to the philosophers, something more is required to restore harmony in Utopia. There must be a different kind of bargain, which recog-nizes a different kind of interest. Those who have been winners must be prepared to sacrifice some of their competitive advantage, and allow those who have been losers a share of the cake.

But it is not enough to try to buy harmony with material concessions. The poor must be included as full members of society; they must be freed from their servile status, not merely granted golden chains. They must be included in the common good, and the new bargain must give them common interests with suburban Utopians in creating good social relations.

Essentially, the suburb-dwellers are in a trap, just as the poor are. So long as their votes (as much as their purchases) are expressions of their material preferences, they will always choose to elect a government which will exclude and oppress the poor. They cannot choose to make themselves worse-off, and the poor better-off, without being shown that it is in their interests to do so. And, since in Utopia only material preferences count as interests, this is logically impossible.

Here the government must take a creative leap of faith. It must risk itself by trying to create the common interests that are so conspicuously lacking in the relations between suburbans and the poor. Technically, the first step in this process involves providing a citizenship share of the national product to all, unconditionally, without work tests or earnings rules. Suburbans will have to pay slightly higher taxes to finance it, but it will give the poor incentives to take all kinds of paid jobs, and those who feel overworked the opportunity to do rather less.

Fortunately for this government (or a new one which is prepared to take the risk), it can make an appeal to the long-term material interests of suburbia. The present system of oppressing the poor is not only expensive in itself, it also represents a barrier to the very flexibility of the labour market on which efficiency and growth depend. The existence of a reliable citizenship share (Basic Income) will allow a faster rate of adaptation of the economy to global forces, and hence eventually a larger cake to be divided among all.

But the philosophers are adamant that the new direction should not depend solely on appeals to material self-interest because that would be self-defeating. They recommend that an old idea of active citizenship participation should be revived, as the basis of a new approach to social relations. The Basic Income provides for the first time a 'social wage' which corresponds with no labour time. In this sense it formalizes the opportunity for citizens to join together to create their own community and to cooperate for the common good. The state should take every opportunity to encourage the creation of common interests in good social relations, in association for cooperative purposes and mutual aid.

Finally, the new direction also points to a new basis for household cooperation. In future, there should be no assumption of female altruism; still less should women's self-sacrifice be compulsory. With the advent of a Basic Income, home-based women would have a small independent income in their own right. Not only would their dependence on men be decreased and their autonomy increased, there would be far more incentives for couples to share the unpaid work in households. This in turn would contribute to a tendency to see child care and other unpaid caring in more collective, cooperative terms, as part of community life, and less as private moral obligation.

Reaction to the philosophers' report is mixed. Many Utopians regard it as euphoric, speculative and unscientific, and there is a strong undercurrent of scepticism in suburbia. The Utopian parliament meets to discuss the report next week . . .

It would be nice to continue the rest of this book in the same vein, and perhaps it would be more instructive if I did so. Maybe it could simply consist of the philosophers' report, set out in full, with appendices. But I lack the wit (or perhaps the nerve) to carry this through. Instead, I shall revert to a more conventional style and content. But I hope this fable will serve as a distillation of the argument and spirit of what follows.

Note

1 Martin Hollis, *The Cunning of Reason* (Cambridge University Press, 1987), ch. 1.

1

Morality and Self-Interest

What makes a good society? Not any longer the heroic virtues of its leaders, nor the divine inspiration of their policies; not even the civic responsibility, nor the universal enlightenment of the electorate. Nowadays society consists of large numbers of people, bound together in a huge commercial and political web, yet somehow also sharing obscure and fragmented moral obligations towards each other.

How much does the good society depend on being organized in such a way that people cooperate for mutual benefit, and how much does it rely on individuals following moral rules? Should people be responsible only for themselves and their immediate families, or should they share in a wider responsibility, with their fellow citizens, for the good of all?

These questions are very old ones, but they are also very urgent and immediate. During the British General Election of 1987, they came to the surface in an argument between the major party leaders about morality. Mrs Thatcher insisted that the essence of morality was that individuals should be free to choose; Mr Kinnock argued that it was about people's relationships with each other, through the state.[1] The dispute seemed to be settled in Mrs Thatcher's favour by the voters, but was their choice a moral one?

It was in some ways surprising to hear an argument about social morality in a modern election. For many years after the Second World War, it looked as if moral arguments had disappeared from politics because various kinds of experts in the social sciences had found ways of managing societies and their problems. Their expertise provided them with technical ways of ensuring that the economy was efficient but dynamic, that intelligence and skill were utilized and rewarded and that people's needs were met.

One reason for the success of Margaret Thatcher's and Ronald Reagan's new approach to government was that these experts had become discredited. Their new approach emphasized individual self-interest and self-responsibility as the basis for prosperity and as a solution to social problems. Political leaders in other advanced capitalist countries increasingly adopted similar ideas and policies.

The first objection to their programmes was that they would not work. This issue is still unsettled. The new approach has had some success in producing economic growth and price stability where previously there was stagflation, but the cost has been high - in Britain, in terms of unemployment, and in the United States, in terms of the national debt. It is still difficult to say whether it can be sustained in the long term.

But as these programmes had some measure of success, and were endorsed by electorates, the objection was increasingly voiced - especially in Britain - that they were immoral. In particular, cuts in social service provision and the privatization of publicly owned enterprises were denounced as favouring the interests of better-off groups over worse-off and the interests of some individuals over those of society as a whole. Opposition has focused on the effects of these policies in undermining the good society and promoting selfishness and greed.

The result is that almost every social phenomenon is now capable of provoking a moral argument, and these arguments all take similar forms. Whether the subject is rising crime, increasing violence, abuse of children, football hooliganism, the spread of AIDS or whatever, one side insists that it is only a moral problem in so far as it reflects standards of individual behaviour or family responsibility, while the other argues that it is also a symptom of a disintegrating social fabric, which is the result of government policy.

One other surprising development has been the re-involvement of the churches in social issues. Whereas religion seemed to have been relegated to the sidelines by the experts who managed society in the post-war era, the outbreak of moral dispute has brought it back into the field of political controversy. But the churches are also deeply divided over these issues, and along lines rather similar to those which divide politicians. In the final weeks of 1987, the British public witnessed the unedifying spectacle of the Church of England split into warring factions over ethical as well as doctrinal questions.

But these disputes do not take place in a social vacuum. Society has already changed a great deal since the post-war era, and the new approach to government has accelerated change. In many ways, leaders like Margaret Thatcher and Ronald Reagan are only expressing the values and standards that already exist in modern advanced Western countries. To some extent, the leaders of the Soviet Union and Communist China seem to be pointing their societies in similar directions.

A new orthodoxy

One of the most important shifts taking place in recent years is an increasing focus on individual decision-making, at the expense of political decision-making. Instead of seeing the good of individuals in terms of government policies, society is seen in terms of the choices made by each of its members. According to the new approach, a good society can only be created and sustained through the millions of such choices being made every minute.

This change in the political world is reflected in present intellectual debates. The most provocative and stimulating new ideas about society have sprung from the attempt to apply basic economic theory to the whole social system.[2] If individuals in their capacities as employers, workers and consumers make 'rational choices', according to consistent preferences, why should not the same bargain-hunting approach be applied to all the other choices they make? Models of society constructed out of rational individual choices have involved political theorists and philosophers in fierce new disputes about the nature of social relations, and even of the individual self.[3]

In all these debates, a thorny issue remains the relationship between morality and self-interest. The bargain-hunter of economic theory is primarily self-interested, apparently incapable of choosing anything that does not best meet his or her personal preferences. Yet clearly no society made up of such individuals could be sustained, or has ever existed. Concern for others, and even apparent self-sacrifice, are features of everyday life, and must be part of any account of the good society.

In this book I shall be concerned with both the 'popular' political debate about this issue, and the academic debate. It seems to me that the latter is (as so often) largely treading in the footsteps of the former, trying to make theoretical sense of the path that ordinary people and folksy politicians have already taken. Accordingly, in this first chapter I shall concentrate on a view of the relationship between morality and self-interest which seems to be becoming very widely accepted as the basis of social relations in advanced capitalist countries – and hence to be very influential in other parts of the world.

My starting point is that there is a *new orthodoxy* on social issues, which insists that they should be explicable in terms of individual choices. This new orthodoxy consists of a set of connected principles, saying how society should be organized, if we take account of both self-interest and altruism as the bases of such choices. When it first appeared as part of a political programme, the then dominant approach to government – social democracy – tended to dismiss it as extreme and irrelevant. But (if nothing else) the electoral successes of those who espouse it demand that it is taken seriously.

The main difference between the academic and the political debates lies in the moral claims made in the name of individual choice. Academic proponents of rational choice theory tend to take a strictly value-neutral stance, as befits those who draw their inspiration from the amoral science of economics. But politicians and their followers – whether of the folksy or the hectoring variety – have strongly emphasized the moral content of their views, and presented the new orthodoxy as being a new social morality.

In my view, the moral claims made in the name of the new orthodoxy are of particular interest, not least because they seem to have been persuasive and politically effective. Even though they lack academic rigour, they seem to demand attention in their own right for this reason. Again, when they were first put forward, it seemed child's play to their political opponents on the left to defeat them. Yet, in practice, the new orthodoxy has seized the 'moral high ground', and is increasingly forcing the left to fight on its territory – that of individual choice - in which it has so far been conspicuously unsuccessful. Indeed, in accusing the new right of being immoral in its policies, the left has exposed its own uncertainties and ambiguities over moral issues.

Here then is a list of the main principles which make up the new orthodoxy, and a brief statement of the arguments for them:

1 *People should be free to choose in decisions about their lives* Each person is the best judge of what is good for himself or herself; therefore, each individual should be allowed to follow his or her plan of action. They should not be forced to do things for the good of society as a whole, or for the good of others, unless this is the only possible way of providing for the good of all.

Because everyone is potentially competing for limited resources, individuals have different interests. The only way to ensure peaceful coordination between all the interests of individuals, and to allow all choice, is through markets, which are systems of exchange which allow for efficient, orderly competition and cooperation, and provide the best results for all.

2 *Individuals are responsible for themselves and for the commitments they make to others* The freedom to choose implies a responsibility for one's own life. People who are the best judges of their own good have a responsibility to provide for their own good, from their own efforts. They have no general right to help from others.

But people may choose to share the whole or parts of their lives with others; they are then responsible to them for whatever commitments they make to each other. Examples of this are the commitments implied by marriage and having children; parents have moral obligations to each other and to their children. But individuals do not have any specific obligations to, or responsibilities for, strangers with whom they have no personal relationship. They may choose to commit themselves to the needs of certain others (such as those they feel sympathy with, or pity for).

3 *People are entitled to what they can legally earn and to the property they can legally acquire* What people earn in competition and cooperation with others reflects their value to society. Hence people's income is a measure of the contribution of their work to the good of others; for example, by creating the wealth that all need for prosperity. They are therefore morally entitled to what they earn.

People should be free to decide how to spend their earnings. This includes the freedom to give their money to those with whom they feel sympathy, or to whom they have commitments, and to bequeath their property as they choose at their death.

4 *The government, which should be chosen by the majority of voters, should provide only those goods which all need, but which cannot be supplied by markets* These include law and order (which assure freedom and fair competition) and defence against aggressors from abroad. The government should punish those who try to acquire resources by unfair means or who threaten peaceful and

orderly relations by violence; it should be ready to punish outside aggressors by waging war.

The government should also meet the needs of those who try to take responsibility for themselves, but who (through illness, lack of ability or misfortune) fail to do so. But it should not assist others unconditionally; they should be required to demonstrate their willingness to take responsibility for themselves, and to honour their commitments to others.

Nowadays, anyone who disagrees with the orthodoxy represented by these principles is swimming against the tide. Not only are most Western democracies ruled by governments which subscribe to some version of them; most people in these societies seem to live their lives by some version of them. Indeed, any middle class person who argues against the orthodoxy is in danger of being accused of hypocrisy because it is probable that their own life reflects these same principles to a great extent.

Obviously, it would be wrong to say that these principles add up to a view which is a new *consensus* because they are fiercely disputed. But they have become an orthodoxy, in the sense that other points of view have to take them into account, and justify themselves in relation to them. Conversely, even the most trashy and prurient publications (such as several popular British newspapers) can lay claim to a spurious legitimacy by appealing to these principles.

Individual interests

A very important feature of the new orthodoxy is the way it deals with potential conflicts between the interests of individuals. As freedom of choice is such an essential aspect of its understanding of a good society, individuals must be allowed to follow their interests as far as possible. In the very abstract model of the economy that it uses, markets lead to the unexpected result that everyone gets the best possible return for their own efforts because impersonal economic forces guide people's transactions with each other towards this outcome. It was an argument first put forward by Adam Smith in the eighteenth century, in his book *The Theory of Moral Sentiments*:

> [The rich] consume little more than the poor, and in spite of their natural selfishness and rapacity, though they mean only their own conveniency, though the sole end which they purpose from the labours of all the thousands whom they employ, be the satisfaction of their own vain and insatiable desires, they divide with the poor the produce of all their improvements. They are led by an invisible hand to make nearly the same distribution of the necessaries of life, which would have been made, had the earth been divided into equal portions among all its inhabitants, and thus without intending it, without knowing it, advance the interests of society, and afford means to the multiplication of the species.[4]

In this model, the interests of the poor are served by a free market system because this provides the maximum growth of prosperity, from which all benefit. But it also allows maximum choice, and hence a system of voluntary exchange relations, which is consistent with morality. The same free choice is characteristic of all the individuals' other social relationships, but here people may be required to sacrifice their interests because non-market relations involve commitments to the good of others, as well as to one's own. Hence moral relations, as distinct from economic ones, imply altruism – a willingness to abandon self-interest for the sake of a duty to someone else.

To mount a successful moral challenge to this theory, its opponents must either show that its outcomes are not morally justified, or that some other form of economic relations is morally superior, or both. But any such challenge must find a way of dealing with the issue of individual interests, and how potential conflicts of these can be resolved. This requires a fundamental analysis of the notion of interests, as well as that of morality.

The moral orthodoxy associated with social democracy was not fundamentally different in these respects from the new orthodoxy. Rather, it argued that markets were not the best way of making society as prosperous as possible, of using knowledge, energy and skill to the best advantage or of meeting needs. It proposed more efficient ways of achieving all these goals, and argued that it was in everyone's interests to organize parts of the economy according to non-market principles, for the good of all. There were indeed some moral arguments for social democracy, but these were not extensively developed or seen as essential for its maintenance.

The theoretical basis for social democratic institutions was that economic growth could be accelerated and sustained by planning and intervention, through state agencies, through public ownership of infrastructural utilities and by various measures of expert management and adjustment. The institutions and processes of social democracy were aimed at achieving a more efficient use of productive resources, and especially at securing full employment; in all these respects it claimed to promote prosperity and to distribute its benefits more surely than markets had done. Because of this claim to greater efficiency and faster growth, it was able to argue that the interests of all but the idle rich were served by its economic system, rather as the new orthodoxy now argues that the interests of all but the idle or unfortunate poor are served by markets.

By a similar argument, the social services could be seen as ways of providing for needs such as pensions and health care which – given the uncertainties that everyone faced during their working lives and family development – represented a prudent fall-back resource for all. Because the costs of administration were low relative to the value of the benefits and services, they could be justified as efficient systems, which were in everyone's interests, so long as all contributed to a pooling of risks. In other words, any moral arguments for the social services as redistributing welfare towards the poor were secondary, or not advanced at all. Indeed, some countries with very extensive and expensive social services, like West Germany and Austria, were more unequal (in terms of final distribution of income) than other countries with much lower social welfare expenditure (as a proportion of national income) like Japan and Australia.[5]

So the arguments for social democracy did not fundamentally challenge the older free market concepts of individual interests and morality which have since been revived in the new orthodoxy. But, because social democracy put more emphasis on the role of the state in managing the economy and in providing social services, it tended to weaken the idea that individuals were morally responsible for their own self-sufficiency and for those to whom they made personal commitments. Instead, this responsibility was shared with others through the state, which took the lead in organizing the economy and the social services, rather than expecting all individuals to plan independently for themselves.

This meant that social democracy's account of morality was ambiguous. On the one hand, it was not always clear whether the systems for economic management and the welfare state appealed to the self-interest of all individuals or were a form of compulsory altruism, imposed in the name of moral values, for the sake of worse-off members of society. On the other hand, it was unclear whether – in important questions affecting society as a whole – the state was to be regarded as the primary moral agent, with the responsibility for providing for the good of all by meeting needs, or whether the individual was still morally responsible for seeking his or her own good, though personal preferences and plans.

Weaknesses of social democracy

As long as economic growth was maintained, unemployment remained low and social services could be expanded to meet increasing needs, social democracy's claims to be the most efficient way of securing the interests of all were credible. Even governments of the right could not afford to risk radical changes in social democratic economic or welfare institutions. But once growth slowed or was halted, unemployment increased and social services became overstretched, these views lost their conviction.

Seen as technical ways of maximizing growth and achieving the best possible distribution for all, social democracy could readily be challenged by market-based approaches. Since the risks of unemployment and poverty were evidently highest among certain fairly well-defined groups in the population, the rest had an interest in limiting the state's expenditure on social provision. Only in countries which were able to sustain economic growth and hold down unemployment by social democratic methods (such as Sweden) was it possible to retain faith in these institutions as serving the interests of society as a whole.

Social democracy has thus been caught between a strategy of continuing to

claim that it represents the most efficient form of economic and social expertise, and one of claiming that the moral role of the state should (on certain
issues) take priority over the choices and preferences of the individual. The
latter strategy has two disadvantages. First, it involves requiring people to act
against their apparent interests, at least in the short run. Secondly, it involves
claiming that the state's agencies are reliable ways of pursuing moral goals, by
moral methods, to achieve a good society.

The first problem is one that is being recognized by the British Labour
Party in the aftermath of its 1987 election defeat. The Labour Party's
campaign was based to a considerable extent on attacking the Conservative
government's treatment of social issues, and the market-based approach to
these, as immoral. Yet the implication of this was that many people on mid-
dling incomes would be required to sacrifice some part of their resources
under a Labour government, for the sake of those worse-off than themselves.
Immediately after the election, several members of Labour's leadership
declared that the party could never win unless it was able to persuade people
in these more advantaged groups that its policies were in their interests.
These arguments were used in support of a new approach (as yet largely
undefined) by the Labour Party, which its advocates called 'socialist individualism', and which promoted (among other things) greater freedom of choice
within the social services.[6]

The second problem has been a long-standing one where social democratic
governments held power for long periods in the 1960s and 1970s. If social
democracy represents a morally superior way of organizing society, then we
would expect this to be reflected in a better quality of social relations. For
example, social problems such as crime, violence, alcoholism and mental
illness might be expected to decrease. In fact, there was little evidence that
they did so; instead, some problems seemed to increase, and new ones
appeared, like drug abuse and child abuse, which critics saw as signs of
alarming deterioration of individual and family responsibility.

Equally damaging was social democracy's failure to respond to social
change in an active and dynamic way. If the state was to be a moral agent,
then it was required also to show some of the qualities of a moral entrepreneur
in the face of change. Yet social democratic governments often appeared blind
to important new social issues, for example, over equal opportunities for
women and for black people, and concerning the environment. They seemed
unable to mobilize potential new moral forces in society such as feminism,
anti-racism or the ecological and peace movements. At times, they seemed
defensively nationalistic in the face of transnational problems.

The success of the new orthodoxy lies in its ability to supply an account of a
good society which is in line with the direction of socioeconomic change, and
which justifies the characteristic morality and lifestyle of the newly prosperous middle classes: 'suburban prejudice made flesh', as it has been aptly
described.[7] It emphasizes the failures of social democracy in order to highlight
the futility of any attempt to resist global economic forces or to moralize

wider social relations. In basing its social relations as much on individual and family responsibility as on market forces, it can claim simultaneously the advantages of freedom in economic transactions and of self-discipline in personal relationships.

It has come as a shock to the left to find that the moral relativism that appeared in the 1960s to be its strength, allowing a diverse collection of ideals and enthusiasms to coexist, and a more complex and apparently tolerant culture to flourish, has now become one of its weaknesses. The new orthodoxy offers a potent mixture of economic diversity – the infinite variety of the market place – and moral certainty. Compared with this, the left seems both drab and confused.

Argument and plan of the book

There are many possible ways of assessing the new orthodoxy, and alternatives to it. My concern in this book is to analyse how individual choice relates to the good of society, and to argue that the new orthodoxy's account of this relation is extremely misleading.

In trying to construct a theory of the good society out of individual self-interest and individual moral responsibility, the new orthodoxy constructs no society at all. Mrs Thatcher betrayed this in a much-quoted statement, during an interview with a women's magazine: 'There is no such thing as society. There are individual men and women, and there are families.'[8] What this phrase was trying to capture was the idea that individuals' choices are directed towards the interests of themselves, and those for whom they feel affectionate or sympathetic concern. What it actually captures is the idea of a society in which people lack any common interests in the good of their community.

I shall argue for a social morality which arises from common interests in the common good. When people act together for the sake of mutual benefits in which they all share, then they are acting both in others' interests (because others gain from their actions) and in their own (because they gain also). Often these benefits are indivisible and qualitative. A good society is one in which people share in a good quality of life, and value their association with each other as members of the same community. The value of shared association cannot be split into individual portions, any more than can the value of a good party, a good meeting or a good religious ceremony.

I shall argue that dividing individual choices into those which are self-interested and those which benefit others is fundamentally misleading. The choices which we make in everyday life are shaped by social institutions like markets, families, voluntary associations, friendship networks, neighbourhoods, communities and political organizations. In most of these, our own interests are not identifiable as separate from those of others, but *inextricably linked with others' interests*. We can only understand and follow our own interests by recognizing our common interests with others.

The individual choice perspective obscures this. Hence the new orthodoxy, because it cannot recognize common interests, systematically erodes those institutions and forms of life which promote the goods of association, mutuality and sharing, and substitutes institutions which favour individualism, privacy and exclusiveness. In doing so, it actually creates interests in selfishness, greed and callousness where none previously existed. Worse still, it creates new coalitions of interests between those with a stake in possessive, materialistic egoism, and against those with no stake in such values, because they are excluded from those institutional systems.

The result is that the new orthodoxy loses sight of society as a system of social relations between people whose interests are linked to each other's, and brings about a society in which all can see only their own competitive interests. Paradoxically, a perspective which tries to overcome the problem of conflicting individual interests ends up by creating a society in which the Hobbesian state of war - a state of hostility of all against all - is brought about.

I shall argue that the good society requires institutions which promote common interests and encourage association, inclusiveness and sharing. When we consider society as a whole, the common interests that people have in certain goods that stem from membership of that society are constituted in citizenship. Where citizens have a common interest in those aspects of social relations which they share together, then this represents the common good. I shall suggest (following Aristotle) that the good society is one which promotes the good of all its citizens, by promoting their interests in the common good. In so far as the new orthodoxy's view of individual choice - both egoistic and altruistic - has rendered these ideas virtually meaningless, I am required to construct my argument rather laboriously, step by step.

In chapter 2, I use the example of a disaster (the sinking of a ferry) to illustrate my concept of common interests. The point about such a situation is that it makes little sense to distinguish between egoistic and altruistic choices, since the survival of each of the passengers depends on the actions of all others. Cooperating and helping each other may allow all to survive, where either selfishness or self-sacrifice would endanger the lives of many. Hence actions which promote a coordinated escape are both self-interested and moral because all have a common interest in the common good (the survival of all) But the new orthodoxy would distinguish between this situation and everyday social life, by arguing that in ordinary (non-disastrous) situations there are no such common interests; instead, because individuals have different preferences and projects, interests diverge. Here I examine in more detail the individual choice model (both popular and academic) of how divergent interests are reconciled through markets and through altruism, and the social morality to which this gives rise.

In chapter 3, I begin my construction of an alternative view of interests. Using Robert Axelrod's demonstration, I shall show that individuals have an interest in cooperating with each other where neither has any prospect of gaining competitive advantage over the other, and where the benefits they gain are mutual. I go on to show (following Michael Taylor) that this form of reciprocity and cooperation was characteristic of social relations in societies without a market or a state, and led to orderly relations which were egalitarian and communal in nature. But the creation of markets and states eroded these common interests in cooperation and reciprocity in relation to many goods, including order and defence. Hence, we must understand competitive self-interested behaviour as a solution to the problem of markets rather than markets as a solution to the problem of competitive self-interest; and we must understand the 'free-rider problem' and the 'public goods puzzle' as issues which arise from political societies, rather than states and public goods as solutions to the problems of cheating.

In chapter 4, I consider a number of systems of social relations (markets, representative democracy, membership groups, reciprocity groups) in a particular combination, presented as a future scenario which might be developed out of current trends in advanced capitalist societies and the new orthodoxy's principles. I argue that this scenario could be seen to be the result of individual choices (economic or democratic), and hence as morally justifiable according to the new orthodoxy. Yet they reflect a very unequal distribution of income and power, such that the members of certain large groups in society would appear to stand to benefit from the redistribution of the assets which cause these inequalities. This raises the question of whether disadvantaged groups can be said to have any interests in or obligations to a whole social system (such as the one in the scenario) and whether an egalitarian redistribution of such assets would be morally justifiable, given that it might have to override the individual choices of a number (perhaps even a majority) of the population.

In chapter 5, I argue that the idea of a good society only makes sense in terms of the common interests of all citizens in a good quality of life. This notion of the good society is part of the republican tradition, and regards the common good as actively created, qualitative and purposeful. In order to enable participation and self-rule, the state must use power to distribute assets and structure interests. This tradition emphasizes that social institutions must allow a debate about justice, freedom and equality, to involve citizens in adapting their society to changing conditions.

In chapter 6, I show that in a modern advanced capitalist country (Britain), a majority of citizens has a material interest in excluding the poor from any share in the assets which give income and power advantages. This leads to a social structure in which the most important division in society is between the relatively comfortable majority and an underclass. Since the latter has no self-interested motive in cooperation or participation, it is perceived by the majority as burdensome and threatening. Welfare provision is gradually transformed into mechanisms for control and punishment, while the passivity of the underclass changes to conflict, crime and disorder.

This division of society into competing coalitions, with no common interests, must soon lead to a deterioration of the quality of life in the new orthodoxy's society. The only way to overcome this which is consistent with the common good is to give the underclass motives to cooperate and partici- pate. The first step is to allow members of the underclass self-interested incentives to enter the employment market, which the new orthodoxy denies them. In chapter 7, I examine a mechanism for this first step towards an alternative model of society – Basic Income – and argue that this is a necessary condition for a re-emergence of common interests in public goods.

However, it is not enough for the state to restructure economic interests in this way. In order to reconstruct the social fabric of our communities, and allow all to recognize an interest in improving the quality of public life, an alternative programme should reassert the value of association and partici- pation. In chapter 8, I argue that only in this way will the new orthodoxy's narrow concern with private goods be corrected.

In chapter 9, I argue that the household, which is glorified by the new orthodoxy as the focus of its values, is increasingly under stress from the contradictions in emerging social relations. In particular, women cannot simultaneously meet the demands on them as exploited part-time employees and as unpaid carers for a growing elderly population. The strain on family relations will reveal the unbalanced emphasis on privacy and exclusiveness, and lead to greater appreciation of the advantages of public and collective provision of care.

Implicit in my argument throughout the book is a view of interests as being much broader than calculated economic advantage, and of morality as social. In chapter 10, I look at the theoretical underpinnings of this view of reason- ing about interests and responsibilities, and suggest an approach based on dialogue between members of a community. In this way, individual calculative and technical rationality is challenged by a debate about social purposes which recognizes common interests in a good society.

Finally, in chapter 11, I turn from consideration of a good society to relations between societies. Since power within nation states derives largely from the threat of conflict between states, the future of social relations is closely linked to that of international relations. But all people share an interest in peace, and increasing interdependence demands some expression for these international common interests. This concluding chapter sketches the prob- lems and possibilities of a common good that includes all humanity.

Notes

1 Speeches during the election campaign made on 5 June 1987. Mrs Thatcher said, 'Choice is the essence of morality. It is the essence of all religion. If you are to take away so much in tax that people don't have choice, to take away from them responsibility for their families and their children, I would say that was the immoral route. And, as I understand it, the right to choice is the essence of Christianity' (*The Independent*, 6 June 1987).

2 See, for example, Gary Becker, *The Economic Approach to Human Behaviour* (University of Chicago Press, 1976); John Harsanyi, *Rational Behaviour and Bargaining Equilibrium in Games and Social Situations* (Cambridge University Press, 1977); Howard Margolis, *Selfishness, Altruism and Rationality: a Theory of Social Choice* (Cambridge University Press, 1982); Mancur Olson, *The Logic of Collective Action* (Harvard University Press, 1965); Amartya K. Sen, *Collective Choice and Social Welfare* (Oliver and Boyd, 1970); Brian Barry, *Sociologists, Economists and Democracy* (University of Chicago Press, 1970); A. Heath, *Rational Choice and Social Exchange* (Cambridge University Press, 1976).

3 See, for example, Martin Hollis, *The Cunning of Reason* (Cambridge University Press, 1987); Amartya K. Sen, 'Rational fools: a critique of the behavioural foundations of economic theory', *Philosophy and Public Affairs*, 6 (1977), pp. 317-44; Anthony Giddens, *Central Problems in Social Theory* (MacMillan, 1979); Jon Elster (ed.), *The Multiple Self* (Cambridge University Press, 1986); R. Harrison (ed.), *Rational Action* (Cambridge University Press, 1979).

4 Adam Smith, 'The Theory of Moral Sentiments', (1762) in H. W. Schneider (ed.), *Adam Smith's Moral and Political Philosophy* (Harper, 1948) pt IV, ch. 1.

5 Francis C. Castles, *The Working Class and Welfare: Reflections on the Political Development of the Welfare State in Australia and New Zealand, 1890-1980* (Allen and Unwin, 1986).

6 Michael Meacher, 'A new vision of socialist individualism', *The Independent*, 16 July 1987. An article expressing similar views by John Prescott appeared in the *Guardian* in the same week.

7 By Brian Redhead, BBC Radio 4 *Today* programme.

8 Margaret Thatcher, interviewed in *Woman's Own*, 31 October 1987.

2

The New Orthodoxy's Good Society

In an ideal world, everyone would cooperate with everyone else because all would recognize that what was good for society was also good for themselves. A perfectly moral world would be one in which nobody ever acted in a way which harmed others, and everybody always acted so as to promote the good of others. If such a Utopian world ever came into existence, it would be a peaceful and harmonious anarchy because there would be no need to force people to cooperate with each other.[1]

It is very difficult to conceptualize the elements that go to make up this notion of a perfectly moral world, and to relate the real world to it. But we need to do so if we are to give an account of the good society. For example, we need to be able to say whether moral relations require continuous self-sacrifice by all, or whether the good of all could be promoted by some form of mutually advantageous cooperation.

The nearest we come to a real-life situation in which large numbers of people cooperate for the good of all is - paradoxically - a crisis or a disaster. For short periods, in the face of some common adversity, people do seem to pull together for the good of all. In Britain, the Second World War produced a spirit of determined cooperation against a common enemy. Although British society was strongly controlled and planned during the war, this would not have been effective without a voluntary commitment by the people to the war effort.

In 1987 a number of large-scale disasters provided examples of ordinary people helping each other during a crisis. The sinking of the sea ferry at Zeebrugge and the fire at King's Cross underground station in London were instances of concerted action, including personal bravery and resourcefulness by members of the public.

Under such circumstances, it seems that people do recognize that there is a common good, and feel drawn to act together. For the purposes of this chapter, it is important to analyse why this happens during a crisis, and what makes it much more difficult to bring about similar unity of purpose and commitment to each other's needs in ordinary everyday situations.

Disasters and the common good

The sinking of the ferry *Herald of Free Enterprise* was a particularly clear

example of the kind of behaviour I am trying to analyse, partly because the
ferry was full of people of different nationalities who were strangers to each
other, and partly because the disaster took place at sea, and so rescue services
took some time to arrive. In spite of the appalling conditions and the extent of
the damage to the ship, by the time rescuers arrived passengers had begun a
concerted effort to reach safety, in which they helped each other, without any
authoritative organization or instruction.

It would be easy to idealize a description of what occurred, and what
follows is in no sense an attempt at an accurate reconstruction. No doubt
many people panicked, and sought safety without regard for others. Immediately after the tragedy, it was said that some trampled over others while trying
to save themselves. No doubt there were even more people who were frozen
into inaction by shock, fear or sheer lack of practical skills. It appears from
this and other tragedies that those who acted most decisively to help others
and to get concerted action started were often people who had had some
training in the armed forces or voluntary emergency services.

In spite of these reservations, there do seem to have been several examples
in different parts of the ship of groups of people who were strangers to each
other cooperating for their mutual safety and survival. It was as if, under these
circumstances, people perceived themselves as in a certain sort of relationship
with each other, and acted together without any prior negotiation or agreement. The features of their cooperation might be summarized as follows:

1 *The common good arose from a shared situation* In this instance, all the
people on the ferry, though they came from different backgrounds and
cultures, were literally 'in the same boat'. Because all were in mortal danger,
all had a need to escape from the ship.

2 *This situation created common interests* Although each passenger had an
individual interest in preserving his or her own life, all had a common interest
in cooperating to help each other to escape. What I mean by a common
interest is that each could quickly assess that an orderly, concerted, combined
effort to survive would be more likely to succeed than a free-for-all, in which
everyone tried to save themselves. For example, if this had occurred, people
would have been fighting each other for the use of articles to construct ways
out, and blocking exits by trying to scramble through them simultaneously.

3 *All cooperated with each other for the sake of the common good* Concerted
cooperation did not imply that everyone tried to rescue everyone else, as this
would have been equally chaotic. Nor did it mean that everyone stood back,
saying to each other, 'After you, Cecil; no, after you, Claude.' It meant that
all were active in a joint effort to get out, which it was in the interests of all to
achieve by cooperation.

4 *Those with special abilities played key roles* The fact that all played an
active part did not imply that everyone did the same thing. Very fit and strong
people built ladders out of furniture, carried small children up them, broke
windows and so on. A very tall man acted as a 'human bridge' over a watery
chasm, allowing others to pass over his body to safety.

5 *Those with special needs received extra help* For example, children and disabled people, who were in no position to save themselves, were given physical assistance by stronger passengers. It was reported that one passenger carried a baby in his teeth, and that another held a small child above his head as the water rose to engulf him.

6 *Existing commitments were recognized* Although everyone cooperated for mutual safety, individuals gave priority to helping members of their families. Some intuitive balance was struck between concern for the good of all and concern for closest relatives.

7 *All shared responsibility for the good of all* Everyone was included in the common good, without regard for their status or origin, and all were jointly responsible to each other for their part in cooperation. Until the official rescuers arrived, and unless a trained member of the crew was at hand, all took part as equals with equal responsibility.

8 *No one was compelled to act against his or her will* Although some people behaved heroically, no one was forced to do so. No individual was sacrificed for the good of others, or used as a means of others' safety, without consenting to this role.

The important feature of the behaviour of the people involved in the disaster was their perception of the situation as one in which the individual good and the common good did coincide, and their spontaneous cooperation for the good of all. When a group of people act in this way, they not only recognize common interests in cooperation, but create common interests by producing mutual benefits.

Where this occurs, there is little conflict between self-interest and the interests of others. It is in people's interests to act together to further the common cause, and to play whatever role their abilities require. For any individual to try to act independently would not only damage others' chances of survival, but probably also his own.

It might be argued that this does not apply to the possibility of a coalition of the strong to save each other at the expense of the weak. It might be in the interests of reasonably able-bodied people to cooperate with each other, and to leave the least able to perish. But this does not allow for the complication of commitments by particular able-bodied people to members of the non-able-bodied group. For example, a very strong or very tall person, whose abilities or capacities might be crucial to the coalition's success, might refuse to cooperate unless his family was among those rescued.

The point here is not whether anyone would make such calculations during a crisis like this one. It is that it is quite easy to conceive of a situation in which everyone had a common interest in cooperating for mutual survival, and that in such a situation the individual's good would not conflict with the common good. Here we have a situation which is similar to the ideal moral world described at the start of this chapter.

The point about this is that it illustrates a relationship between morality and self-interest which is quite different from the new orthodoxy's account.

The actions of the people who cooperate to bring about their own survival are moral because they promote the good of all, harm no one and exclude no one. Yet they arise from common interests in survival, not from individuals sacrificing their own interests to those of others.

It is true that examples such as the ferry disaster contain instances of special heroism, where an individual risked or lost his or her life to save another. In this sense, some individuals clearly do sacrifice themselves for others' good. But if this occurs as part of a scheme of concerted cooperation within a group, it cannot be understood as an isolated act of bravery. When a group is cooperating to achieve the common good, and each member's role is in line with his or her abilities, what they do can only be understood as part of that cooperative effort. Indeed, heroism seen simply as risk-taking would be counterproductive of the common good, unless it arose directly from the needs of a member of the group, and the role of the heroic person. In this sense, individual acts are morally praiseworthy mainly in so far as they contribute to the common good, rather than because they involve self-sacrifice. Indeed, if an act of heroism subsequently turns out to have contributed to the survival not only of the group, but also of the hero, it is no less heroic.

Problems of cooperation

In the everyday life of modern society, there seem to be no such common interests, and hence no such common good. One reason for this is the sheer size and complexity of society. There is no way that an ordinary person can look around and recognize what needs to be done for the good of all, or how he or she can contribute to it. There are just too many people, doing too many different things, and no one has a clear enough picture of the intentions or needs of the rest to be aware of where the common good lies. Even if everyone made a concerted effort to find out, the scale of the exercise would probably make it self-defeating.

A second reason is that people want different things for themselves, and each may have a different idea of his or her own good. People make their own plans of life, and choose projects (long-term goals, leading to programmes for action) and commitments (relationships with others for common purposes). The new orthodoxy points out that the notion of the individual as a moral agent implies that a rational, mature person has the capacity to make such plans, to choose such projects and commitments and to recognize that others are doing the same. Hence there is not, except in a crisis when all are faced with death or injury, any single common good that all can pursue cooperatively. Instead, there are potentially as many different goods as there are individuals.

Thirdly, there is only a limited quantity of natural resources in the world, there is only a limited amount of time in each individual's life and each has only a limited amount of energy. All these have to be divided between a much larger number of possible combinations of uses, purposes and outcomes. Ultimately, a finite process of production, exchange and distribution must be decided, and this must bear some relation to all the potentially competing life-plans, projects and commitments of all the individuals in society. Clearly, it is unlikely perfectly to satisfy all the aspirations of each person, and will lead to conflict and disorder unless some systems can be discovered for coordinating these, so that a series of orderly and peaceful compromises is reached; this is probably the nearest that can be approached to voluntary cooperation, and hence to the moral ideal described at the start of the chapter.

Fourthly, no single system of coordination is likely to prevail for every kind of good and every relationship between individuals in a large society. For reasons of scale and diversity, there are likely always to be a variety of systems of social relations coexisting, for the production and distribution of different goods according to different criteria. For example, even the most tyrannical state would find it difficult to organize people's personal relationships with each other, even if its rulers were convinced that a certain disposition of friendships, marriages and neighbourhood groups was essential for the common good. Equally, even the most fervent supporters of markets have stopped short of suggesting that political office should be allocated by means of the price mechanism or that religious salvation should be treated as a commodity to be bought and sold. In the last resort, even in a society where one formal system predominates for most goods and in most social relations, informal alternatives are likely to survive.

The new orthodoxy asserts that this combination of factors - size, the individual as a moral agent, finite resources and plurality of systems of relations - points towards a division of society into spheres of cooperation, each with its characteristic way of harmonizing potentially conflicting individual interests. In this way it is able to construct a version of the common good, and hence a moral theory, which is plausible, and which - by virtue of its emphasis on individual choice and voluntarism - bears some relation to the ideal presented in this chapter's opening paragraph.

Economic cooperation

The new orthodoxy places special importance on markets as systems for coordinating diverse individual plans in large-scale societies. This is partly because it claims that they are the most efficient ways of bringing prosperity to society as a whole, and including all in its benefits. But it is also because it argues that markets are morally superior to other economic systems because they allow more freedom of choice, and because they create common interests in cooperation.

First, the new orthodoxy argues that markets are the best ways in which individuals and commercial enterprises can signal to each other about their plans and projects, so that these can be coordinated with each other. They are morally superior because they allow mutual adjustment without restrictions of choice or authoritative allocation; in this sense they allow 'order without commands'.[2] The rules of markets apply to all participants, and allow them to rely on each other's collaboration to a considerable extent, while rewarding initiative and foresight.[3]

Secondly, markets create common interests, in the sense that there can be no transaction between buyer and seller unless both are getting something that they want.[4] Purchasers can influence producers, through market preferences, to produce what they want; employers can influence employees, through wage rates, to develop skills and diligence needed in production; conversely, producers and employees will only supply their products or labour power if the price or wage offers sufficient inducement. Thus, where there is division of labour and limited resources, each has an interest in providing something that someone else requires for the pursuit of his or her good. In supplying commodities for sale, the seller is necessarily providing for the buyer's good, or no purchase would take place; in buying commodities, the buyer is necessarily providing for the seller's good, or there would be no sale. Hence, it is claimed, the market creates mutual benefits and promotes the common good.[5]

As presented by some theorists, this makes market transactions sound very much like the relations between the victims of a disaster, but this is misleading. Markets are sytems which not only start from the assumption that individuals are self-interested in a competitive way, they *require* them to be self-interested in a competitive way, in order to achieve what they are claimed to achieve.[6] In the highly idealized model on which all the claims of market efficiency are based, individuals and enterprises are assumed to have consistent and fully ordered preferences (they know exactly the order of priority of all their wants), perfect information (the price and quality of everything that is available, and how these relate to their wants) and unerring powers to compute the utility of each unit in terms of its price. They all aim at the maximum satisfaction of their preferences; if they do not, then they reach an inferior outcome, and the whole system falls short of the efficient allocation of resources which is its major claim. In other words, self-interest is built into the assumptions of the system, and without the striving for competitive advantage which is its hallmark, many of the fortunate results – for example, products becoming cheaper over time, super-profits of monopolies being gradually eroded – would not follow.

Obviously, there are many economic theories which do not make these assumptions, or which modify them substantially, in order to reach a model which is closer to the real world. For example, if competition is imperfect, and hence people's information is incomplete, then individuals may prefer to 'satisfice' (hedge their bets) rather than trying to maximize.[7] More important, when an enterprise is made up of a number of different departments, with slightly different goals, then the way it acts may necessarily be a compromise between these goals. But even when the theory is developed to take account of organizational behaviour, it is still an analysis of how to gain competitive advantage, and the consequences of such attempts. 'Satisficing' is an adaptation to a situation in which maximizing is too risky a strategy, and organizations are no less in the business of bargain-hunting than individual consumers.

On the other hand, economists also recognize that not all bargain-hunters are choosing for themselves alone. The unit whose preferences are being expressed in choices may be a household or even a group. Some theories gloss over this problem, but others regard group-orientated choices as being quite different from self-interested preferences. For example, Margolis argues that all individuals have both egoistic and altruistic utilities, and an unconscious internal mechanism for allocating resources between them, such that they move towards an equilibrium, based on a 'fair share' between self-interested allocations and those which benefit others.[8] But if such a mechanism could be relied upon, then there would be no problem over how to reconcile self-interest with the good of all: Utopia would indeed be within our grasp, and much of the new orthodoxy's rhetoric would be redundant. This idea will be further discussed in the next chapter.

So we may conclude that, if markets do lead to the common good, it is through the efficient operation of impersonal economic forces and not through their moralizing properties. As Adam Smith remarked, 'It is not from the benevolence of the butcher, the brewer or the baker that we expect our dinner, but from their regard to their own self-interest. We address ourselves not to their humanity but to their self-love, and never talk to them of our necessities but of their advantages.'[9]

While it is true that buyers and sellers must fulfil each other's wants for a market transaction to take place, it can hardly be said, for instance, that an employee is concerned for the good of an employing multinational company or a shopper for the good of a supermarket. The whole point of markets is that they make transactions impersonal, so that the parties need not be concerned for each other's good, but only for the most favourable terms they can get. To buy in a village shop because one is concerned for the welfare of the shopkeeper is a clear example of non-market behaviour. Adam Smith justified markets by showing that other forms of transaction, like begging or flattering, which depended on appeals to the good of the parties, were very time-consuming and hence inefficient.[10]

For all these reasons, it is more accurate to describe the ways that markets operate as Adam Smith did; they enable orderly and efficient relations between large numbers of people in the provision of certain goods, in situations where there are resource limitations and a division of labour, through self-interested decisions in which the good of others is not intended. In such circumstances, their advantage is that they channel self-interested competition (which is already assumed to exist as a feature of the situation) in order to achieve forms of cooperation. The way that this creates common interests is quite different from the way that this is done in the disaster example.

In that example, a market solution would require us to assume that some people (the strong) had the capacity to get out, perhaps by hiring equipment from others (rescue services). The weak would then pay the strong to carry them to safety. This would certainly be an alternative way of achieving cooperation and a mutual interest in the survival of passengers (or at least those who could afford to pay to be rescued), by mobilizing the self-interest of all the parties. It would also furnish a very graphic demonstration of why we do not use markets as a way of organizing certain goods, such as emergency services.

Political cooperation

Because of the problems of cooperation in large groups, with differing preferences and finite resources, the new orthodoxy argues that markets are the best ways of providing most goods because they allow freedom to choose according to self-interest, yet promote efficiency and prosperity from which all benefit. Hence the definition of the common good in the economic sphere favoured by the new orthodoxy is the sum of all the individual rights of people in society.

But it is forced to recognize that there are some goods which cannot be best provided in this way. It is of the nature of some goods that they cannot be divided up in such a way as to exclude those who do not pay for them. Hence, since markets only work through self-interest, and since it will be in every individual's interests not to pay for a service, but to leave it to others to pay, it will not be in the interests of any enterprise to provide it.[11] These goods include some which are in everyone's interests (such as defence against attack by members of other societies) and some which are essential to the functioning of markets themselves (such as laws which prohibit theft, force and fraud). A self-interested individual will want the advantages of being a member of a society in which there is defence against outside aggression and laws protecting orderly markets, but will prefer to enjoy these benefits without paying for them (to be a 'free rider') so long as he or she cannot be excluded by virtue of non-payment.

This leads to a justification of the state as a system for providing these 'public goods' in such a way as to change people's interests, and give them a common interest in the goods which are necessary for a free and prosperous society, but which cannot be supplied by markets or by any other form of coordinated self-interest. It was Thomas Hobbes who first pointed out that competitive individuals would be led to create a structure of authority under which all would be compelled to obey the law,[12] and even though subsequent thinkers have rejected the authoritarian conclusions he drew from this, a similar argument has often been used to justify the limited authority of a liberal democratic state. In such theories, any powers of compulsion which restrict individual choice are seen as regrettable, but military forces and law enforcement agencies are examples of public goods which enable individual freedom and market exchange, but which could not arise without the state.

The recognition that the state can alter people's interests by the way in which it provides public goods creates a problem for those who adopt this line of argument. If the state can create a common interest in the public goods of defence and order by compelling all to contribute, then it can also create a common interest in other social goods by similar means. For example, social services, or food subsidies or minimum wages might be provided in such a way as to create common interests in these as public goods. All these might seriously disrupt the workings of markets, which are seen as the only reliable basis for the common good in the economic sphere.

The new orthodoxy sees the main purpose of democracy as being to guard against this danger. It is indeed possible for politicians and employees of state agencies to use their power and authority to alter incentives so that it is apparently in people's interests to contribute to many non-market goods through taxation. Indeed, the new orthodoxy regards the whole social democratic edifice of economic management and all its social institutions as having been just such a manipulation of incentives, so as to create an apparent common interest in a system which was monstrously inflationary and inefficient.[13] But democracy allows defenders of freedom and efficiency to show that these apparent common interests are in fact illusory, and are really constructed so as to enhance the interests of politicians, bureaucrats and state dependants. The new orthodoxy claims that democracy allows individual voters to strike at these corporate state interests, and to bring about a return to market methods, which ultimately secure the common good, by creating common interests in free choice, efficiency and prosperity.

But this attempt to restrict the political sphere to goods which cannot be supplied by markets is problematic. Once we recognize that the state and the market are alternative ways of structuring people's interests, we see that there is no such thing as 'individual self-interest', in the rather abstract sense that the new orthodoxy might suggest. The structuring of interests which is achieved by the market is only possible because of the state's authority, which creates an interest in a certain kind of order (defence of property, enforceable contracts, prohibition of violence etc.). So it is wrong to see interests as 'given'; they are created by the systems we adopt for producing the various goods we seek, and the ways we cooperate with each other. Once we recognize interests as created in this way, and as altered by the combinations of systems that make up society, this has important implications for the common good, which will be discussed in the next chapter.

Meanwhile, the new orthodoxy uses its political power to dismantle social democratic institutions, and return many publicly owned utilities and services to private enterprise, on the grounds of efficiency and freedom of choice, because they have become potentially profitable. It is interesting that in Britain so far these have mainly been state monopolies which were established in the nineteenth century (for example, gas and telecommunications) rather than those created by post-war social democratic governments.[14] In these ways, the interests of individuals are indeed being restructured, and a way of analysing these will be proposed in chapter 4.

Responsibility and altruism

The new orthodoxy's conception of rational adult individuals as moral agents, capable of forming their own life plans, and choosing projects and commitments, implies that each such person is responsible for his or her own good. Not only should all individuals be free to seek their own good in their own way; they should also be responsible for following through their plans, and taking the consequences of their choices.

The advantage of markets in relation to this idea of moral agency is that they provide incentives for individuals to look after themselves, and to make themselves useful to others.[15] People know that they can do best for themselves by doing, making and selling things that others want. It is therefore in their interests to be as useful as possible to other people, and markets reward them accordingly. This gives them the message that the world does not owe them a living, but that they can earn a living by effort and skill.

In this respect, advocates of the new orthodoxy see market relations as 'natural', in the sense that people living in a state of nature would have to work (hunt, grow crops or whatever) to stay alive. Markets remind people that there is still this connection between what they choose to do and their subsistence, even in a complex society. They have no moral claim on each other, other than the claim they can make by being of service to each other, and being paid for that service, unless they are victims of some identifiable misfortune.

Here again, the structure of relationships and interests that is characteristic of market societies is projected onto 'nature'. What the new orthodoxy describes as natural is the individualism of market relations. In reality, the 'state of nature' was (and is) communal rather than individual, and people did have a claim on each other, by virtue of membership of the same community. Market relations destroyed these communities, and restructured interests in the way described. The implications of this will be discussed in chapters 3 and 5.

The new orthodoxy recognizes that individuals make commitments to each other of a non-commercial kind, and it sees these as involving mutual obligations which are moral duties. For example, marital relationships mean that parents are jointly responsible for children's upbringing, and kinship relationships involve responsibility for the care of elderly people. In these transactions, individuals may well have to sacrifice their interests at times for the good of family members, for example, in caring for a handicapped child or disabled relative. Within families, individuals have duties to be concerned for the good of each other.

These moral obligations arise from the closeness of family relationships, and from the common interests created by shared lives.[16] Whereas markets allow self-interested cooperation between strangers, family relationships are commitments to common purposes, sustained by affection as well as duty. Because feelings of sympathy and solidarity between family members are seen as 'natural', once again this form of relationship is taken to reflect a social order which has its origins in biological and psychological features of universal 'human nature'.

In this theory, market relations are sustained by mutual self-interest, reinforced by law, but family relations are based on emotion, trust and promises. The duties associated with these relationships have to be learnt, and hence standards of personal behaviour (self-discipline, consideration for others, mutual assistance) are derived from childhood and family experiences, and maintained by the shared lives of family and kinship groups. Similar relations can be extended to wider groups only where there are similar feelings and shared values, though basic self-sufficiency and respect for others can be carried over into public life.

Individuals can discharge their moral duties to each other in family life either by direct unpaid labour or through providing by means of markets. For example, a moral agent has fulfilled his or her duties as much by paying for a nanny, a nurse or a gardener as by performing the tasks associated with these roles. The new orthodoxy does not necessarily prescribe rigid gender stereotypes - male breadwinners, women housewives - but it seems to accept uncritically the fact that in practice only better-off people can afford to pay others to do what is traditionally regarded as 'women's work'.

According to the new orthodoxy, altruism is characteristic of groups in which there are these bonds of feeling and trust. In a good society, the individual's private relationships will be the moral sphere, in which duty and self-sacrifice are required, but wider social relations can only be sustained by a combination of self-interested market transactions and legal controls. These elements go to make the best possible combination of freedom, efficiency and concern for the good of others.

Social services

This leads to a far more restrictive attitude to the provision of social services than was characteristic of social democracy. It means that these are limited to services that the market cannot supply, and to individuals who cannot provide for themselves by their own efforts or whose families do not provide for them from a sense of love and duty.

This follows from everything in the previous sections. The state is only required to use its power so as to alter incentives, and construct common interests, where people do not have a self-interested motive to provide a social good. But markets already give people a motive to look after themselves, and a means of obtaining the services they need to do so. Hence the state is only required to provide non-market services for those who would otherwise be left out.

For example, insurance provides a market system for supplying health care for most needs. If risks of long-term illness, disability and handicap are excluded, a high proportion of the population can afford the kinds of premium that such insurance requires.[17] So state health services, financed out of taxation, should be confined to those long-term risks and to acute services for people who are unable to afford to insure themselves. Even though this approach to health care has not been accepted in Britain, it is urged on the government by many theorists within its own school of thought.

Poverty poses a rather different problem. Although various forms of insurance and saving are ways in which individuals can meet their own needs during periods of unemployment and in retirement, there are some who do not earn enough to live on when in full-time work, let alone when they are out of it. Here the new orthodoxy insists that the state should only provide income support for those in 'genuine need', who have tried to be self-sufficient, and not for those who have made no effort to support themselves and their families. To do otherwise would be to undermine the natural requirement imposed on people by the laws of the market, to make themselves useful to others and not to expect to get something for nothing.

The solution adopted by the new orthodoxy is to impose a test on those who apply for financial assistance from the state.[18] For people who are old, sick or disabled, this test is designed to show that they are incapable of paid work, and that they do not have sufficient income or savings to provide for themselves. The 'means test' is therefore not simply a way of rationing assistance, to save state expenditure; it is also a way of testing who is in 'genuine need'. Obviously, it is rather a crude test because it does not determine how people came to be in this financial situation, but it is the simplest way of distinguishing a group for which the state should take some responsibility from the rest.

In the case of able-bodied people, the test has to take a different form because it is designed to find out whether they are being sufficiently diligent in trying to support themselves and their families by paid work. In the case of those with low-paid jobs, they are assumed to be doing their best, and so are given extra assistance if the family income falls below a certain level. But in the case of those who are unemployed, there is a greater problem in devising a suitable test.

One way is to try to ask questions, and set tasks, which find out whether the claimant is really available for employment and actively seeking it. But in the United States, and now increasingly in Britain, this is seen as insufficient. Another approach is to require the claimant to do a form of 'training', or work for the state, as a condition for receiving any assistance. The system of 'workfare' - compulsory work as a condition of entitlement to benefits - is seen as morally justified because no individual has a claim on others' help without demonstrating a willingness to do something in return.

According to the new orthodoxy, these tests should reduce the number of people who depend on state financial assistance to the minimum, and increase the number of those who have the advantages of the market to the maximum. But paradoxically this is not necessarily so. The problem is that the provision of means-tested benefits restructures the incentives of the poor, so as to reduce self-interested motives in improving their earnings. Especially when the with-drawal of benefits is combined with the imposition of income tax, individuals and households may face a situation in which they are no better-off, or only very slightly better-off, by earning more. Hence there may come to be a large sector of low-paid people, who are trapped in poverty by the very tests that try to exclude those 'not in genuine need'.

At the same time, once the state adopts schemes for requiring claimants to do work in exchange for benefits, it comes to be in the interests of those who use such workers (including the state itself) to get work done by this method, rather than employing people who have to be paid wages, holiday pay, taxes, etc. So the restructuring of interests that occurs through workfare schemes can also lead to the creation of a large class of paupers, who are compulsorily employed under non-market conditions. These difficulties weaken the new orthodoxy's claim that its system gives all members of society common interests in the common good. They will be examined in more detail in chapters 4 and 6.

A good society?

The new orthodoxy's claim to being a moral theory rests on its reconciliation of cooperation and self-interest. It argues that, since all individuals have potentially competing views of their own good, and since altruistic cooper-ation is only possible in small groups bound together by mutual affection and trust, markets are the best way of creating common interests. They allow a form of cooperation which stems from self-interest, and encourage both self-sufficiency and the pursuit of usefulness to others. Since being a moral agent implies free choice, this combination of systems of cooperation in the differ-ent spheres allows the best form of society because it involves least compul-sion for the sake of the common good.

The most obvious criticism of the new orthodoxy is that it relies too much upon self-interest, and upon the economic sphere, to shape society and to determine individuals' life chances. In so doing, it justifies the advantages of the economically successful, and condemns those who are unsuccessful to poverty and disadvantage. Far from being a moral theory, it is obtuse in its deafness to the moral claims of justice, equality and need, all of which demand a quite different distribution of wealth, income and power.

But advocates of the new orthodoxy argue that these supposed aspects of the common good are very loosely defined. Their own theory is a carefully constructed version of the nearest approximation, under present conditions, to a society based on peaceful voluntary cooperation. The systems of the dif-ferent spheres are designed to give the greatest possible freedom of choice to individual moral agents, consistent with the greatest good of all (defined as the sum of individual rights).

This challenges opponents to show that any other form or pattern of distribution or system of relations could be spontaneously established; or that any compulsory redistribution of assets could be justified in terms of a moral principle. If an alternative theory accepts that markets are the only possible spontaneous form of orderly self-interested relations in large groups, and that any other system must rely either on compulsion to reconstruct interests, or on altruism, it is required to provide a moral justification of redistribution or a plausible account of an altruistic society.

For an example of the first kind of alternative, let us take the most influential theory of justice which might be put up as an argument against the new orthodoxy. According to Rawls's theory, one of the two crucial tests of whether a particular distribution of assets in society is fair or not, is whether any inequality is to the advantage of the worst-off group.[19] This criterion is adopted as a result of a thought experiment, in which people (or potential people) have to choose a social system, in ignorance of which particular endowments of intelligence, skill, attractiveness, health and fortune fate would deal them when they entered the real world. It is argued that, if people had to risk the possibility of being among the worst-off, they would choose a system which gave them the security of limiting inequalities in this respect. Many authors have adopted Rawls's arguments to justify social democratic institutions and social services.

But the new orthodoxy would not accept this as being a moral argument, and with some reason. In effect, it reduces the choice of a constitution, and the institutional arrangements of a society, to a single decision by individuals devoid of human characteristics, in a situation of total ignorance about themselves. This then becomes a permanent constraint on all their subsequent choices, and a universal rule governing the whole social system.

The new orthodoxy would argue that such embryonic people would not be regarded as moral agents because they would not be in a position to formulate a view of their own good. When we talk about the good of society, we mean the good of real-life people and their actual plans and projects. This means taking into account people's real material interests, not hypothetical ones. So a moral theory should be concerned with chosen cooperation between people, given their actual characteristics and the opportunities and resources available, rather than what they might be committed to do through some prenatal decision. It is this robustness of the new orthodoxy's appeal to the real world of people with dissimilar endowments and preferences that gives it much of its appeal.

Alternatively, another approach would be to try to construct a theory in which people choose to sacrifice their interests for the good of others. It is frequently argued, for instance, that survey evidence under Mrs Thatcher's government points to a greater willingness to sacrifice income for the sake of an improved health service, or even for the sake of relieving poverty, than the government's policies allow. But such evidence would be an unreliable basis for a social system, since this willingness to make sacrifices might be very temporary and conditional, as the fate of the welfare state in many Western countries has shown. If people really want to do these things, they can make voluntary contributions to relevant charities.

The new orthodoxy would argue that for thousands of years philosophers and rulers tried to construct ideal societies in which the social system was sustained by individuals' regard for the good of others. Some of these were religious societies, which attempted to create the Kingdom of God on earth, and others were humanistic. In the modern age, such attempts are doomed to failure because of the very nature of large-scale commercial societies. The attempt was finally abandoned with the failure (or modification) of the Enlightenment's project in the eighteenth century. The only modern choice thus lies between a system based on freedom and self-interest and one based on compulsory altruism.

Conclusions

In this chapter I have tried to set out the moral arguments for the new orthodoxy, and to show that the task of refuting them is not as easy as is often assumed. It provides a plausible account of the links between individual freedom, self-interest and morality within the context of a modern capitalist society.

I have shown that the new orthodoxy's theory of the good society is one in which voluntary cooperation for the good of all is established by means of different systems of social relations in a number of different spheres. The primary sphere is the economic one, in which a common interest in order and prosperity is created through markets; this system works for society as a whole. On a much smaller scale, shared lives, affection and trust allow altruistic cooperation in families and voluntary associations. But the political sphere is a residual one, reserved for the compulsory creation of common interests in goods not supplied by markets or households. These include social services for what the new orthodoxy describes, in a deeply patronizing phrase, as the 'least fortunate members of society'.

The problem for opponents of this theory is to construct an alternative social morality which, starting from individual moral agents in pursuit of their own good, arrives at a system of voluntary cooperation. If they accept that self-interested individuals can only cooperate through markets, and that other forms of cooperation require altruism, then it is difficult to refute the view that the new orthodoxy maximizes voluntary cooperation. They are then left with the difficult problem of constructing moral justifications for compulsory self-sacrifice. This, for instance, is the problem that seems to confront the British Labour Party at present.

The line that I shall take is a different one. I have shown in this chapter that the market model of self-interest requires all to seek the maximum individual advantage in relation to each other – 'looking after onself' is necessarily construed in terms of competitive advantage. Unless people do this, the advantages of the market (in terms of efficiency and prosperity) do not arise. But this does not imply that seeking competitive advantage is the only possible form of spontaneous self-interested cooperation in large groups. I shall argue that other kinds of cooperation are self-interested under certain conditions, and that to equate self-interest with competitive advantage is therefore misleading.

Outside the institutions of market exchange, we take part in social relations in which our own interests are not separate from those of others, but linked with them. We can only recognize and follow our own interests by understanding how the groups, associations and communities of which we are part give us common interests with others. Hence it is in each individual's interests to act so as to contribute to the group's purposes and to promote its ends. This does not require special motivation (altruism), but rather special conditions, which lead to particular institutions concerned with negotiating and sharing.

By focusing on individual choices, using the paradigm of the bargain-hunter in the market, the new orthodoxy is able to reduce all social relations to a series of calculated moves (ultimately capable of being expressed as mathematical formulae) in an impersonal competitive game. If the whole of society were indeed such a game, then the analysis would be valid. But the trick behind the scenes is to project economic rules onto other social relations, and then insist that only economic analyses can explain the players' moves.

This trick has been very successfully used by the new orthodoxy to change social relations in two directions. First, it justifies extending market systems into areas of social life which were previously governed by other (non-competitive) rules, insisting that only competition can ensure order and cooperation. Market apologists introduce the gambling casino and thank the roulette wheel for having created an orderly system of betting, when people might otherwise have been at home wagering their Sunday dinners or at church betting on which hymn numbers would come up next week.

Secondly, having reduced society to millions of isolated bargain-hunters (or gamblers), it then insists that they must show great moral responsibility in taking care of themselves and others. Having destroyed the systems through which it was actually in their interests to do so, it now exhorts them to sacrifice themselves for the good of others, pointing out that their strongly competitive instincts require this special kind of ethical motivation if society is to function for the good of all.

I shall argue for a re-emergence of social relations (which are largely invisible to the method of analysis that starts from individual choices in market systems), and for a restoration of their priority as aspects of the good society. But first I must show that such forms of self-interested cooperation are possible.

Notes

1   See for instance, Reinhold Niebuhr, *Moral Man, Immoral Society: a study in Ethics and Politics* (Scribner, 1932), ch. 1.

2   F. A. Hayek, *The Constitution of Liberty* (Routledge and Kegan Paul, 1960), p. 159.

3   Ibid., p. 160.

4   H. B. Acton, *The Morals of Markets: an Ethical Exploration* (Longman/Institute of Economic Affairs, 1971), pp. 16-18.

5   Ibid.

6   Although Acton presents his argument in the form of the previous paragraph, he acknowledges that 'for the system to work, even altruistic people have to look to their own benefit' (Ibid., p. 16).

7   Herbert Simon, 'From substantive to procedural rationality', in S. Latsis (ed.), *Method and Appraisal in Economics* (Cambridge University Press, 1976).

8   Howard Margolis, *Selfishness, Altruism and Rationality: a Theory of Social Choice* (Cambridge University Press, 1982).

9   Adam Smith, *An Inquiry into the Nature and Causes of the Wealth of Nations* (1776), ed. R. H. Campbell and A. S. Skinner (Clarendon Press, 1976).

10 Ibid., bk II, ch. 1.

11 Mancur Olson, *The Logic of Collective Action* (Harvard University Press, 1965).

12 Thomas Hobbes, *Leviathan* (1651), chs XIII-XIX (Collins, 1962).

13 Acton, *The Morals of Markets*, pp. 16-18.

14 James Foreman-Peck, 'Thatcher, the not too eminent Victorians, and private ownership', *Guardian*, 7 August 1987.

15 Acton, *The Morals of Markets*, ch. 4.

16 This kind of argument was first developed by David Hume and Adam Smith.

17 Ralph Harris and Arthur Seldon, *Overruled on Welfare* (Institute for Economic Affairs, 1979)

18 Acton, *The Morals of Markets*, p. 45.

19 John Rawls, *A Theory of Justice* (Clarendon Press, 1972).

3

Cooperation and Self-Interest

My aim in this chapter is to show that a system of voluntary cooperation between self-interested people is in principle possible, and that such a system could exist without a market or a state; but that the formation of markets and states creates systems of interests which erode that form of voluntary cooperation. I shall then analyse the forms of non-market, non-official cooperation that are to be found in modern large-scale societies, and show that they need to be understood in rather different terms from those of the simple communities of pre-commercial and pre-political society.

The point of all this is to show that the new orthodoxy's accounts of cooperation, self-interest and altruism are all misleading, and point to a wrong notion of the place of morality in society. Instead of seeing self-denying altruism as the only alternative to competitive self-interest, we should see the behaviour that is generally taken to be morally praiseworthy – caring, sharing, generosity, peacemaking and so on – as reflecting the kind of cooperation which is self-interested under certain circumstances.

In order to take this line of argument, I must set myself against a tradition of thinking which is much more powerful and long-standing than the new orthodoxy itself. This is the tradition of starting any analysis of society and its institutions from the standpoint of an individual whose interests are already determined by his or her participation in a large-scale commercial nation state. This convention has understandably become the starting point of economics, and particularly the study of models derived from the market hypothesis; but it has also, less excusably, been the starting point of political philosophy and science, which analyse society as made up of individuals with ready-made interests, as citizens and as participants in the economy.

We can trace this tendency at least as far back as Hobbes, whose picture of human nature as essentially competitive and potentially conflictual was clearly and unapologetically derived from the European society of his day, yet he presented it as having universal and timeless application.[1] As a result, his account of the destructive consequences of individual self-interest, and hence the need for the state, put the cart before the horse; he (and others since) have not considered the possibility that these aspects of human nature are the products of societies presided over by states, rather than fixed characteristics of human beings.

The tradition which started with Hobbes has accordingly taken little account of other social sciences, and particularly social anthropology, whose studies of systems of cooperation might have led to a different understanding of self-interest and of altruism. It ignores the rather obvious point that, if human society had really been as violently competitive as its account suggests, then it would have been unlikely to have evolved and developed, as a system for group living, to the point where markets and states could come into being. Individual self-interest would constantly have frustrated the possibility of those very kinds of cooperation which the new orthodoxy sees as the basis of modern society.

In my alternative account, therefore, I shall pay considerable attention to what we know about cooperation in simple societies, which had neither markets nor states, and to the transformation of interests that has taken place as a result of the emergence of those newer systems. These original forms of cooperation also give important insights into the dynamics of membership groups, which are their equivalent in modern society, and which will be the subject of the second part of the chapter. This in turn will form the first part of my alternative account of the nature of social morality and its place in modern society.

Cooperation between individuals

The first step in my argument is to show that self-interested individuals will cooperate with each other under conditions which are different from those of the commercial market. In particular, I want to demonstrate that cooperation does not depend on making competitive gains at the expense of others or on accumulating advantages over others.

Such a demonstration has been carried out by the American political scientist, Robert Axelrod.[2] He conducted two computer tournaments, designed to test the comparative success of various strategies in a large number of two-player encounters in a simple game. The game, a variant of 'Prisoner's Dilemma', was designed to symbolize self-interested individuals' choices in transactions with others, in which there were opportunities to try to gain competitive advantage or to draw a smaller benefit from cooperation. The two players were given choices of two moves, symbolizing respectively exploitation/defection (A) and cooperation (B). If the first player chose A and the second B, then the first scored five points and the second none – the second had therefore been 'taken for a sucker'. If both chose B, then both scored three points, which represent the benefit of cooperation; and if both chose A, then both scored one (a 'stand off').

In a short game between two players, both would probably have played A on every move, but a longer game of 200 moves offered opportunities for stable cooperation to be established, and hence for higher scores to be achieved. However, it seemed obvious that the highest scores of all would be

recorded by players who feigned cooperation, but occasionally or systematically defected, thus taking the other for a sucker.[3] When Axelrod invited
contestants to enter their computer programmes for his tournament, and
offered a prize to that which recorded the highest score, it seemed that such
opportunistic strategies were likely to be the most successful, and accordingly
many entries adopted this approach.

The surprising result of the first tournament was a victory for a simple
programme called 'Tit for Tat', which opened with a cooperative move, and
after this simply reproduced on the following move whatever the other
programme did in response to its current move. Hence 'Tit for Tat' scored
highly when paired with programmes that were basically cooperative, but was
not easily exploited by programmes which attempted to take advantage by
occasional or frequent defections. Indeed, all the programmes which were
basically cooperative, in the sense that they never defected first, were
relatively successful, and these eight occupied the top positions among the
contestants.

The programmes which tried to gain big pay-offs by playing others for
suckers were all grouped at the bottom of the league, with scores substantially
behind those of the top eight. This was because the cooperative programmes
scored highly with each other (and so gained the benefits of cooperation),
whereas those that attempted to exploit frustrated each other and lost
opportunities to gain from cooperation by provoking retaliation.

Axelrod then organized a second tournament, in which the results and
a detailed analysis of the first were available to contestants, including information about the reasons for successes and failures. Far more entries (62 in
all) were received, and people from a wide variety of academic (and gaming)
backgrounds submitted programmes. Even though 'Tit for Tat' was known to
be the programme to beat, and many contestants must have taken account of
its strategy in order to try to emulate, surpass or counter its success, it was
once again the winner. Once again, cooperative programmes which never
defected first were more successful (all but one of the top 15 programmes),
and would-be exploiters were less successful (all but one of the bottom 15).[4]

It is important to recognize what this experiment showed and what its
limitations were. The way in which the game was set up encouraged players
to be self-interested (winning was the objective and the player with the
highest score was the winner). In this sense it was a competitive game. It also
gave players the opportunity to try to take advantage of each other, and hence
to gain competitively through exploitation/defection. The prospect of this
advantage was enough to tempt around half the contestants to enter programmes which were opportunistic, in the sense that they sometimes defected
first, and it also meant that basically cooperative programmes had to guard
against attempted exploitation.

The interesting thing about the result was that the programme which won
never tried to gain advantage over any other, and never actually scored more
than the programme it was playing with; it won because others did badly with

each other, not because it beat anyone, and because it was not seriously exploited by anyone. It always applied the same simple rule to its interactions, which was reciprocity; it was cooperative and minimally retaliatory. It therefore maximized the gains of cooperation, but avoided the losses of mutual recrimination.

In many ways this was very different from the standard account of how self-interest can lead to voluntary cooperation through markets, and from the new orthodoxy's account of the reconciliation between free choice and cooperation. Those accounts seem to imply that the whole motive for entering into transactions is to maximize individual gain through competition, and thus to achieve cumulative advantage. The cooperation which is achieved within the system is a by-product of competition, not an aim of the participants. The whole point about the 'invisible hand' explanation of how markets lead to optimum outcomes is that they do so without any individual or enterprise intending the good of any other, and each striving only for his or her own good.

The terms of Axelrod's game broke down this distinction between self-interested intention and cooperative outcome by giving a moderate benefit for cooperation. In this way, his game rewarded a rule of conduct which was neither conventionally egoistic nor conventionally altruistic, but which sounded quite like a simple morality. He summarized it as follows:

1 *Don't be envious.* Comparison of success is irrelevant; it is best for both players to do well.
2 *Don't be the first to defect.* Withdrawing from cooperation provokes retaliation, and cooperation my be difficult to restore.
3 *Reciprocate both cooperation and defection.* This maximizes benefits, but minimizes exploitation.
4 *Don't be too clever.* Complex strategies are self-defeating, simple ones are easy to 'read' and more productive of trust.[5]

This suggests that what we have come to see as self-interest (the pursuit of individual advantage through competition with others) is only one form of self-interested behaviour. Those who followed its dictates in Axelrod's game (e.g. by opportunism) thought they were acting in their own interests, but turned out to be wrong; this form of egoism was self-defeating. It also suggests that the new orthodoxy's claim that self-interest can only lead to cooperation through markets is wrong. The behaviour that it calls self-interest (or 'rational egoism') is the *consequence* of the way that markets structure rewards and allow the exchange of goods and services. Rather than markets being a solution to the problem of egoistic, competitive human beings, egoism and competition are solutions to the problems of living in commercial societies.

One important feature of these societies which was absent from Axelrod's game is the possibility of carrying over competitive gains (whether these result from luck or skill) into the next round of interactions with others, and ultimately of converting these into assets which give additional competitive advantages. In Alexrod's game, even where one player was scoring more points than the other, this made no difference to their opportunities in the next move; in this sense, both were always equal, and both faced exactly the same choices and constraints at every stage of the game. His experiment showed that, far from the possibility of such cumulative advantage being a necessary condition for cooperation among self-interested individuals, as the new orthodoxy would claim, the absence of it is one of the factors which can allow cooperation under competitive conditions.

But it is also very important to recognize the limitations of Axelrod's demonstration. The most serious of these is that his game consisted of encounters between individuals - a series of two-player games - whereas markets can be represented as multi-player games. Hence, markets appear to be much better representations of large, impersonal societies and the social relations that characterize them. In the next section I shall suggest ways in which it might be possible to develop Axelrod's account of the possibility of stable cooperation, and of its spontaneous development in societies made up of two-person interactions, into systems of cooperation between groups.

Secondly, Axelrod's demonstration shares a limitation of the market account of cooperation; both are entirely abstract formulations, with no substantial content. Both may therefore turn out to be unreliable guides to real-life interactions and their outcomes. We need to have much clearer ideas about the processes of cooperation, their efficiency, effectiveness and so on.

Thirdly, whereas we know a great deal about how the abstract market model applies to the problems of producing and exchanging material goods and services, and most of what we know suggests that it is a highly efficient system of allocating resources under certain conditions, we know much less about how Axelrod's demonstration might be applied to those same activities. In the following section and in chapter 4 I shall suggest that there are strong reasons for doubting whether cooperation, in Axelrod's sense, is an efficient system for maximizing outputs under modern economic conditions. However, some forms of cooperation, I shall argue, are necessary conditions for a good society.

Reciprocity and cooperation

Although Axelrod's demonstration was abstract, and conducted only in terms of two-person transactions, it seems probable that it contained at least some of the necessary elements for stable cooperation between groups of self-interested individuals. This is because two-person and two-group reciprocity have been apparently universal features of those societies which for millennia existed without a market and without a state: simple, traditional societies. The simplest of these, hunter-gatherers, were (and in a few places still are) communities in which forms of reciprocity provided the basis of harmony within the group.

Anthropologists have distinguished between several forms of reciprocity in such societies, of which two are the most important for our purposes.[6] The first is *generalized reciprocity*, in which people give gifts and perform services for each other unconditionally, in the general expectation that similar gifts and services will at some time be returned, but without any specific requirement of when or how much or even ultimately whether this does occur. This takes forms which are recognizable in modern society, including help, care, generosity, sharing and hospitality.

The second is *balanced reciprocity*, which is a direct exchange of gifts or services, which are of roughly equal usefulness, and where there is an expectation that the reciprocal offer will be made in a fairly short time. If the gift or service is not returned in a balanced way, within the usual period, then the relationship is disrupted; hence this form of reciprocity is conditional and temporary.

Axelrod's rule of 'Tit for Tat', which was the most successful of the cooperative strategies, sounds very much like balanced reciprocity, since cooperation was conditional on an immediate response in kind, and retaliation followed instantly and automatically where there was a single defection. In this sense, 'Tit for Tat' was the equivalent of 'an eye for an eye and a tooth for a tooth', since it never forgave a defection until a new offer of cooperation was forthcoming.

However, Axelrod did distinguish certain circumstances in which a more generalized reciprocity (which forgave single defections by 'turning the other cheek') was actually more successful than 'Tit for Tat'. His rule of always reciprocating both cooperation and defection was qualified by the important proviso that 'the precise level of forgiveness that is optimal depends on the environment. In particular, if the main danger is unending mutual recriminations, then a generous level of forgiveness is appropriate. But if the main danger is from strategies that are good at exploiting easygoing rules, then an excess of forgiveness is costly.'[7]

Indeed, to illustrate this point, Axelrod showed that a programme he called 'Tit for Two Tats', which allowed one defection without retaliation, would have won his first tournament (in which the exploitative programmes were relatively crude), but did only moderately well in the second round because there were sophisticated programmes which were aimed at taking advantage of forgiveness. In other words, something more like a New Testament version of acceptable retaliation (given that we only have two cheeks) is the most successful strategy of self-interest in social environments where there are no individuals seeking out such patterns in order to exploit them.

This is not altogether surprising. Both in simple societies and in the modern world, people are most likely to engage in generalized reciprocity among known and trusted kin and friends; indeed, anyone who was unwilling to overlook a single lapse as uncharacteristic would be regarded as a rather fierce and forbidding friend or kinsman. Balanced reciprocity is more commonly the rule among acquaintances or neighbours. But the importance of Axelrod's demonstration, and its link with the studies of simple societies, is again in showing that such ways of behaving are self-interested, in the sense of rational choices for the individual, and do not require an entirely different motivation (altruism) from that which informs actions in all other spheres (egoism).

However, these two-person reciprocal transactions are not the only feature of cooperation within simple societies; in fact, it is probably easier and clearer to refer to these transactions as 'reciprocity', and to reserve the term 'cooperation' for joint activities which involve groups of people engaging in purposeful work, from which all can expect to benefit. In these many-person organized activities, problems about self-interest arise which are not dealt with in Axelrod's game. These concern the incentives for 'free-riders' to try to do less than their share of the work, and to try to gain more than their share of the benefits. As in the way that the free-rider problem is a feature of market systems, the difficulties are clearest in the case where the goods produced by cooperation are such that no individual can be excluded from benefiting from them, such as defence, law and order and a healthy environment.

Once again, there is no shortage of anthropological and historical evidence that for most of the history of mankind, people have in fact cooperated in hunting, in building shelters, in settling disputes and in protecting their communities from outside attacks. Nor is it difficult to see why, in the absence of differentiated economic and social roles, and of a state which had a monopoly of organized force, it was in their interests to do so.

However, this form of cooperation for mutual benefits by all the members of a group is only a rational choice for each individual (or household) if all others take their share of the burdens and efforts required. Hence, as Michael Taylor has pointed out in his account of self-governing communities, the individual's cooperation is conditional on others' participation, which needs to be ensured, both by checking that it does occur and by exhortation or shaming if it does not.[8] Hence Taylor argues, and it has been widely accepted, that the voluntary cooperation which provides such public goods as order, defence and communal buildings, from which all members of simple societies benefit, requires small, face-to-face communities. Only if individuals can reinforce informally the obligations on all others, through personal relations, will it be in their interests to contribute to these public goods.[9]

In reality, systems of reciprocity and cooperation are intertwined in simple societies; for example, cooperation in hunting, and both sharing food and giving food are almost universal features.[10] In many, members of the community present crops or animals to a chief, who has no formal power, but who acts as a focus for both cooperative activity and reciprocity by redistributing these donations to members.[11]

Taylor points out that, in so far as each individual has an interest in sustaining the cooperation of all others in the community, none has an interest in gaining competitive advantage over the rest. This is because cooperation depends on maintaining a rough equality between all the participants. Hence, any individual who does gain a chance advantage will usually choose to share his gains with others.[12] This corresponds with Axelrod's finding that attempts to gain competitive advantage are counterproductive in an environment in which cooperation gains modest rewards and opportunism provokes instant retaliation.

The other reason why competitive behaviour is often disadvantageous in simple communities is that there is neither the technology nor the social system to turn gains into advantageous assets. Surpluses of food, for example, can neither be stored nor sold; they cannot be turned into better tools, or used to obtain more or better land, since there are neither innovations nor markets.[13] The result is that those who have access to better resources or more labour power simply work less, or share what they have with others who are less favourably endowed.[14] This corresponds to the rule in Axelrod's game that competitive gains cannot be translated into cumulative advantages, so that the would-be defector or exploiter has more to fear from retaliation than to gain from opportunism.

Finally, the other threat to cooperation in simple communities comes from their growth beyond the size at which informal methods of monitoring each others' cooperative efforts can be sustained, and where competition and defection become more prevalent. Where this occurred in simple societies, and where land and other resources were plentiful, a group formed a new community by moving to other territory, thus defusing conflict over work-shares and competition for resources.[15]

In this section I have tried to show that the rule of behaviour embodied in Axelrod's 'Tit for Tat' reciprocity, whose basis he summarized in terms of what sounded like a simple morality, corresponds closely with the self-interested cooperative actions of individuals in simple communities. In modern terms, we might characterize behaviour which consistently shares resources, meets others' needs and refrains from opportunism and competitive advantage-seeking as moral because it is so different from what we recognize as self-interested behaviour in modern society (or at least in its economic sphere). But in the circumstances of simple communities, where relations between individuals could readily be represented in terms of Axelrod's game, such rules of conduct are self-interested, rational choices and lead to spontaneous non-market cooperation.

States and markets

For as long as hunter-gatherer communities could continue to split and move into new territory, human beings could establish self-interested systems of cooperation without authority.[16] If it had not been in individuals' interests either to share or to go their separate ways, then millennia of such communities, based on persuasion without power, would have been impossible. But in various parts of the world, further splitting-off was blocked, either because of geographical barriers or because the land was too poor to sustain life.[17] At this point, it seems that two adaptations in social relations took place, more or less simultaneously.

On the one hand, crops were cultivated, which allowed a territory to support a larger population. On the other, some tribes began to compete with others for territory by warlike means.[18] Up to this point, it seems that hunter-gatherers probably had the technological knowledge to grow crops, but had chosen not to, preferring their existing lifestyle and diet: the only advantage of agriculture being that of providing more food from a given area.[19] Similarly, war appears to have been unknown because communities were able to sustain their separate identities with little more than ritual threats and because the spoils of war were negligible.[20] But as soon as one tribe organized for war, it gave others in the region little choice but to do the same.[21] In organizing for inter-communal conflict, human society began for the first time the struggle for power which has characterized it ever since.

These two developments were obviously linked and interdependent. The institutional arrangements for arming and sustaining warriors (government) required the extraction of a surplus from food production, which was made possible by agriculture and exchange.[22] The existence of fixed territorial systems of food production and markets made conquests attractive, since the conquering tribe could exact a tribute in food (or eventually money) to feed a larger army.[23] In order to resist the threat of conquests, communities needed to be larger (and hence organized round more efficient food production made possible by markets) and better defended (which required an authoritative organization and the penetration of power into communal life).[24]

With these enormous institutional changes in the structure of human societies, individual interests were fundamentally altered. Whereas individuals had had an obvious interest in cooperating to provide communal facilities, they now had an apparent interest in trying to minimize their contribution to the state, unless they were forced to do so (the free-rider problem). If a household or a village could avoid providing food or soldiers, but gain the benefits of state defence and order, then it would be rational to choose to do so. Whereas individuals had had an obvious interest in sharing before, they now had an apparent interest in accumulating property and maximizing competitive advantage.

So the human dilemma that Hobbes identified as part of the 'state of nature' – that competitive, power-seeking individuals had no interest in cooperation, in keeping promises, in telling the truth and no reason to trust each other – was in fact a product of the institutions of the market and the state. In the 'Leviathan trap', no individual has a reason to choose the first cooperative move because all must expect to be exploited, so there is no end to mutual mistrust and conflict.[25] Hobbes's answer was an all-powerful state, which enforced cooperation by punishing defection. But it was the state which, by turning cooperative goods into public goods, and protecting accumulation rather than sharing, actually created the 'Leviathan trap'.

We can therefore trace to this crisis in human history the oldest forms of social conflict - between rulers and ruled, and between rich and poor. Though the two are obviously linked, it seems that the former was the older and more fundamental division because power (based on military might) can ultimately overcome wealth unless it is deployed for defensive purposes: in ancient terms, Genghis Khan could conquer Imperial China; and in modern terms, West German colour televisions and BMWs could not stop Russian tanks reaching the Rhine.[26] But rulers' interests, and hence the relations between power and wealth, depend on the nature of the society that is ruled.

If an economy is efficiently organized, and the latest technology is being used to maximize the social surplus, then it is in the interests of rulers to 'sell' public good to society, through taxes, and to minimize overt coercion, which would merely provoke resistance and tax evasion. But if an economy is backward, and its economic potential is not being fully exploited, then it is in rulers' interests (whether they are external conquerers or internal ruling factions) to use compulsion to restructure it, to create new institutions, interests, public and private goods.[27] The latter applies as much to a colonial power's reorganization of a Third World economy in line with capitalist priorities as to Stalin's forced collectivization and industrialization of the USSR or to Mrs Thatcher's dismantling of British social democracy.

Within the economy, competitive advantage was attained by those who could convert gains into productive assets. But eventually a whole structure of institutions was created - property, enterprises, skills, jobs - through which gains could be consolidated and protected. The possession and defence of assets became part of the competitive struggle, and large coalitions of interests (classes) formed around the broad movements of these contests. Individual interests refer to positions in relation to these assets, as well as to market choice.

There is no single, simple formula to explain the relation between the sets of interests created in a social system based on markets and the state. Power-based relations (domination) and asset-based relations (exploitation) can combine in many forms. In the simplest of these, the system of rule is militaristic and supports rich warlords in their coercive economic exploitation of the peasantry. Under early capitalism, political domination was separated from exploitation, and the new class of industrialists paid the state to provide a legal and infrastructural system which allowed them to manufacture for profit. The modern state 'sells' a much larger volume of public goods directly to individuals, who pay either through taxes (the system developed under social democracy) or through tight controls over work and wages (that of existing East European socialism).

From these combinations arise all the paradoxes of modern social relations. Hobbes thought that there were 'natural laws', that individuals should keep the peace, treat others as they wish to be treated, respect promises and so on;[28] yet he considered that they would only keep these under threat of punishment. On the one hand, every society praises voluntary cooperation as the basis of the best social order; yet all recognize that rational individuals will not choose to cooperate under their systems. Instead, all rely on some combination of compulsion and competition to achieve their major goals, and appeal to morality for whatever is left. Even in those matters which affect groups living closely together, reciprocity, trust and cooperation are seen as requiring self-sacrifice, and those social goals which cannot be achieved through markets – whether the proper care of children or the avoidance of unsightly litter – are enforced by law and official intervention.

Membership and sharing

Yet clearly reciprocity, sharing and cooperation do occur in modern societies, and not merely through institutions with strong values of self-sacrifice. On the contrary, cooperation is still self-interested under certain circumstances, which depend on the interests created by markets and the state. Although the major social systems have eroded common interests in the goods created by simple communities, groups, associations and organizations still flourish, and provide many of the goods which individuals value.

Since Hobbes, both political and economic theory have been concerned with explaining how particular combinations of coercive and competitive relations occur, the institutions to which they give rise and how these serve individual and group interests. They have also argued over the justification of particular distributions of resources and assets, and over why – despite the predominance of compulsion and competition within the social order – individuals should choose to share and cooperate with others within certain forms of association.

The theoretical approach to these issues which underpins the new orthodoxy is based on the simple idea that society's institutions, and the combination of systems which compose social relations, can be explained, analysed and criticized in terms of choices by self-interested individuals. Yet within the theoretical literature there is very little agreement over how to take the very first step in such an analysis: extending it from the economic sphere into political and social systems.[29] For example, there is a puzzle about the fact that fairly large proportions of the electorate actually turn out and vote at an election, since – for an individual who calculated his utilities in the market manner – the effort of getting to the polls is so great in relation to the potential effect of a single vote among so many thousands.[30]

The key to unlocking these puzzles lies in modifying the idea that individuals calculate their utilities in isolation, like someone drawing up a shopping list before going to a supermarket in a strange town. Much of social life is not like this; we are directly involved with others, discussing, negotiating, bargaining, arguing, listening, writing and reading others' views. As part of this process, we are able to draw up our own terms of participation in social systems, and agree them with others. Associations and communities are not like shops precisely because there is not a price list of the goods we can select according to our preferences; rather, we participate in creating goods, which only come into existence through a rather messy process, in which how we contribute, debate and compromise is more important in determining the outcome than our calculated preferences or the time and energy we allot. We cannot (for example) understand membership of a tenants' group in the same terms as subscribing to a national charity, since what the group is and does depends on how the members act together and define their mutual interests.

Individual choice models deal in pure private goods (which are bought and sold in markets) and public goods, which are 'bought' by isolated social actors in a large anonymous, market-like society. The puzzle is then to explain why individuals seem to make choices in which they could have done better by ignoring the effects of their decisions on others. Hypotheses about altruism or unconscious group-orientated mechanisms (implanted by evolution or an innate sense of fair play) are then introduced to explain these apparent anomalies.[31] The choices cease to be puzzling once we see that people perceive themselves as members of groups with common interests, who can act together to create goods of their own and share them according to their own criteria.

So I am arguing that people can and do cooperate in the creation of the common good because they have an interest in enhancing the quality of their life together. We do not yet live in private cells, sealed away from the influences of others, from which we send telecommunications about our preferences, ordered from an electronic price list and delivered by remote-controlled transport modules. We do not subscribe to others' needs by banker's order, nor yet by lighting a candle for them in our cells. We inhabit (for much of our lives) a public domain, which we share with our neighbours and fellow citizens. We only know about our needs and theirs through our relations with them in this domain, and so we only know about our interests through discussing the problems and possibilities which our shared world gives us. In all this, we and they have common interests in the common good.

But clearly we do not all have the same interests. As successful or unsuccessful bargain-hunters in the economic sphere, we acquire income, wealth, skills and other assets. These, and our roles in formal systems, shape our interests in public goods, both those provided by the state and those supplied through voluntary organizations. Because of markets and political systems, we do not meet as equals in the public domain, but as bearers of assets and roles and with the interests these give us.

Interests, assets and power

In a society which is organized around accumulating material assets and political power, interest groups (people with common interests) form around the possession of material wealth and political influence. In competition for advantage, coalitions of interests are formed, and individuals perceive their choices in terms of membership of these groups and coalitions. Under these circumstances, membership groups seek to exclude non-members from the benefits of belonging to groups with a share in an asset which gives a material or power advantage.

As markets and political systems have become more important features of social relations, and as informal communal cooperation has dwindled in its apparent significance (because its contribution to social life is not measurable in terms of money or power), so exclusive membership groups have tended to replace inclusive communal groups. This in turn has meant that state-provided public goods have been created as substitutes for informal communal goods, and that political societies have used the terms of citizenship as substitutes for the common interests of communities.

Here is a brief example. In rural England, between the thirteenth and sixteenth centuries, a growing commercialism and extensive private property rights coexisted with continuing communal institutions.[32] On the one hand, there was a flourishing market in land, and a substantial proportion of those who owned land were rich enough to employ paid labour. On the other, those who owned no land had enough continuing common rights and - especially after the Black Death - were in sufficiently short supply as labourers to gain a subsistence living. Central government was remote and unreliable, so these rather isolated village communities had to preserve ways of getting by during bad harvests, epidemics or natural disasters. There is plenty of evidence that these took the form of sharing between all members of the community, and especially the sharing of foodstuffs which would (under normal circumstances) have been marketed.[33] By the second half of the sixteenth century, the process of commercialization had gone so far, local economies had been so absorbed into the national economy, labourers had become so vulnerable to inflation and to fluctuations of demand for their services, that common interests in the local community were in danger of breaking down. At this point, an increasingly ambitious and interventionist central government stepped in to order each parish to provide relief for the poor (and punishment for the idle), using a compulsory public system to replace the previous voluntary communal one.

Exclusive membership groups are organized so as to reserve for their members the benefits of their cooperation; and so as to defend common interests in a resource, asset or status. Business people form chambers of commerce, professional people form associations to promote their interests, and workers with common skills form trade unions. Many of the rules governing these groups are designed to forbid members to compete with each other for the sake of individual short-term advantages. Lawyers and doctors are not allowed to advertise, trade unionists are not allowed to blackleg or accept work at less than the union-negotiated rate of pay, and claimants' union members are not allowed to collude with official distinctions between 'deserving' and 'undeserving' claimants or to undermine each other's claims.

But exclusive groups also often provide their members with the kinds of benefits which were previously created by inclusive communities. They allow individuals to pool risks, and share the advantages that flow from cooperation, and from their common resource or skill. They appeal to common interests, so as to provide mutual support and to redistribute between more and less fortunate members.

The rules of membership groups are concerned with fairness rather with maximization. They define the contributions that are required of members and the benefits they can receive, but seldom define the latter in terms of the former. Rules of fairness are often complex, involving rights (benefits derived from the terms of membership), merit (benefits connected with special efforts on behalf of the group or achievements from which the group has gained advantage) and needs.[34] For example, the early trade unions, friendly societies and cooperatives had complex rules, which broadly embodied the principle that members should contribute when they were in work and benefit when they were unavoidably out of work, but with special provisos about workers sustaining the standards of the trade and provision for special hardship and exceptional need.

All this implies that individuals in complex modern societies continue to have common interests with others which allow them to cooperate in ways which are quite unlike markets or political systems and which concern formal or informal ways of sharing and helping each other. But it also implies that there is a serious problem in such societies over relations between such interest groups. This is because large-scale societies are organized around competition for money and power, and common interests (in groups and coalitions of groups) are shaped by this search for competitive advantage.

Conclusions

In this chapter I have argued that cooperation is in individuals' interests, where they can retain basic equality in their relations (competitive advantage cannot be accumulated), where relations can be negotiated (rather than coercively imposed) and where individuals or groups can withdraw and form new cooperative associations if negotiations break down. In other words, cooperation depends on equality, 'voice' (participation) and 'exit' rights. Where these exist, rational individuals will choose to cooperate in creating common goods.

I have also argued that competitive (market) and coercive (power) relations undermine the possibility of cooperation, and gradually replace communal societies by the familiar modern economic and political systems. The supposed impossibility of self-interested cooperation, other than in impersonal market exchange or compulsory public goods, is in fact a creation of modern social relations.

Does this men that material accumulation and power-seeking must necessarily supplant cooperation and sharing in all social relations? Not necessarily.

It might be possible to use power to create common interests in cooperation and sharing, by bringing about conditions favourable to the recreation of communities and mutal assistance. Under these circumstances, the scope for self-interested cooperation would be increased.

Clearly, from the history of modern societies, market relations have offset power relations and vice versa. State power has been used to prevent accumulation of private wealth (especially in existing socialist countries) and market systems have replaced state services (in Western countries, and most recently also in Eastern Europe). But there have also been attempts to redistribute wealth and power for the sake of greater equality, to enable participation, cooperation and a sense of membership and fairness.

Here again we run into a paradox because justice and fairness have traditionally been seen as *alternatives* to power, or ways of reducing the corrupting effects of power. On the one hand, the use of coercive power ('might is right') is taken to be the opposite of justice. But, on the other, justice requires equality, and where there is no equality, power relations prevail. Thucydides reported that the Athenians, in ordering the Melians to surrender (they were later slaughtered), pointed out, 'You know as well as we do that right, as the world goes, is only in question between equals in power, while the strong do what they can and the weak suffer what they must.'[35] If power is the mark of inequality, and justice requires equality, how can power create justice?

The answer is presumably that it can only do so if the powerful recognize that their own institutions of rule are in some sense self-defeating, or if the powerless take power from their rulers and share it more equally. But in a market economy, political power and wealth are likely to be linked, if not actually coordinated. Hence, issues over the redistribution of power also raise questions about the redistribution of material assets.

Democracies are systems in which each adult person has a small stake in political power, through the vote. They probably owe this historically to the need for modern societies to engage their citizens as active participants in mass warfare.[36] But modern voters have material interests in the economy and in public goods (as taxpayers and as consumers). If justice is concerned with the good of all (rather than with that of particular interest groups), then democracy will only deliver justice if a majority of voters have an interest in the common good.

This brings us neatly back to the question of individual choice. The new orthodoxy insists that in politics, as in economics, any enduring system must appeal to the self-interest (and the self-responsibility) of a majority of individuals. In the next chapter, I shall consider what this means in terms of modern society.

Notes

1 'in the first place, I put for a general inclination of all mankind, a perpetual and restless desire of power after power, that ceaseth only in death ... Competition of riches, honour, command, or other power, inclineth to contention, emnity, and war: because the way of one competitor, to the attaining of his desire is to kill, subdue, supplant or repel the other' Thomas Hobbes, *Leviathan* (1651), ch. XI (Collins, 1962). This was the basis of his famous description of the state of nature as a state of war 'where every man is enemy to every man' (ch. XIII).

2 Robert Axelrod, *The Evolution of Co-operation* (Basic Books, 1984).

3 The scoring was arranged so that the players could not do better still by taking turns to exploit each other, so that an even chance of exploitation or being exploited was not as good an outcome as consistent cooperation. Players communicated only through their moves, and hence the only available data to any programme was past interactions with the same player. Hence the strategy which worked best depends on the strategy of the other player. This meant that, in a long series of moves, the future was important, and pay-offs for each move could only be assessed in the light of this likely pattern of future interaction.

4 Axelrod also held subsequent hypothetical tournaments with the same 62 programmes, but with the least successful contestants progressively eliminated, and found that the successes of the first tournament were cumulative. The only opportunistic programme in the top group was eliminated once the weaker programmes disappeared (Axelrod, *Evolution of Co-operation*, p. 52).

5 Ibid., p. 110.

6 See, for example, Marshall Sahlins, *Stone Age Economics* (Tavistock, 1974), ch. 5.

7 Axelrod, *Evolution of Co-operation*, p. 120.

8 Michael Taylor, *Anarchy and Co-operation* (Wiley, 1976), ch. 3.

9 Michael Taylor, *Community, Anarchy and Liberty* (Cambridge University Press, 1982), pp. 65-94.

10 See, for example, Marcel Mauss, *The Gift: Forms and Functions of Exchange in Archaic Societies* (1925) (Routledge and Kegan Paul, 1969), and Colin Turnbull, *The Forest People* (Cape, 1961).

11 See, for example, Raymond Firth, *We, the Tikopia* (Allen and Unwin, 1936); Douglas Oliver, *A Solomon Island Society* (Harvard University Press, 1955); and E. E. Evans Pritchard, *The Nuer* (Clarendon Press, 1940).

12 Taylor, *Community, Anarchy and Liberty*, pp. 103-4.

13 Sahlins, *Stone Age Economics*, pp. 76-7.

14 A. V. Chayanov, *The Theory of Peasant Economy* (Irwin, 1966).

15 Taylor, *Community, Anarchy and Liberty*, pp. 135-6.

16 E. R. Service, *The Hunters* (Prentice-Hall, 1966). 'There is no pecking order based on physical dominance at all, nor is there any superiority-inferiority ordering based on other sources of power such as wealth, hereditary classes, military or political offices' (p. 88).

17 E. R. Service, *Origins of the State and Civilization: the Process of Cultural Evolution* (Norton, 1975).

18 M. N. Cohen, *The Food Crisis in Prehistory: Overpopulation and the Crisis of Agricultural Growth* (Aldine, 1965).

19 Ibid., p. 15.

20 Service, *The Hunters*, p. 60.

21 A. B. Schmookler, *The Parable of the Tribes: the Problem of Power in Social Evolution* (University of California Press, 1984). 'Imagine a group of tribes living within easy reach of one another. If all choose the way of peace, then all may live in peace. But what if all but one choose peace, and that one is ambitious for expansion and conquest? ... Power can be stopped only by power, and if the threatening society has discovered ways to magnify its power through innovations in organization or technology (or whatever), the defensive society will have to transform itself into something more like its foe in order to resist the external force' (p. 21).

22 For the Marxist view of states as arising from surpluses and from class formation, see Frederick Engels, *The Origin of the Family, Private Property and the State* (1893) (Lawrence and Wishart, 1972). For the view that military power led to intensification of production, see Sahlins, *Stone Age Economics*, chs 1 and 2, and M. D. Sahlins and E. R. Service (eds), *Evolution and Culture* (University of Michigan Press, 1960).

23 G. Lenski, *Power and Privilege: a Theory of Social Stratification* (McGraw-Hill, 1966).

24 R. Carneiro, 'A theory of the origin of the state', *Science*, 169 (1970), pp. 733-8; M. H. Fried, *The Evolution of Political Society* (Random House, 1967).

25 Martin Hollis, *The Cunning of Reason* (Cambridge University Press, 1987), ch. 3.

26 Schmookler, *The Parable of the Tribes*, pp. 57 and 111.

27 Ibid., pp. 47-52.

28 Hobbes, *Leviathan*, ch. XIV.

29 See, for instance, J. Harsanyi, *Rational Behaviour and Bargaining Equilibrium in Games and Social Situations* (Cambridge University Press, 1977); A. K. Sen, 'Rational fools: a critique of the behavioural foundations of economic theory', *Philosophy and Public Affairs*, 6 (1977), pp. 317-44.

30 Howard Margolis, *Selfishness, Altruism, and Rationality: a Theory of Social Choice* (Cambridge University Press, 1982), p. 17 and ch. 7.

31 Ibid., chs 3-6.

32 Alan Macfarlane, *The Origins of English Individualism: the Family, Property and Social Transition* (Blackwell, 1978).

33 Sidney and Beatrice Webb, *English Poor Law History: Part I: The Old Poor Law* (1929) (Cass, 1963), ch. 1.

34 Bill Jordan, *Rethinking Welfare* (Blackwell, 1987), ch. 3.

35 Thucydides, *The Peloponnesian War*, trans. Richard Crawley (Modern Library, 1951), V, 90.

36 Samuel Bowles and Herbert Gintis, *Democracy and Capitalism: Property, Community and the Contradictions of Modern Social Thought* (Routledge and Kegan Paul, 1986), ch. 2.

4
Exploitation and Domination

We are now in a position to look at individual choices from a very different point of view. We have seen that people's interests are not 'given'; they are neither biologically determined, nor driven simply by their subjective 'desires'. Still less are they constrained by fundamentally competitive or power-seeking 'instincts'. But they are constrained by social institutions.

These institutions did not evolve through individual choice; they were not selected by our ancestors as the most promising avenues of progress. Rather, they were forced upon human societies by the pressures of food scarcities and overpopulation. Once adopted, both markets and states shaped the interests of individuals and groups, requiring them to accumulate territory, wealth and skill, and to defend these by the use of power. We can only understand individual choices in the light of these (unchosen) economic and political systems; conversely, we can only understand many social activities and associations as attempts to overcome the constraints imposed by these systems.

In this chapter, instead of considering individuals' interests within the rules of the competitive games, I shall look at how it might be in individuals' interests to change the rules of the games. If we think of choices only within the constraints of competition for material advantage and power, then we will quite artificially limit the scope of possible options. But as soon as we grant the possibility of changing the rules, of abolishing certain institutions or creating new ones, then people can be seen to have rather different (and more radical) interests. The history of political and moral thought is largely the story of such exercises – of writers imaginatively changing the rules, and seeing what would happen to those whose choices were most constrained under existing institutions.

In crude terms, what we mean by power is the ability to impose one's choices on others. But, as Lukes has pointed out, the institutional use of power allows some people to determine the range of choices open to others.[1] In this chapter I shall be concerned with the power to choose the rules of the game, and by doing so to limit other people's options. The imaginative exercise (thought experiment) lies in thinking what those people would choose to do if they were not constrained by the rules made by the powerful.

Such a thought experiment is necessarily 'counterfactual'; it involves suspending the realities of everyday existence. After all, power-holders themselves

did not invent the rules of the games that they impose; they in turn are constrained by institutions and by the historical evolution of societies. But (as
a counter to the notion of competitive market and political choices as necessary and 'natural') it is instructive to consider what individuals and coalitions
might do in the absence of the institutional power which rules out certain
choices.

The way the experiment will be conducted is as follows. First, I shall set out
a 'future scenario': an imaginative construction of a future advanced capitalist
society, in which trends already evident in the new orthodoxy will be carried
towards their seemingly logical outcome. The aim is to highlight some of the
social issues emerging in modern Western societies (by exaggeration), and to
identify some of the interest groupings (in terms of assets giving advantages)
which seem to be developing in such societies.

Secondly, I shall analyse the choices that individuals and coalitions within
these institutional positions would make if they were free to change the rules
of the game. In this way, we can not only identify which institutions determine individual choices and how, but also which social actors have power
over which others. In other words, we can see which have 'chosen' participation in social systems (in the sense that they have an interest in the continu-
ation of the rules) and which have 'constrained' participation (in the sense
that they would benefit from a change in the rules).

Finally, I shall consider whether the changes in the rules which would
benefit the constrained participants would be morally justifiable, and on what
grounds. This will lead to a fuller discussion of the concepts of membership
and citizenship.

A future scenario

What follows is a rather stark model of how an advanced Western society
might look by the end of this century. It is deliberately set out in such a way as
to exaggerate and highlight some features of the kinds of societies promoted
by the new orthodoxy, so as to take these towards their logical conclusions.
Hence it is not a prediction about future societies, but a representation of
what such societies might be like if the new orthodoxy were taken at its word.
It is provided in order to raise the issues about chosen and constrained
participation in social relations which are the subject of this chapter.

Here are the possible major sectors of such a society:

1 *The financial sector* This is a large and growing sector, consisting of
banks, insurance companies, pension funds and the headquarters of international enterprises, most of whose production sites are located abroad in the
newly industrializing countries. An efficient financial sector provides
relatively high salaries for a large proportion of professional, managerial and
white-collar workers in our future society.

2 *The industrial sector* Since most labour-intensive manufacturing takes place in the newly industrializing countries, this sector has shrunk to the point where it is providing only 20 per cent of total employment in the economy, and consists mainly of high-tech manufacturing, using robots and microelectronic processes. As a result, jobs in this sector are relatively highly paid, and workers are predominantly white, male, trade-union members.[2]

3 *Private services* Since many of the services previously provided through the state have been privatized, and since employment in such fields as retailing, leisure, catering, personal and domestic services has continued to expand, this sector now provides much the largest source of employment in the economy.[3] The scope for expansion in this sector faced limits arising from difficulties in improving productivity, especially in personal-service occupations; hence greater efficiency and competitiveness was achieved by flexible use of labour power. In the main, this consists of employing a workforce made up of married women and young people, paid wages considerably below those of industry and below subsistence level; this is possible because these people live as part of family units. There is also a very extensive use of part-time, casual and short-term contracts, which reduces the employment costs associated with pension rights, sick pay, holiday pay, redundancy entitlements, etc. Hence the typical worker in this sector is a low-paid, part-time worker, a married woman, the wife of a white industrial worker or public sector manager or administrator.

4 *The public sector* As a result of the changes mentioned above, this sector is far smaller than previously, and employment in it has been transformed. On the one hand, there are managers, supervisors and administrators, with roughly the same pay and conditions as their counterparts in private services (i.e. considerably worse-off than those in the financial or industrial sectors). On the other hand, there are the workers who are providing the residual services for poor people (those services which it was not economic to provide on a market basis, and for those people who cannot afford marketed services). As a result of diminished industrial employment, and the possibility of providing private services through low-cost employment schemes, there remains a large number of unemployed, unskilled, prime age males, often of low educational attainment, or residents of poor neighbourhoods. Because of institutional racism, barring them from decent jobs and housing, many of the latter are black. In order to provide 'training' and 'employment' for this large group, public sector schemes have been developed for all those out of work for over three months. Because of the possible disincentive efforts of unconditional benefits, participation in these forms of 'training' and 'employment' is a requirement for all those able-bodied people claiming social assistance benefits. Hence anyone refusing the 'offer' of a place on one of these schemes loses their entitlement to benefits.[4] This 'workfare' system of compulsory recruitment has become the major route into 'employment' in the public sector. Hence the typical public-sector employee is a black resident of a very poor neighbourhood, doing compulsory low-paid work for the state.

5   *The disabled* This group consists of people with physical or mental handicaps, and elderly people who lack adequate occupational or private pensions. (Those who can pay for the care services they need out of household income really belong in the private services sector as its clients.) They are the clients of the public sector, but constitute a sector of their own because they receive their income from the state in the form of means-tested social assistance payments.

6   *Informal carers* This sector is made up of those people who provide family care (euphemistically known as 'community care') to disabled people, and those providing full-time unpaid care to children. These constitute a separate sector because their title to means-tested benefits (if any) stems from their caring role; alternatively, they are wholly dependent on income from a wage-earning member of the household. Most are the spouses of disabled people or married women whose husbands' earnings are insufficient for them to afford private care services.

Assets and advantages

It is not difficult to imagine that such a society might result from the self-interested choices (both economic and political) of individuals in a present-day advanced capitalist country (such as Britain). It represents, if you like, the kind of institutional pattern of enterprises, employment, public services and family provision which might evolve from a combination of private preferences, electoral and political decisions in the next ten years.

Yet it also seems obvious that some individuals in this future society would enjoy enormous advantages over others, and that people in the disadvantaged categories would not choose to occupy these roles if they had any alternative. In other words, even though the institutional arrangements of the future society might quite feasibly be the result of self-interested choices from within the constraints of present-day institutions and roles (and hence in terms of present-day interests), they could not be seen as 'chosen' by a large proportion of the social actors in the system.

So the question is whether we can specify any way of saying which actors are so constrained by the choices available within social institutions that they would have an interest in creating quite different institutions (providing different choices), and which have such opportunities within this particular set of arrangements that they would oppose any such change. If we can find such a way of distinguishing between categories to those with an interest in changing the rules, and those with an interest in keeping them, then we will have discovered which have chosen and which constrained participation.

A promising approach to this question can be found in the work of John Roemer, in his book *A General Theory of Exploitation and Class*.[5] Roemer's test for whether a particular individual or coalition was *exploited* by another was whether the former would be better-off if the assets relevant to their productive relations were shared out equally, and the individual or coalition then withdrew with their share from the institutional arrangement under which they participated in the system. Conversely, those who would be made worse-off would be *exploiters*. (If it could be shown that some people had an interest in sharing and withdrawing, then clearly others were exercising power in such a way that this option was not open to them because they had an interest in continuing the system.)

Roemer showed that it was possible to devise games which corresponded to each of the major historical modes of production (feudalism, capitalism and socialism) which in turn would yield distinctions between those who were exploiters under each system, and those who were exploited. This enabled Roemer to provide a mathematical demonstration, for example, that under perfectly competitive capitalism, workers could be better-off by withdrawing with their per capita share of wealth, while capitalists would be worse-off; from this he concluded that the existence and extent of capitalist exploitation could be identified, under its own highly abstract assumptions.

This insight was further developed by Erik Wright in his book *Classes*, by showing that Roemer's theory is most useful as a test for identifying exploitation in abstract economic models, but that the definition of exploitation can be stated in terms of the causal influence of the distribution of various assets on the distribution of income.[6] If the unequal distribution of certain assets influences people's incomes, then those who gain from this are exploiters, and those who lose are exploited. This means that exploited people have an interest in redistributing these assets so as to share them equally among all eligible individuals, while exploiters have an interest in keeping the existing distribution.

The difficulty is that these theories have already stretched the conventional meaning of 'exploitation' well beyond its normal limits. As the term is commonly used, exploitation occurs where someone performs a service for someone else, who gets a benefit from that service *and* exerts power over the service-provider. Yet even in Roemer's original account, there were examples of exploitation with no such relations.

In the expanded use of the term, exploitation implies only that some people gain income advantages from the unequal distribution of certain assets, and others lose by this inequality. As we shall see, this allows (as cases of exploitation) social relations which do not involve direct exchange of labour, and assets which are not used in production. The main objections to doing this arise from the analysis of class, which was one of Roemer's original concerns, and which has occupied many of those who have developed his work.[7] Wright argues that the concept of class should be restricted to those groups generated by inequalities in income which stem from unequal ownership of productive forces.[8] But for my purposes this restriction is unnecessary, since my concern is to distinguish between those who have an interest in changing the rules (institutions) and those who have an interest in keeping them. If some of the categories identified in this way stem from non-productive assets, such as colour and gender, then this is important.

But these same unequal holdings of assets also give rise to advantages in terms of power, as well as income. One of the reasons why the exploited cannot change the rules, by altering the institutions through which they lose materially, is that they lack the power to do so.[9] Hence we can identify a second aspect of social relations which may result from unequal distribution of these assets, which will be called *domination*. If equalization of assets would give some people less power, they are dominators, if it would give them more, they are dominated.

This now enables us to distinguish between chosen and constrained participation in a social system. We can define chosen participation as that which someone has an interest in doing under the current distribution of assets, and constrained participation as that which someone does, even though they would have an interest in an egalitarian redistribution of an asset relevant to this system of social relations, and usually because they have no access to the resources they need other than through this system.

What follows is a list of those assets which, in the future scenario, seem to influence the distribution of income and power, and hence to distinguish between two categories of people: those who would lose from equalization of shares of the asset (and therefore have an interest in those institutions which lead to the unequal distribution) and those who would gain, in income and in power, from an equal sharing out of the asset (or from the abolition of the advantages associated with it).

1 *Wealth* In the future scenario, people who own productive resources have incomes from capital assets, and those who do not lack such an income. Accordingly, wealth is an asset which distinguishes between a category of people who would be better-off through redistribution which shared wealth equally among all, and those who would be worse-off. The rich also have better access to positions of authority within the state, and the poor are more likely to be under the control of state agencies, as claimants or 'workfare' employees; hence the poor would gain power from an equalization of wealth.

2 *Control* Bosses control productive processes; workers are controlled. The former organize the division of labour and coordinate productive activities, and this control gives them income advantages over the latter. Managers have power over workers and businessmen have influence over political decisions.

3 *Skills* People who can acquire training in skills get income advantages, especially in the financial and industrial sectors; the unskilled have restricted economic opportunities. Skilled people are able to reach positions of authority in the economy and the state.

4 *Jobs* The institution of employment provides people with full-time, permanent jobs with an asset in terms of income, sick pay, holiday pay, pension rights and prospects of training and promotion. All those who do not have full-time jobs, including part-time casual and short-term workers, are disadvantaged by lacking this asset, and have an interest in a redistribution of

employment. Jobs provide access to authority positions, and hence confer power advantages. For example, people in jobs have the opportunity of gaining positions of power through trades unions and trades councils (for example, positions on social security appeals tribunals).

5 *Maleness* Because men have better access to employment and higher earnings, maleness is an asset which gives its holders income advantages; women have an interest in abolishing the connections between maleness and these advantages. Men have greater opportunities of gaining power in every sphere.

6 *Whiteness* White people, who form the majority, deny black people access to well-paid jobs; hence, whiteness becomes an asset with income advantages, and black people have an interest in dismantling institutional racism by abolishing the connections between colour and these advantages. Similarly, white people hold power over black people in every sphere.

For each of these six assets, it seems that we can now identify a group of people who would be better-off by changing the rules of the game, so as to share out the assets in question, and hence the income and power advantages that stem from them. This, of course, would imply a radical change in the social institutions which the new orthodoxy has promoted. Could such a change be justified?

Disadvantage and redistribution

From the argument of the last section, all that we can say about the future scenario is that certain groups in such a society are exploited (in terms of income distribution) or dominated (in terms of power distribution) because they have an interest in the redistribution of the assets which cause these inequalities. But to be able to say this would not convince an advocate of the new orthodoxy that we had identified a route towards a better society than the one which was set out in the scenario, for the following reasons:

1 Advocates of the new orthodoxy would point out that, although the equal distribution of these assets would make certain groups better-off, it would make other groups (the exploiters) worse-off. Hence, any such redistribution has to be justified in terms of some principle.

2 In the new orthodoxy, the primary principle is freedom of choice, and the individual must be free to follow his or her interests, in order to be regarded as a moral agent. Even though we have shown that some people's participation in this society would be constrained, in the sense that it would be in their interests to redistribute certain assets equally, this redistribution would violate the freedom of choice of the advantaged, since no one should ever be compelled to act for the good of others.

3 Even though the distributions of assets in the future scenario can be shown to cause exploitation and domination, they can also be shown to have

come about by processes which are orderly and peaceful (markets, democratic elections, voluntary agreements, fulfilment of moral obligations). All these processes are consistent with freedom, as defined by the new orthodoxy, which would maintain that freedom under the constraint of exploitation or domination is still superior to the compulsion that would be involved in egalitarian redistribution of assets.

4   According to the new orthodoxy's principles, people are entitled to the property they own, the salaries they earn, the jobs they get or the power they hold by legal means (i.e. competitively, democratically or by agreement, according to the sphere). Redistribution offends against this principle of entitlement, by imposing some arbitrary pattern (such as equality) on distributions, which cannot be justified. If free choice is to be respected, this principle of entitlement to the results of market competition and voluntary agreement must also be respected.[10]

There are plenty of weaknesses in this argument, which need not concern us here.[11] But a stronger challenge to those who are defining exploitation and domination in terms of inequalities in the distribution of assets is to construct arguments for the abolition of these inequalities which do not fall foul of their own standards. For example, how is it possible to bring about an authoritative redistribution of wealth, control, skills, employment, gender and racial assets without substituting new forms of exploitation and domination? Roemer's own analysis of East European socialism shows that it is characterized by skills and status exploitation, and Wright's that it contains organizational exploitation; most analysts would concede that it embodies domination by bureaucrats and members of the Communist party.

Furthermore, it is not at all clear what (if anything) follows from the identification of exploitation and domination in our scenario. Here the advocates of the new orthodoxy would be right to insist that there must be some principle according to which these supposed evils should be reduced. Roemer attempts to do this in relation to exploitation, by appealing to an 'ethical imperative'. He argues that exploitation which is 'socially unnecessary' (in the sense that its elimination would not alter the incentives and institutions of an economy in such a way as to make the exploited worse-off) should be abolished because failing to abolish it would retard 'self-actualization'. In other words, exploitation impedes the economic development that can provide a greater number of people with the material means to choose and follow their life plans. But this appeal to a moral standard comes as a rather unexpected afterthought to his analysis; it is not at all clear why we should apply this particular ethical imperative, rather than (for example) those of the new orthodoxy, to the social relations he has identified.

Redistribution and membership

A more promising approach to this problem seems to lie in the recognition that any notion of egalitarian redistribution appeals implicitly to a concept of *membership*. For example, the definitions of exploitation and domination rest on an imaginary process of giving each member of society an equal share in such assets as wealth, control or employment opportunities. The idea of sharing such assets has no place in a set of principles such as the new orthodoxy because it is constructed entirely in terms of individuals competing for resources and power, and a secondary altruistic morality. But the ways of getting things done that I identified in chapter 3 included membership, along with reciprocity, as the cooperative survivals of the archaic social systems which were described at the start of the chapter.

The new orthodoxy regards the state as an authoritative way of providing public goods in cases of market failure and to deal with 'externalities': by-products of private transactions, such as pollution. But the state might also (or alternatively) be seen as a way of creating common interests in public goods which could be voluntarily supplied, through cooperation. In this case, it would be concerned with bringing about conditions in which people would have interests in working together for the good of all. In this way, the state becomes a kind of membership group for all members of society, sharing common risks and pooling their resources, rather as other membership groups do.

Indeed, this is the only way in which we can make sense of the traditional concern of political theory with ideas of justice, freedom and equality. The language in which we discuss the rights and duties of citizenship is that of a membership group, in which individuals are supposed to cooperate together for common purposes, and to share burdens and benefits fairly, by agreement. It speaks, therefore, of a community bound together by the recognition of interdependence, and of shared needs, whose terms of membership allow negotiated solutions to common problems. In other words, despite the reality of power in large, plural, anonymous societies, both the theoretical and the rhetorical vocabularies of politics appeal explicitly to the common good, in terms of citizenship as membership.

Clearly, there is a perpetual tension between individual interests and common interests in large-scale societies with power-based political systems. The history of liberal political thought and practice is one of a series of balances or accommodations[12] between these two, in which ruling groups seek to justify their own power by permitting a range of individual freedoms which are consistent with the national interest, while at the same time building support for their rule from the most influential interest groups. The new orthodoxy is the latest example of such a balance. Its terms of citizenship are captured in the phrase 'the property-owning democracy', and it thus appeals to the self-interest of those who have this stake in its system to cooperate against those with no such interests. Membership is defined in terms of possession of private goods (explicitly shares and houses, but implicitly also jobs and possibly whiteness), excluding from full citizenship those with no such stake in the system.

By contrast, social democracy's form of citizenship, and hence terms of membership, concerned public goods, based on compulsory contributions. The remarkable convergence of advanced capitalist societies in respect of welfare states – institutional arrangements for including organized labour movements in the political process and providing social services on a redistributive, membership basis to most citizens – suggests that post-war economic conditions in most of these countries (with the partial exceptions of the United States and Japan) made such developments self-interested for the major coalitions in these societies. In Britain, continued loyalty to the National Health Service by a large majority of the population, in spite of its growing costs, and the expansion of private medical care schemes, implies that it still functions as a membership group for British citizens, and that this reflects the interest that most people have in retaining a good quality service for primary health care and for chronic conditions (especially those of old age) which insurance-based schemes have difficulty in providing at reasonable costs.

But the future scenario also shows how the new orthodoxy's principles undermine these welfare systems, by promoting competition between individuals and between enterprises over public goods that were formerly seen as benefits of membership. It indicates that, if these changes continue in the same directions as they are taking at present, the result will be a society in which the membership benefits of citizenship will be minimal for a considerable proportion of the population. Whereas some interest groups will have a strong interest in the social order, there will be a considerable minority of people who are exploited and dominated in several dimensions of their social interaction, and whose participation in society is therefore constrained in every respect. It would seem very appropriate to refer to such people as an 'underclass'.[13]

Does this imply that a majority of citizens will have an interest in a radical redistribution of assets if the future scenario comes into being? Not necessarily, as I shall show in chapter 6. Just as social democracy was able to construct majority interests in public goods, so the new orthodoxy has been able to build a majority stake in private goods. It is quite possible that a coalition of support could persist, despite the exploitation and domination that have been identified, because a majority would have more to lose from sharing with the underclass than to gain from sharing with the advantaged.

But this identification of interests purely in terms of income and power obscures the possibility of membership based on common interests, and of citizenship which builds active and participatory cooperation. In order to see this, we need to find a way of recognizing certain kinds of interests which the new orthodoxy's principles make invisible. This will be the subject of the next chapter.

Conclusions

I started this chapter with the idea of a thought experiment which would help identify interests of a different kind. Given that our interests are shaped by social institutions, how can we tell when people have an interest in changing these, and when they are simply getting by as well as possible within their constraints?

The future scenario provided an exaggerated version of the new orthodoxy's good society, and one which might have been developed from its principles. The idea of sharing out assets provided a way of distinguishing those groups with an interest in maintaining these institutions, and those with an interest in changing them.

But radical change, based on the redistribution of assets, involves over-turning established ideas of ownership and entitlement, and overriding the interests of the rich and powerful. Whereas the new orthodoxy can justify its institutions as having arisen from individual choices, such a redistribution appears coercive and arbitrary.

Another approach to the problems of exploitation and domination lies in the idea of membership. Here sharing is justified by the fact that it creates common interests among citizens of the same society, based on ideas of justice, freedom and equality. Citizenship might allow the members of a large community to cooperate for the common good. In the next chapter I shall investigate this possibility further.

Notes

1 Steven Lukes, *Power: a Radical View* (Macmillan, 1974).
2 Even with 'neutral' assumptions, the main source of an anticipated expansion of some 1.5 million jobs in the British economy between 1986 and 1995 is in business and miscellaneous services (1.4 million), with an anticipated loss of 0.5 million jobs in manufacturing. See Institute for Employment Research, *Review of the Economy and Employment, 1987* (University of Warwick, 1987).
3 Employment in all services in most advanced industrialized countries of the Western world now stands at between 60 and 65 per cent of the employed work-force, of which between a quarter and a third is part-time, mainly by women, in such countries as Britain, The Netherlands, Denmark and Sweden. In most Western European countries, employment in *public* services exceeds employment in manufacturing industry; in Denmark it is more than double. The assumption behind this scenario is a shift from public to private service employment. It is also a shift from full-time to part-time, and from male to female employment. See J. Atkinson and N. Meager, *Changing Working Patterns: How Companies Achieve Flexibility to Meet New Needs* (National Economic Development Organization, 1986).
4 Already in 1987 in Britain, there were about 700,000 people at a time undergoing 'training' or 'employment' in one or other of the Manpower Services Commission's Special Employment Measures. In 1988, the government plans to withdraw supplementary benefits from young people who refuse places on the largest of these, the Youth Training Scheme, and to change the system of 'payment' on the other major scheme (previously called the Community Programme) to relate it to the benefit level, plus expenses. This seems to point the

way towards making all benefits conditional on accepting offers of such schemes. A large proportion of Community Programme projects are already located in public services or in voluntary agencies providing social care. As employment in public services is gradually reduced, and as private services expand, it would seem logical to increase the use of such schemes in the provision of public services.

5   John E. Roemer, *A General Theory of Exploitation and Class* (Harvard University Press, 1982), pt III.

6   Erik O. Wright, *Classes* (New Left Books, 1985).

7   See, for example, Jon Elster, *Making Sense of Marx* (Cambridge University Press, 1985), section 6.1, for a very different development of Roemer's theory of exploitation and class.

8   Wright restricts his account of exploitation to influence on income distribution of unequal distribution of ownership over people (feudal exploitation), unequal distribution of the means of production (capitalist exploitation), unequal distribution of skills (socialist exploitation) and unequal distribution in organizational assets (organizational exploitation). But in his article 'A revolution in class theory' (*Politics and Society*, 15, no. 4, 1987, pp. 453-82), Philippe Van Parijs argues that both maleness and whiteness confer specific advantages in the labour market, and should therefore be seen as assets relevant for defining exploitation. He goes on to argue that having a regular job is also an asset that gives clear income advantages, which are of increasing significance in modern advanced economies. His most novel proposal is of a category of 'job exploitation', which I am adopting as one of my kinds of exploitation here.

9   Van Parijs, 'A revolution in class theory'. He points out, however, that this requires a well-defined concept of power; for example, we must be able to say whether someone's power (command over others) has increased or decreased under changed circumstances, and power itself must be distinguishable from the assets that confer it; for example, rights such as ownership or a managerial role are distinct from the actual giving of commands. Presumably this could be shown by demonstrating that some people with these assets do not get things done by giving commands, but get them done in other (e.g. cooperative) ways.

10 This general line of argument against compulsory redistribution, against patterned distributions, and in favour of an entitlement concept of justice, is that taken by Robert Nozick in *Anarchy, State and Utopia* (Blackwell, 1974).

11 For example, an entitlement theory could be constructed which allowed unequal holdings of wealth, and unequal incomes, but not income inequalities that stem from wealth inequalities: Roemer's is such a theory. See Robert J. van der Veen and Philippe Van Parijs, 'Entitlement theories of justice: from Nozick to Roemer and beyond', *Economics and Philosophy*, 1 (1985), pp. 69-81.

12 See, for instance, Samuel Bowles and Herbert Gintis, *Democracy and Capitalism: Property, Community and the Contradictions of Modern Social Thought* (Routledge and Kegan Paul, 1986). They mention as accommodations between personal and property rights the Lockean (representation tied to property), the Jeffersonian (wider distribution of property rights), the Madisonian (creating political divisions between those without property) and the Keynesian (incorporating those without property into the political process). See also A. O. Hirschman, *Exit, Voice and Loyalty* (Harvard University Press, 1970).

13 See, for instance, Ralf Dahrendorf, 'The underclass and the future of Britain', Tenth Annual Lecture, St George's House, Windsor Castle, 27 April 1987.

5
Citizenship and Social Morality

At the end of chapter 4 we seemed to have reached an impasse. On the one hand, the new orthodoxy was insisting that the distribution of assets which resulted from market-based transactions was justified, and that public goods were only needed where markets failed; hence, the social institutions which evolved through self-interested economic and democratic choices were appropriate for a good society. On the other, the future scenario, taken together with the thought experiment, was suggesting that substantial groups in such a society would suffer (or were already suffering) exploitation and domination, and that a significant minority would be relegated to the position of an underclass, with no self-interested motives for participating in any social sphere. How can we decide whether the redistribution of all or any of the assets which give income and power advantages would be for the common good?

In this chapter I want to locate this question within a long debate about social morality. I shall argue that there is a tradition which has identified membership of society - citizenship - as the basis of the common good, and hence as indispensable to any form of social morality or good society. According to this tradition, the state must ensure that certain assets are distributed in such a way that all citizens have an interest in contributing to, as well as benefiting from, particular social goods. Of course, historically, those bound together by sharing in these goods were not necessarily all the people living in that society, and political power was used to exclude and subjugate groups (women, workers, slaves) not seen as fit for citizenship. The challenge is therefore to see whether this active and egalitarian concept of community can be extended to include all the adult members of a large-scale modern society.

In this tradition, what was meant by citizenship was the sharing with others of the burdens as well as the benefits of certain aspects of social life, so that particular goods could be provided in the ways specific to membership groups. In order to achieve this, the assets most relevant to these goods had to be equalized, or at least made subject to an equal division among equal contributors, to promote sharing and mutual responsibility.

What morality *meant*, in this tradition, was precisely these forms of sharing and mutuality in public goods. There was no clash between citizenship obligations and the duties of private morality because there was no such thing as private morality. People's responsibilities to their fellow citizens, as members of the same society, *were* their moral responsibilities. In this sense, the membership group that provided these goods replaced the archaic community as the basis for cooperation, and the virtues of the good citizen were the kinds of behaviour required to provide public goods.

The great revolution in moral thinking which occurred in the eighteenth century (at first largely confined to Britain and the United States, but gradually spreading to the rest of Europe) was that no such public morality was necessary or possible, and that it could be replaced by a combination of commercial relations and private morality. This was the ancestor of the new orthodoxy, and it allowed much greater inequalities in assets to be morally justifiable.

With this change, the notion of citizenship, while still defining what members of society had in common, came to be quite separate from the idea of morality; and instead of trying to ensure that citizens had an interest in the common good, the state was mainly concerned with allowing them to pursue competitive advantage. The result was that citizenship lost its connections with both morality and self-interest, and came to be exclusively concerned, in liberal theory at least, with the relationship between individual liberty and political authority.

The moral ideal of citizenship enjoyed a brief revival in Britain during and immediately after the Second World War, when its connection with the common good and with social morality was reasserted, though not in a very systematic way. But this revival of the tradition was not developed, and soon decayed. Social democracy did little to promote it because it was more concerned with the expert management of society than with encouraging people to share and support each other in active ways.

In this chapter I shall try to resurrect the traditional association between citizenship and morality, by showing that any effective moral critique of the new orthodoxy must appeal to the concept of citizenship, and that any moral justification of egalitarian redistribution must be based on an attempt to create a common interest in the provision of certain social goods, by ending specific forms of exploitation or domination. This will allow me to propose ways of determining when the egalitarian redistribution of assets would lead to a better society.

Because this view of citizenship as common interest has become largely unintelligible in the language of modern social relations, and is dismissed as fantastical by the new orthodoxy, this chapter will necessarily be an exercise in intellectual archaeology, containing more quotations and references than the rest of the book. The aim is to revive a tradition which has survived - rather like the household articles of earlier civilizations - only in a fragmented form though, unlike these, it is still used by moderns in everyday contexts, largely for rhetorical and polemical purposes. For those with no taste for such exercises, this chapter may be one to skip; a summary of the argument is contained in the conclusion to it.

The republican tradition

The tradition which I want to discuss has a certain continuity and several common features, even though the differences between the authors who can be identified as members of it are as great as the similarities. I have called this the republican tradition, and traced it to classical Greece, though important aspects of it are to be found within a Christian tradition, and among writers from monarchical societies (such as seventeenth- and eighteenth-century Britain). My purpose is to extract features of the tradition, as they appeared in different centuries, so as to build up a picture of its view of citizenship, and to show (very briefly) how this was supplanted by the liberal tradition.

Although the republican tradition can be traced to Plato, its clearest classical exposition is provided by Aristotle. Without attempting to summarize his political theory, I shall simply sketch those elements which seem particularly relevant to the idea of citizenship in the republican tradition.

1 A political community is a shared project; in this sense it is an association, like a household or a membership group, of people committed to a common purpose, to provide themselves and each other with certain goods. 'Every polis (or state) is a species of association . . . all associations aim at some good; and the particular association which is the most sovereign of all, and includes the rest, will pursue this aim most, and will thus be directed to the most sovereign of all goods.'[1] 'All associations are in the nature of parts of the political association. Men journey together with a view to some particular advantage, and by way of providing some particular thing for the purpose of life; and similarly the political association seems to have come together originally, and to continue in existence, for the sake of the *general* advantage which it brings.'[2]

2 The people who join together to form a political community have a bond to each other; sharing is an essential part of this relationship. 'Every form of friendship involves association . . . The form of friendship which unites fellow citizens - or fellow tribesmen, or fellow voyagers - is more in the nature of a pure association, since it seems to rest on a sort of compact.'[3] 'Not being self-sufficient when they are isolated, all individuals are so many parts all equally depending on the whole (which alone can bring about self-sufficiency). The man who is isolated - who is unable to share in the benefits of political association, or has no need to share because he is already self-sufficient - is no part of the polis, and must therefore be either a beast or a god.'[4]

3 The political community aims to achieve the common good of its members. Every activity and association has aims and purposes, and the state has the aim of achieving what is good. 'The good life is the chief end, both for the community as a whole and for each of us individually.'[5] 'In all arts and sciences the end in view is some good. In the most sovereign of all the arts and sciences - and this is the art and science of politics - the end in view is the

greatest good and the good which is most pursued. The good in the sphere of politics is justice; and justice consists in what tends to promote the common interest.'[6]

4   Membership of a political community (citizenship) is an active, not a passive process; the members must rule themselves. 'He who enjoys the right of sharing in deliberative or judicial office (for any period, fixed or unfixed) attains thereby the status of a citizen of his state.'[7] 'The citizen in this strict sense is best defined by the one criterion, "a man who shares in the administration of justice and the holding of office".'[8] 'Claims to political rights must be based on the ground of contribution to the elements which constitute the being of the state.'[9] 'When the condition of a state is constructed the ruler shares in the general benefit by virtue of being himself a member of the citizen body.'[10]

5   Power used to activate commitment to the common good is self-rule, the collective ability to achieve the goals of the community. Power used by individuals or groups to rule over others for their own advantage is tyranny. 'Those constitutions which consider the common interest are *right* constitutions, judged by the standards of absolute justice. Those constitutions which consider only the personal interests of the rulers are all *wrong* constitutions, or *perversions* of the right forms.'[11] Men are 'drawn together by a *common interest*, in proportion as each attains a share in good life (through the union of all in a form of political association).'[12]

What is striking about these ideas is that the state is treated as being an association, much like those modern membership groups in which people commit themselves to the shared pursuit of excellence in some form of much-loved game or much-prized expertise. Alasdair MacIntyre refers to these associations as 'practices', and defines them as involving standards which are intrinsic to the activities, and which are constantly extended.[13] 'A practice involves standards of excellence and obedience to rules as well as the achievement of goods. To enter into a practice is to accept the authority of those standards and the inadequacy of my own performance as judged by them.'[14] Furthermore, the goods pursued in practices 'are indeed the outcome of competition to excel, but it is characteristic of them that their achievement is a good for the whole community who participate in the practice.'[15] In other words, the pursuit of the good created by the association is for the benefit of all, and all members rule and are ruled by each other in relation to standards of excellence.

But Aristotle makes it clear that there is nothing altruistic about this association. The goods provided by the political community are essential to human life, and the benefits of citizenship are mutual. He also makes it clear that the common good is not something that is achieved by individuals setting aside their own interests - it is the common interest. A good constitution is one which ensures that all citizens continue to have a common interest in the good of all, and do not use political power to further the interests of particular cliques or groups (such as the rich).

He discusses various ways in which this can be done (and was done in the Greek city states) including equalization of property, sharing income and giving military service, but reaches no definite conclusions about these. Later writers following in the same tradition were more prescriptive about ways in which participation in and contribution to the common good was best achieved, and how forms of equalization among citizens could maintain the practices of their association (self-rule and justice).

For example, Machiavelli was both more sophisticated and more pessimistic about the relationship between the common interest and the interests of individuals and groups. He believed that there was a cycle of good governments replacing bad and vice versa. A bad, power-seeking tyrant was overthrown by citizens who 'conducted themselves according to the laws they laid down, subordinating all of their advantage to the common good, and with the greatest diligence cared for and preserved things private and public'.[16] But the next generation, 'refusing to content themselves with equality among citizens, but turning to avarice, to ambition, to violence against women, caused a government of the best men to become a government by the few, without having any regard to civil rights'.[17] His proposed solution to this cyclical pattern was to have a 'mixed government', made up of princedom, aristocracy and popular government, such as republican Rome had been; 'the condition of that republic became firmer, since then all of the three types of government had their shares.'[18] Rome's liberties were preserved by continuous strife between the people and the senate, each guarding its share of power. 'The aspirations of free people are seldom harmful to liberty, because they result either from oppression or from fear that there is going to be oppression.'[19] Whereas nobles long to rule, the people merely long not to be ruled. 'Hence, if the common people are set up to guard liberty, it is reasonable that they will care for it better, and since they cannot seize it themselves, they will not allow others to seize it.'[20]

Thus Machiavelli saw the state as constantly having to preserve a balance between competing interests in order to create a common interest in freedom and good government. He also thought that the state should keep its citizens ready for military action in defence of their country, or to expand its territory, and that this demanded an active, participatory citizenry, which made good government more difficult.[21] The most favourable circumstances for good government occurred when the citizens were hard-working (because they were relatively poor), freedom-loving and militarily active. But even favourable circumstances and a good constitution would not guarantee good government over time because circumstances changed. Hence Rome, which had 'the basic organisation of the government or of the state; and after that the laws which, along with the magistrates, restrained the citizens',[22] fell into corruption, because Roman victories abroad made the people complacent, and they allowed powerful rather than good men to take office. But with this corruption of the people, 'basic customs' which once were good for Rome became bad for it, and the constitution was undermined. Machiavelli's notorious advice to princes is probably best understood as a guide for a new ruler in a corrupt state, where power alone could, through a type of moral entrepreneurship and innovation, recreate a common good. In such circumstances, the prince should be guided by 'reasons of state', the interests of society as a whole, as brought into being by an innovative ruler.[23]

Although Rousseau's account of the origins of society was utterly different from Aristotle's, he was equally concerned that the citizens of a state should be able to form a general will for the common good. But whereas Machiavelli was chiefly concerned with the corrupting effects of greed for power, Rousseau was concerned with those of greed for possessions. Differences of property divided society into classes with opposing interests; this made its members incapable of forming a general will. Hence the state should take over the property of its citizens, and distribute it so that all could be small independent producers. As far as land was concerned, 'a man must occupy only the amount he needs for his subsistence', so that 'no citizen shall ever be wealthy enough to buy another, and none poor enough to be forced to sell himself' (as a waged labourer).[24] This would prevent dependence and exploitation. 'It is one of the most important functions of government to prevent extreme inequality of fortunes; not by taking away wealth from its possessors, but by depriving all men of the means to accumulate it; not by building hospitals for the poor, but by securing the citizens from becoming poor.'[25]

But Rousseau was writing in the context of an emerging commercial society, in which material interests in competitive gain were not so lightly dismissed. He recognized that there would be, in such societies, a perpetual tension between cooperative common interests and competitive self-interest. This was not so much a conflict of interests as a conflict of priorities between different kinds of interest.

> For every individual as a man may have a private will contrary to, or different from, the general will that he has as a citizen. His private interest may speak with a very different voice from that of the public interest; his absolute and naturally independent existence may make him regard what he owes to the common cause as a gratuitous contribution, the loss of which would be less painful for others than the payment is onerous for him.[26]

In other words, individuals are always in danger of relapsing into competitive self-interest, if they are not involved as active members in processes which identify and pursue their common interests with others. Social institutions (including, so Rousseau thought, compulsion) should ensure that people were constantly reminded of their citizenship, and of the general interests which were fostered by public life, and which withered if citizens reverted to a pursuit of individual gain. It was in the nature of commercial life that it obscured common interests in the quality of life, and elevated private material advantage, a tendency which the good society would seek to offset.

I have argued that what all these theories have in common is the concept of citizenship as concerned with the common good, defined as a good shared with others, including a quality of social life that is created by a certain form of participation together in a political association. Citizenship implies that a political community is both a 'practice' (in MacIntyre's sense) and a membership group, with shared benefits and burdens. It provides a way of getting things done in society which has some of the qualities of community, some of membership and some of reciprocity.

But this does not imply, as the quotations from all the authors show, that appeals to the common good are appeals to individuals or groups to act against their interests. They are arguments for states to organize their societies in such a way as to allow or enable citizens to have a common interest in providing certain goods in this way. They all assert that, if states do not organize their societies in this way, then relations between citizens will deteriorate to such an extent that the quality of life will become extremely poor for all, and there will be no justice, and little freedom or harmony. In other words, it is in the long-term interests of all to be members of a society with this form of citizenship. In this sense the republican tradition recommends a social morality which is self-interested; citizenship provides the bridge between individual interest and the good society.

In modern, large-scale societies, consisting mainly of commercial and power-based social relations, the need for state action to promote common interests is greater, not less, than in older times. Because markets and states have invaded more and more spheres of social relations, competitive self-interest and passive withdrawal both threaten the ideal of participation in the creation of shared goods. But the interests that all individuals have in a good quality of life need to be made explicit; they can only be realized through action for common purposes. In the absence of this active concern for the aspects of life that citizens share together, social relations degenerate into corruption (politics as the pursuit of power for the sake of group interest) and individual self-seeking.

Economic self-interest

The republican tradition has been persistently misrepresented as demanding that individuals *sacrifice* their interests to the common good, and as demanding that morality should triumph over self-interest. To quote one modern source among many, William Connolly writes:

> To appeal to the common good is to appeal to a set of shared purposes and standards which are fundamental to the way of life prized together by participants. The participants have an obligation to respond to these appeals, even when the net interest of everyone, when each consults only his own interest, moves in another direction . . . The citizen with civic virtue is asked to give presumptive priority to those dimensions of his own good shared with others, even though such a priority could not be justified by reference to his net interests taken alone.[27]

Yet, as we have seen, all republicans insist that the common good is the same as the common interest. One reason why this misrepresentation is so easily accepted by modern readers is that the concept of interests has come to be associated solely with economic interests. It is as if all other possible meanings of the term have disappeared, so that the notion of an interest in the quality of life, or in conviviality, or in community, for example, is rendered meaningless. Even an interest in freedom becomes difficult to define, unless it is in the freedom associated with market choices. Hence the idea that only market preferences are self-interested becomes tautologous – only market interests count as interests. Interests which arise from any other ways of getting things done, and especially the kinds of common interests identified by the republican tradition, are defined as not being interests.

This change in the concept of interests, which led to the republican ideas of self-interest and common interest being engulfed by that of economic interest, occurred in the eighteenth century. A. O. Hirschman has chronicled the change from a moral and political use to one in which interest is associated purely with material gain.[28] But he has also shown how the thesis that is closely associated with Adam Smith, that commercial relations lead to good government and a good society, was advanced by others earlier in the century. Montesquieu wrote that 'the spirit of commerce brings with it the spirit of frugality, of economy, of moderation, of work, of wisdom, of tranquillity, of order, and of regularity. In this manner, as long as this spirit prevails, the riches it creates do not have any bad effect.'[29] He argued that potentially greedy and unjust rulers were restrained by the fact that commercial wealth could (as capital) flee a badly governed country; thus 'it is fortunate for men to be in a situation in which, though their passions may prompt them to be wicked, they have nevertheless an interest in not being so.'[30] But although Montesquieu thought that economic interest was a far more effective means of moderating political behaviour than moral argument, he simultaneously regretted that commercial relations led to an erosion of hospitality and other moral virtues.[31]

Hume was another whose view of interests as purely economic allowed him to construct a theory of social relations in which the pursuit of wealth was one of the major factors leading to order and harmony. 'Avarice, or the desire of gain, is a universal passion which operates at all times, in all places, and upon all persons.'[32] This made it more predictable and regular than the other 'passions' (emotions). As a 'calm but strong' passion it could master other, more disruptive ones. Hume's equation of avarice with interest allowed him to conclude in his essay 'Of Interest' that 'It is an infallible consequence of all industrious professions, to . . . make love of gain prevail over the love of pleasure.'[33] This was the key to his argument that egoism could be channelled to sustain good government, even in large commercial societies in which 'every man must be supposed a knave'.[34] By contrast, morality for Hume came to be associated with those feelings which led individuals to act against their interests on account of their sympathy and concern for others, and to follow rules of conduct which demanded altruism.

These writers prepared the way for Adam Smith's famous invention of the Invisible Hand, both by equating interests entirely with material gain, and by suggesting that commercial relations were an orderly and peaceful way of securing cooperation between potentially conflicting interests. What Smith did was to develop a far more systematic account of how the division of labour and free trade (both internally and externally) could be in the interests of all groups within society, and could contribute to better government, without any individual intending the good of any other.[35]

But Smith, especially in his earlier writings, was still sufficiently influenced by the republican tradition to lament the loss of some of the features of pre-commercial societies. The division of labour, which gave workers repetitive simple tasks, made them stupid and dull;[36] the pursuit of wealth made the better-off lazy and luxurious, and rendered them unsuited to military service, and unappreciative of culture or education.[37] Furthermore, like Hume, he was by no means convinced that capitalists made good citizens. He regarded commerce and manufacturing as necessary conditions for good government, but not sufficient ones; it could only be achieved by 'mixing' commercial interests with more traditional agricultural and authoritative ones. This was because there had to be some direct link between the principles and insti- tutions of commerce and those of government. 'The proprietor of stock is properly a citizen of the world, and is not necessarily attached to any particular country.'[38] Capitalists had to be drawn into the state and the land, by acquiring ownership of estates, and by gaining office, if liberty and utility were to inform society as a whole, and government in particular.[39]

None the less, the influence of the republican tradition was greatly reduced by this new view of social relations. For example, modern scholarship has shown that although several of the Founding Fathers were steeped in that tradition, Montesquieu and Hume were the authors most read in the American states in the period before their Revolution.[40] Iain Hampsher-Monk has pointed out the remarkable similarities between the American Constitution and Hume's 'Idea of a Perfect Commonwealth'.[41]

Instead of seeing politics as a balance between the particular interests of individuals and groups, and the common interest of all in the state, the political theories that derived from this school of thought saw politics as a balance between individual *rights* (civil and political liberties enabling economic liberty) and the state's *authority* (necessary to secure these rights, and to provide the public goods that individual economic interests would not supply). In this view, citizenship meant no more than the bundle of personal and property rights bestowed by the law and constitution on individual members of society.

Republican and liberal citizenship

At this point it will be useful to contrast the views of citizenship which are characteristic of the republican and liberal traditions. In particular, it is important to clarify the idea of common interests between citizens in a modern context, and show how a republican view of citizenship deals with the apparent irreconcilability between individual economic interests and the common good.

I have argued that the republican tradition regards a political association or community as a 'practice' in MacIntyre's sense. Unfortunately, examples of practices chosen by philosophers to clarify this term are usually very orderly, reflective, artistic and exclusive activities, like embroidery and chess. To illustrate the concept in relation to modern society it is more instructive to choose an example like football – a sport which in most parts of the world contains elements of big business, with highly paid players and a large commercial penumbra, but which also comprises an extended range of unglamorous professional, semi-professional and local amateur leagues, and an even larger fringe of informal and *ad hoc* matches.

Despite this diversity and complexity, the expressions 'the good of football' and 'the interests of football' are quite widely used by players, administrators and commentators, as if people involved in football at every level were members of a community which shared a common good. If we try to analyse what these expressions mean, it seems clear that they do not simply refer to promoting excellence in the playing of the game, or even in the spirit which the game is played (as some philosophers' analyses of practices might suggest). They also include some reference to the relations between the parts of the complex system, such that what happens in the glamorous upper echelons (and in the commercial spin-offs from it) produces advantages and benefits which are shared by the rest of the community, and contributes to 'the health of the game at its grass roots'. Conversely, the 'good of football' requires that local amateur players learn skills and disciplines, and have the desire and motivation to improve their standards, so that there is a constant supply of talented youngsters to the professional game.

This does not imply that there are no tensions and conflicts between the economic interests of the big-business sector and the common interests of the football community. Successful players and clubs, individually and in coalition, often strive to accumulate greater advantages over less successful ones. But there are important limits to these processes beyond which they become recognizably self-defeating. The 'interests of football' are visibly damaged when self-interested economic maximization causes harm to other parts of the footballing community.

Suppose, for example, that a consortium of the few rich clubs was able to set up a superleague, with a very lucrative television contract for a channel devoted exclusively to its matches; suppose also that this consortium made a deal with the firms organizing football pools to concentrate their profits on this sector of the game. In the absence of any mechanism to share these competitive gains with clubs in the lower leagues, these would simply go out of business, destroying the intermediate steps on the ladder between the amateur and professional games. Eventually, people in parts of the country with no superleague clubs would lose the habit of going to watch matches, and in the long term this would effect the number of people playing. Finally, as ordinary people turned to other sports, television audiences for superleague football would dwindle.

Arguments such as these can be applied to every aspect of football, from crowd behaviour to rules which discourage goal-scoring. Hence the interests of football require a continuous review of what is happening in the whole community to ensure that the quality of relationships (involving administrators, players and spectators) is being sustained or improved. The good of football cannot be measured solely in terms of the profits of top clubs or even the combined salaries of all the professional players.

The republican tradition sees citizenship in this way; economic self-interest cannot provide the basis of social relations, and it must be contained within the framework of a community of common interests. Power in society must be directed towards ensuring that common interests are recognizable, and that people have opportunities to act upon them. Once the members of a community cease to recognize that they have interests in common, it is unlikely that power can be effectively used to compel them to participate or contribute, and the republican tradition would argue that attempts to use power in this way would be corrupt.

To return to the superleague example, the new orthodoxy's parody of the liberal tradition might argue that the rich consortium, as the 'wealth creators' of football, were entitled to their advantages, and were only required to contribute in a limited way to the public goods (law and order) supplied by the Football Association. Indeed, if football were society, the new orthodoxy would argue that amateurs had a duty to go on playing the game, even when the wealth creators had removed their motives for doing so; and that clubs in the lower leagues could justifiably be compelled to play it according to the requirements of power-holders, in return for minimal financial support, even when they had no market incentives for doing so.

Liberals have recognized this weakness in their own tradition, and have countered it in a number of ways. First, they have emphasized personal rights, and especially civil and political rights, as vital elements in citizenship, giving individuals protection against arbitrary coercion, and against interference in their private lives. But those on their own do not provide positive reasons for including individuals in the common good, or define good social relations by showing how they give an improved quality of life to all. Nor do they place any duty on the state to promote the common good (in the same sense as 'the good of football') by ensuring that the benefits of advances in the most prosperous sector are shared by all.

Towards the end of the nineteenth century, the New Liberalism in Britain was a philosophical attempt to remedy these shortcomings. It reintroduced a concept of the common good, in an attempt to transcend individualism and appeal to a collective notion of citizenship. For its original protagonists, like T. H. Green and Bernard Bosanquet, the common good was a purely moral concept, derived from Hegelian Idealism; the sense of community was to be restored within existing economic inequalities, and individual freedoms still rested on property entitlements. For other theorists, such as D. G. Ritchie and L. T. Hobhouse, politicians like H. H. Asquith and R. B. Haldane, and reformers like W. H. Beveridge, state intervention was a legitimate means of improving material conditions.[42] The common good required a social minimum standard of living for all, underpinned by welfare reforms. The Liberal legislation of 1906-11 paved the way for social democracy.

Citizenship in social democracy

The phenomena of the inter-war years - mass unemployment, totalitarian government, genocide - revived concerns about citizenship in the liberal world. Total warfare and the success of wartime planning and rationing made feasible the idea of redistributing assets. Under the influence of liberal technocrats like Keynes and Beveridge, state power was used in new ways, in the name of social democratic citizenship.

All over Europe, organized labour movements were given a share of political power on the assurance that the state would maintain full employment and create social services to sustain living standards outside the labour market. Economic management and limited public ownership were the means of sustaining employment for the whole male workforce, and income tax and compulsory insurance the means of providing services. The effects of these measures on distributions of assets were relatively modest compared with the disruptions of war, but they were seen as establishing important new principles because they acknowledged the state's responsibility for creating new forms of equality among citizens.

For example, in Britain Beveridge regarded the commitment to ensuring full employment (which he assumed would provide an adequate household income through male wage packets, when combined with universal new child benefits) as crucial for citizenship.[43] In speeches at the time he made explicit comparisons between the efforts required to win the war and those needed to conquer social problems,[44] and saw the state as creating social solidarity for both purposes. Its responsibility for full employment should be as clear as that for defence.[45] The social services were necessary to secure 'the essential freedoms of mankind',[46] which included freedom from the giants of Want, Disease, Ignorance, Squalor and Idleness.[47]

Beveridge's vision of society as a purposeful association appealed to a common interest in eliminating social evils, which he endowed with monstrous personae, in explicit comparison with the Fascist enemy abroad. In this way he was able to argue that new state institutions, such as a National Investment Board[48] and a National Health Service[49], would be consistent with the traditions of liberal democracy. The interests of a good society, purged of those evils, overrode 'sectional interests',[50] and he claimed the battle for the welfare state as 'a revolution'.[51]

But once the state had struck against these evils, it was not clear from Beveridge's account how citizens were meant to act together for the common good, or how the institutions of the welfare state encouraged the democratic participation that was supposed to be the hallmark of post-war society. T. H. Marshall argued that new 'social rights' gave people something new in common as citizens, as well as reducing risks and insecurity.[52] 'Equality of status is more important than equality of income', he wrote, and the welfare state treated all citizens as belonging to one class.[53] In Marshall's analysis, social rights supplemented civil and political rights as individual liberties which underpinned self-interested economic participation; in his later writings on social policy, Marshall made little reference to citizenship.[54]

By far the most imaginative and creative writer about social democratic citizenship was Richard Titmuss, whose emphasis on the moral dimension of membership of society was much more explicit. For example, he spoke of the goal of social welfare provision as being 'to universalise humanistic ethics and the social rights of citizenship',[55] and the socialist ideal of equality as being concerned with reuniting ethics with politics.[56] The welfare state was moral because it was concerned with the good of all citizens, and not just sections or group interests; it grew out of working-class membership systems for mutual aid, such as friendly societies, but extended their principles to the whole of society.[57] It was therefore concerned with giving the benefits of membership groups to strangers, through strangers.

However, Titmuss was far from clear in his account of the relationship between market-based and citizenship-based systems or the purpose of the latter. I have argued that in citizenship-based systems, the state distributes assets in such a way as to give all an interest in participating in the production of certain goods. So, for example, the state might equalize assets to ensure that all contribute to, and benefit from, a healthier society. Titmuss was a very strong advocate of equality, in assets, income and power, and thought that the state had a moral obligation to achieve this. But as a result he often wrote as if equality were an end in itself, and as if the social services were a means of achieving it. He described the activities of the social services as if they were aimed at correcting the inequalities of market-based outcomes. But in citizenship-based systems, equality is the means to the end of voluntary cooperation in sharing certain social goods, not an end in itself. What Titmuss often described were systems which perpetually intervened compulsorily to alter the results of market distributions, rather than ones which created a basis of equality from which voluntary cooperation could take place.

Furthermore, Titmuss sometimes described the social services as a form of altruism, and sometimes as enabling altruism.[58] In so far as altruism consists of acting against one's own interests, the former is inconsistent with the claim that the social services are citizenship-based. If citizenship is, like the mutuality of membership groups, based on common interest, then it is not altruistic. The social services may enable altruism, if Titmuss's favourite example of the British Blood Transfusion Service is at all typical. He contrasted the voluntary giving of the British system (an example of generalized reciprocity) with the market-based American system, where blood was treated as a commodity with a price.[59] The gift of blood may indeed be altruistic in the British example, if blood donors never imagine that they will benefit from the service. Alternatively, it may be regarded as an excellent example of a citizenship-based service, where all are potential beneficiaries or contributors and at any one time some are actively contributing and some actively benefiting. But the fact that some contributors quickly become beneficiaries (like Tony Hancock in the famous television programme) does not mean that the system is not a moral one. Systems which give people a common interest in cooperation are as moral (in the republican tradition) as those in which some sacrifice their interests to others, and a great deal more reliable. Altruism, as I shall argue later, is best understood as the extension of membership benefits to non-members, or giving membership benefits in the absence of a membership group.

The concept of social morality

At the start of this book I asked the question: what makes a good society? I shall now argue that this question only has meaning within something like the republican tradition that I have described in this chapter, and within a concept of citizenship as having a common interest in the provision of certain social goods. Any other system for getting things done in society as a whole cannot give rise to a significant concept of a good society.

This is because no other kind of system claims to distribute assets according to moral criteria or to seek moral ends. Take, for example, the new orthodoxy's claim that its principles lead to a good society. The system of social relations sanctioned by the new orthodoxy amounts to nothing more than an endorsement of market processes and outcomes, and the authoritative provision of certain other goods. These systems are claimed as morally justified because they result from free choice, and because individuals are entitled to what they gain by legal means. But free choice is nothing more than individual preference, based on competitive self-interest, and the claim to entitlement is nothing more than an attempt to resist any distribution other than the one that results from this version of free choice. There is nothing moral about either the process or the outcome. Citizenship-based systems, by contrast, provide ways of getting things done which involve members of society in shared commitments to the common good, and hence in fulfilling moral responsibilities to each other. This simultaneously allows us to speak of a good society (one in which citizens are committed to the common good) and of a good citizen.

Equally, of course, there can be no valid claim to being a good society from one in which the state distributes assets entirely according to non-moral criteria, or one which seeks no moral ends. Take, for example, a socialist society, which decided to end capitalist exploitation because it was a 'fetter on the development of productive forces' (this was Marx's own reason for ending exploitation).[60] Distribution of wealth, jobs, social services and so on would then be made on the basis of unfettering the development of productive forces (roughly what was attempted in the USSR from the time when Stalin assumed leadership). But neither the distributions nor the ends adopted would be moral in nature, nor would they necessarily try to give all citizens an interest in the common good; indeed, they might involve the 'dictatorship of the proletariat', and the deliberate exclusion of certain groups from any share of power or any benefit of membership.

A good society need not provide all or even most of its goods by citizenship-based systems, as the republican tradition indicates. The best balance between the various ways of getting things done will be discussed in chapter 7. But it is required to be concerned for the common good, by ensuring a common interest in social relations such that what citizens have in common outweighs what divides them. As Machiavelli pointed out (but as T. H. Marshall did not), institutions which provide a common interest in a good quality of social life under one set of circumstances do not necessarily provide for the common interest as these circumstances change. Hence, for example, the post-war social services provided a form of citizenship that was quickly eroded by socioeconomic change, just as republican Rome's citizenship had been.

In a rather strange way, the new orthodoxy does implicitly recognize that only citizenship-based systems can claim to produce a good society. This recognition is implied in the term 'property-owning democracy'. It is a concept which tries to link market-based systems and asset distributions with the ideal of citizenship. It appeals to the notion that every citizen could come to be a property-holder, and that this would give them a common interest in the social order, and a common basis for participation in all social relations. If there were any sincerity in the appeal to this ideal, then it would lead to the question of how government could actually distribute property to all citizens, to bring about the equivalent of a Jeffersonian distribution of land.[61] But the new orthodoxy prefers to leave this as a possible outcome of market relations at some remote future date. In the meanwhile, of course, as the future scenario of chapter 4 indicated, the new orthodoxy finds nothing morally repugnant about growing inequalities in wealth and other assets.

The same point is made in a rather different way by examining recent attempts in the United States to postulate a theory of social obligation which is consistent with the new orthodoxy. It is, of course, a major principle of the new orthodoxy that moral obligations are confined to the private sphere, and that the economic sphere is governed by the preferences which stem from individual interests. But, as we saw in chapter 4, many people – especially those who are poor, black, unemployed or single-parent claimants of social assistance – are so disadvantaged in all their social relations that they have no interest in participation. On the contrary, they have an interest in remaining as passive claimants of assistance. This means that the new orthodoxy requires a theory of social obligation to justify compelling such people to work, as a condition of receiving assistance. The theory advanced is that all citizens owe each other a duty to work as their contribution to the common good. On the face of it, this looks like a citizenship-based concept, since the duty is placed on all, and all are supposed to have a common interest in contributing to a productive system from which all benefit. But this is not a case. Consider this passage from Lawrence Mead's book _Beyond Entitlement: the Social Obligations of Citizenship_:

> Under current conditions . . . society's interest in work can be greater than the individual's, especially in the case of 'dirty', low-paid jobs. For both rich and poor alike, work has become increasingly elective, and unemployment voluntary, because workers commonly have other sources of income, among them government programs . . . Nonwork is most serious among the disadvantaged . . . For the nondependent nonwork may not pose a public issue. For the dependent, however, government probably must enforce work as a condition of support if it wants to advance integration. For recipients, work must be viewed, not as an expression of self-interest, but as an obligation owed to society.[62]

In other words, people who are rich enough to be able to afford not to work do not have an obligation to work, but can choose to work if it is in their interests to do so. But people who are so disadvantaged that it is not in their interests to work _at all_ are obliged to work because it is in the interests of others (the taxpayers, the rich) that they should do so. This is transparently nothing to do with a citizenship obligation. The only way to create a citizenship obligation to work would be to create a common interest in the provision of certain goods through _all_ contributing part of their working lives to producing this good (as, for example, in a citizenship obligation to do military service).

Individual morality and the common good

Advocates of the new orthodoxy would object to the argument of the previous section on the grounds that a good society can (and should) be founded on individual morality. If everyone were self-disciplined, if every household were self-sufficient and if all treated each other with respect, then each could seek his or her own good in accordance with individual, personal preferences. Sharing and mutual help outside the household would be matters for individual conscience.[63]

But this kind of individualism can give rise to no account of the good society, nor indeed of any society at all. The very notion of a society (or community, or association) is impossible to define, except in terms of what individuals have in common or share. It implies, at the very least, that they occupy a common territory, use a common language or are ruled by a common government; it often also implies that they share values and customs.

Similarly, it is impossible to define belonging to a society except in terms of membership, which implies a mutual bond of solidarity, loyalty or benefit, within a system of social relations. Philosophically, the existence of language and the fact that people understand each other implies shared 'forms of life', which are only intelligible as public, not private.[64]

Rules (whether legal or moral) can only be understood as arising from forms of association, involving membership. The same is true of rights. In this sense, the community is logically prior to the individual. As Aristotle says, 'the polis exists by nature . . . and it is prior to the individual . . . the polis is a whole, and individuals are simply its parts. Not being self-sufficient when they are isolated, all individuals are so many parts all equally depending on the whole (which alone can bring about self-sufficiency)'.[65] In other words, the starting point of any account of social relations is the group (household, community or society), rather than the individual, and rules are derived from their association. All religious systems of morality were prescriptions for behaviour in specific societies, aimed at improving the quality of social relations in those societies.

The morality promoted by the new orthodoxy is an adaptation of one such system (Christianity) to a society based on economic exchange between individuals, treated as owning themselves and their property. The kind of morality this produces is inevitably a set of prescriptions about refraining from interference with others, respecting privacy and exclusiveness and achieving self-sufficiency. It regards each individual's good as his or her own property, and forbids anyone else from invading or usurping it, except under certain strictly defined conditions, or with his or her full consent. The state is treated as having authority over each individual or household, rather than as being the authoritative expression of community and membership.

Because it denies the existence of membership and community, the new orthodoxy's morality cannot relate the good of the individual to the good of society. The plight of any one person may evoke the compassion of another, and hence an act of charitable self-sacrifice; but this is not because of any bond of membership between them. Sharing with others can never be for the sake of common interests in a better society because there are no such things.

So moral individuals are trapped within their ethical rules as much as within their self-interested preferences. Following these rules, they can only choose to sacrifice their interests for the good of other particular individuals; they can never choose to promote better social relations for the sake of the common good. Seeing goodness only in terms of rule-following and self-sufficiency, they cannot will the state to establish systems of sharing, which create common interests, because these would violate their own principles.

This means that if, through an unintended consequence of economic development, a minority faces barriers to self-sufficiency and property-ownership, individuals among the majority cannot choose to redistribute their assets through the state; they must rely on private enterprise and private charity to bring about change. And if these fail, and the minority becomes rebellious and lawless, then they must treat them as criminals, coerce and punish them. The behaviour of an excluded minority cannot be taken as an indication of deteriorating social relations, and a need to strengthen membership bonds through sharing; it can only be interpreted as rule-breaking.

We can perhaps best consider the contrast between republican and liberal-individualistic notions of morality in terms of the Kantian imperative of respect for persons: that we should always treat other people as ends, and never as means to ends. In the liberal tradition this is a rule of conduct, against which individuals should test their actions in any situation. But I would argue that mutual respect between people can be better understood as a shared common good, in which both parties of a dyad, or all parties of an association, have a common interest.

The republican tradition insists that individuals are not self-sufficient: they can only meet their needs through their relations with others. Hence they do not live in isolation, but in groups, such as households or communities. It is through the experience of exchanging services and sharing things with others in such groups that we learn how to treat others, by learning what it feels like to be treated in various ways by them. We only have a concept of moral obligations by belonging to groups, and finding out from living with others what is involved in doing things jointly with them. One of the first things we learn is that the quality of life in any group depends on the way people treat each other, and that all have an interest in treating each other with respect, and attending to each other's needs. This is the qualitative equivalent of Axelrod's finding that, where there is a moderate pay-off for cooperation, everyone has an interest in reciprocity, and no one has an interest in being the first to defect.

Hence the common good of reciprocity, in which all have a common interest, is prior to the individual good. It is only through the creation of the common good of mutual respect for people that any notion of an individual person can have any meaning, in moral terms. Without mutual respect at the level of the basic unit of society, there would be a free-for-all; strength, force or cunning would prevail, or the group would simply split up into isolated, hostile, competing individuals. If cooperative relations with others are to be possible at all, then there must be mutual respect, and it is only under the umbrella of this common interest in respect for persons that the notion of individual needs and preferences, within a system of social interaction, can grow. Similarly, a wider political community must establish a common good of mutual respect as a necessary condition for the good of the individual to have any shared social meaning.

The republican tradition regards the quality of life in a political community as depending on shared commitments to common goods, of which basic mutual respect is the primary one. The liberal tradition regards it as depending on individual rights, from which moral rules follow. This debate will be followed up in more detail in chapter 10. But the relevant difference here is that the republican tradition insists that social relations depend on shared commitments, stemming from common interests, and not just from laws. In the future scenario, we considered a society in which some citizens had no interest in participating in any of the formal systems of society - nothing to contribute and nothing to gain. Hence they had no shared commitment to their fellow members, and no reasons to treat them with respect, so the laws made by powerful people to constrain them and force them to work would be coercive and oppressive. Within the republican tradition, this would be a corrupt society.[66]

Conclusions

I have argued that the concept of a good society only makes sense in terms of a shared common good, and that this in turn depends on all the members of society having common interests in aspects of their lives together. But any notion of common interests implies a particular kind of good or goods, with the following characteristics

1 The common good is *actively* created by citizens participating together in some shared process.
2 The common good is *qualitative* rather than simply quantitative. All share in a whole quality of social relations which is not susceptible to quantitative division.
3 The common good is *purposeful*, and the means of achieving it must be adapted over time, if social and economic change are not to undermine it.
4 The common good requires *power* to be used to structure interests and distribute assets, so as to create conditions for active participation and self-rule. But power used to further the interests of individuals and groups corrupts society and destroys the common good.

This view of the common good involves recognizing that the public domain - people's life together as part of the same society - demands a shared debate, negotiation and decision-making over issues of justice, freedom and equality. It requires institutions (which have to be adapted and maintained) through which common interests can be identified and created. Unless these common interests are fostered by active participation, individuals will relapse into competitive self-interest, and elites will use power on behalf of interest groups.

These aspects of the common good explain why the British social democratic version of citizenship was rather partial and short-lived. It was inspired by the experience of wartime solidarity and struggle, where citizenship did indeed have these qualities of shared activity, and special quality of social relations; and a purpose, defined mainly by the nature of the common enemy. The political characteristics of the common interests created by the war against Fascism were *ad hoc* and transient, and both Beveridge and the Labour government made some effort to design institutions which would perpetuate some of these qualities and goals in peacetime, but with limited success.

In those countries of Western Europe which adopted more 'integrated' welfare state systems, and especially Scandinavia, a more purposeful approach to the institutions of social welfare was followed.[67] In Sweden particularly the idea of citizenship has proved to be the focus for policies which have retained a commitment to full employment and to generous social services, by constantly adapting to changing economic conditions.[68] But in other countries, slow growth and mass unemployment created apparent conflicts of interest between contributors to and beneficiaries of the welfare state.

The new orthodoxy, with its blend of individual self-interest and individual morality, cannot show why citizens following its rules should redistribute assets for the common good. Because it can recognize no common interests, it cannot justify the use of state power to promote fairness and equality for the sake of better social relations. Hence, even if society becomes divided into antagonistic sectors or classes, to the detriment of prosperity as well as harmony, it cannot show why it would be in the interests of all to promote social justice.

It is now time to return to the problems that we left at the end of chapter 4. Given the kind of society that now exists in most Western countries, can we recognize a common good in which all citizens have an interest?

Notes

1 Aristotle, *Politics*, translated by Ernest Barker (Oxford University Press, 1948), bk I, ch. I, s. 1.
2 Aristotle, *Ethics* (Heinemann, 1926), bk VIII, ch. IX, s. 4.
3 Ibid., ch. XII, s. 1.
4 Aristotle, *Politics*, bk I, ch. II, s. 14.
5 Ibid., bk III, ch. VI, s. 4.
6 Ibid., ch. XII, s. 1.
7 Ibid., ch. I, s. 12.
8 Ibid., s. 6.
9 Ibid., ch. XII, s. 8.
10 Ibid., ch. VI, s. 9.
11 Ibid., s. 11.
12 Ibid., s. 3.
13 Alasdair MacIntyre, *After Virtue: a Study in Moral Theory* (Duckworth, 1981), p. 175.
14 Ibid., p. 177.
15 Ibid., p. 178.
16 Niccolo Machiavelli, 'Discourses on the first decade of Titus Livius', in *Machiavelli: the Chief Works and Others*, translated by Allan Gilbert (Duke University Press, 1965), ch. 2, p. 198.
17 Ibid.
18 Ibid., p. 200.

19 Ibid., ch. 4, p. 203.
20 Ibid., ch. 5, p. 205.
21 Ibid., ch. 6, p. 204.
22 Ibid., ch. 18, p. 241.
23 J. G. A. Pocock, 'Custom and grace, form and matter: an approach to Machiavelli's concept of innovation', in Martin Fleisher (ed.), *Machiavelli and the Nature of Political Thought* (Atheneum, 1972), p. 159. See also Friedrich Meinecke, *Machiavellism: the Doctrine of Raison d'Etat and its Place in Modern History* (1924) (Routledge and Kegan Paul, 1957).
24 Jean-Jacques Rousseau, *The Social Contract* (1762), in *The Social Contract and Discourses* (Dent, 1952), bk I, ch. 9, p. 20, and bk II, ch. 11, p. 45.
25 Rousseau, 'Discourse on political economy' (1755), in *The Social Contract and Discourses*, p. 267.
26 Rousseau, *The Social Contract*, bk I, ch. 8.
27 William Connolly, *Appearance and Reality in Politics* (Cambridge University Press, 1981), p. 91. See also, for example, Brian Barry, *Political Argument* (Routledge and Kegan Paul, 1965).
28 Albert O. Hirschman, *The Passions and the Interests: Political Arguments for Capitalism before its Triumph* (Princeton University Press, 1977).
29 Charles Louis Montesquieu, *The Spirit of the Laws* (Collingwood, 1923), V, 7.
30 Ibid., XXI, 20.
31 Ibid., XX, 2.
32 David Hume, *Essays Moral, Political and Literary* (1742), (Oxford University Press, 1963), p. 175.
33 Hume, *Essays*, pp. 309-10.
34 Hume, *Essays*, p. 42.
35 As Hirschman points out, whereas Montesquieu and Hume thought that the desire for material gain would improve the political order by modifying and taming the passions, Smith virtually equates the interests and the passions, especially where, in *The Wealth of Nations*, he describes how market societies work to the advantage of all. 'It is thus that the private *interests and passions* of individuals naturally dispose them to turn their stock towards the employments which in ordinary cases are most advantageous to the society. But if from this natural preference they should turn too much of it towards those employments, the fall of profit in them and the rise of it in all others immediately dispose them to alter this faulty distribution. Without any intervention of law, therefore, *the private interests and passions* of men naturally lead them to divide and distribute the stock of every society, among all the different employments carried on in it, as nearly as possible in the proportion which is most agreeable to the interests of the whole society' (Adam Smith, *The Wealth of Nations* (Clarendon Press, 1976), bk IV, ch. vii, s. c.88, emphasis added).
36 Adam Smith, 'Lectures on Justice, Police and Revenue' (1762) in H. W. Schneider (ed.), *Adam Smith's Moral and Political Philosophy* (Harper, 1948), bk II, ch. ii, s. 3.
37 Ibid., p. 257.
38 Smith, *The Wealth of Nations*, bk V, ch. ii, s. f. 6.
39 Ibid., bk V, ch. ii, s. k. 80.
40 J. G. A. Pocock, *The Machiavellian Moment: Florentine Political Thought and the Atlantic Republican Tradition* (Princeton University Press, 1975).

41 Iain Hampsher-Monk, 'European republicanism and the political thought of the American Constitution', Address to the 22nd International American Studies Seminar, Kangwanda, Korea, 30 October 1987.

42 For a full account of the New Liberals' version of the common good, see Andrew Vincent and Raymond Plant, *Philosophy, Politics and Citizenship: the Life and Thought of the British Idealists* (Blackwell, 1984).

43 William Beveridge, *Full Employment in a Free Society* (Allen and Unwin, 1944), pp. 134-5.

44 John Clarke, Allan Cochrane and Carol Smart, *Ideologies of Welfare: from Dreams to Disillusion* (Hutchinson, 1987), p. 88.

45 Beveridge, *Full Employment in a Free Society*, p. 29.

46 Beveridge, *Social Insurance and Allied Services* (1942) (Cmd 6404, HMSO, 1966), para 409.

47 Ibid., para 8.

48 Beveridge, *Full Employment in a Free Society*, p. 160.

49 Beveridge, *Social Insurance and Allied Services*, paras 426-39.

50 Ibid., para 7.

51 Ibid.

52 T. H. Marshall, *Citizenship and Social Class* (Cambridge University Press, 1950).

53 Ibid., p. 56.

54 See, for instance, T. H. Marshall, *Social Policy in the Twentieth Century* (Hutchinson, 1970).

55 R. M. Titmuss, 'Social welfare and the art of giving', in B. Abel-Smith and K. Titmuss (eds), *The Philosophy of Welfare: Selected Writings of Richard M. Titmuss* (Allen and Unwin, 1987), p. 122.

56 Ibid., p. 126.

57 Ibid., p. 122.

58 See, for instance, 'The gift of blood', in B. Abel-Smith and K. Titmuss (eds), *The Philosophy of Welfare: Selected Writings of Richard M. Titmuss* (Allen and Unwin, 1987), p. 190.

59 Ibid.

60 Karl Marx, 'Critique of the Gotha Programme' (1875), in N. J. Smelser (ed.), *Karl Marx on Society and Social Change* (University of Chicago Press, 1973), p. 200.

61 Thomas Jefferson, 'Notes on Virginia' (1784), in Andrew Lipscomb (ed.), *The Writing's of Thomas Jefferson* (Jefferson Memorial Association, 1903), vol. 2, pp. 229-30.

62 Lawrence M. Mead, *Beyond Entitlement: the Social Obligations of Citizenship* (Free Press, 1986).

63 See for example Mrs Thatcher's address to the General Assembly of the Church of Scotland, *The Guardian*, 23 May 1988.

64 Ludwig Wittgenstein, *Philosophical Investigations* (Blackwell, 1953).

65 Aristotle, *Politics*, bk I, ch. II, s. 14.

66 Of course, the republican tradition defined certain people who lived within the territory of a state as not being citizens, notably women and slaves.

67 Ramesh Mishra, *The Welfare State in Crisis: Social Thought and Social Change* (Wheatsheaf, 1984).

68 G. Esping-Andersen and W. Korpi, 'Social policy as class politics in post-war capitalism: Scandinavia, Austria and Germany', in J. H. Goldthorpe (ed.), *Order and Conflict in Contemporary Capitalism* (Oxford University Press, 1984). They describe the Swedish government's strategy as 'to introduce a new set of citizen rights to collective capital ("economic citizenship") as a means of resolving the existing contradictions between social citizenship with full employment and economic growth' (p. 196).

6

The Morality of Exclusion

We are now caught in a number of interlocking puzzles. The new orthodoxy tells us that its good society is constructed out of the self-interested and self-responsible choices of individual members of society. I counter that these choices misconstrue both interests and responsibilities; we can only understand these by recognizing how our lives are shared with others in our community. I also suggest that a large proportion of people – perhaps even a majority – are exploited and dominated in one sphere or another of the new orthodoxy's social system. Why then do we not recognize our common interests in a different kind of society, and vote to change our social institutions?

In this chapter I shall show why it does not seem to be in the interests of the majority of members of an advanced capitalist society to share out crucial assets in an egalitarian way. If we follow the new orthodoxy in recognizing only competitive material gain as self-interest, then the majority would be worse-off as a result of an equal redistribution of all assets. Instead, it is in their interests to form a coalition (including many individuals who are exploited and dominated in several spheres) against those who have little or no interest in participating in the economy or the political system because they have no chance of gaining competitive advantage within existing social institutions.

Using Britain as an example, I shall show that the most important asset giving income advantages turns out to be a full-time job. Although a minority of the adult population have such a job, a majority have an interest which is linked to one, either by sharing a household with a full-time employee or by having a pension drawn on one. Hence the majority seem to have an interest in a system which reserves full-time employment mainly for one group (skilled white males), creates an exploitative form of exployment for a second group (married women and young unskilled workers) and excludes a third group (mainly comprising black people, residents of deprived areas, disabled people and their carers).

The exclusion of this third group (the underclass, which also comprises retired people without savings or occupational pensions) is a direct result of the new orthodoxy's way of calculating interests, and encouraging accumulation of private goods. The new orthodoxy has reinforced the majority interest in excluding the minority by rewarding those in full-time work (for example, by tax cuts) and by promoting ownership of shares and houses.

At the same time, it has reduced the importance of public goods, and tried to undermine reliance of the majority on them. For example, the Thatcher government has encouraged British taxpayers to see the National Health Service as expensive (even though better-off people, who consult doctors more often, get more treatment and live longer to receive it, get most for their money,[1] and the NHS is probably the most cost-effective health service in the world). The government seems, in refusing to fund further increases in state health care, to be determined to make the majority more reliant on private, insurance-based systems, and hence to reduce majority interests in a public good. It is even prepared to risk short-term unpopularity for the sake of its long-term goal: a society in which those linked to full-time employment have an interest in providing for themselves, out of their earnings, all those goods which they do not supply for each other on an unpaid basis in households.

But this restructuring of majority interests has important implications for the minority. New social institutions have been created to deal with the fact that exclusion from links with full-time employment gives people no interest in, as well as no opportunity for, social participation. The provision of public assistance (means-tested benefits) was recognized as causing a passive and resentful form of dependence. The next step was to provide large-scale state schemes for low-paid, part-time work, such as those of the Manpower Services Commission in Britain. When few of the 'employees' of these schemes got jobs in the market, the emphasis shifted to 'training'. As the limitations of this approach became clear, because of the disincentives and poverty traps faced by members of the underclass, the government is drawn towards coercive measures, forcing claimants off benefits and making participation in 'training' compulsory.

The final outcome of the new orthodoxy's programme is a division of society into a majority with a stake in assets giving income and power advantages (albeit unequally distributed within this group) and a minority who are excluded from any share of these assets. This involves the use of power to coerce and harass the underclass, and to consolidate the interests of the majority. In this system, representative democracy becomes the instrument of a corrupt form of rule.

Finally, I shall show that the underclass comes to have an interest in active and lawless resistance, such that the lives of the majority are constantly disrupted and made insecure and anxiety-ridden. At first, the majority sees its interests as lying in further repression of the minority, for example, by increased expenditure on police and prisons. It is only after a serious deterioration in the quality of life that the whole system can be seen as self-defeating. Interests in the common good, made invisible by the new orthodoxy's methods of accounting, become recognizable only when the public domain has deteriorated into an arena for war between individuals and classes.

Economic interests and the underclass

The first part of my argument consists of another imaginative exercise (thought experiment). It involves a process rather like the one in chapter 4 in which we identified exploitation and domination. The question to be answered is this: who would be better-off, and who worse-off, if *all* the assets identified as relevant in the distribution of income and power were shared out equally among the relevant candidates?

In this way, I shall show that – because of the way in which households are composed – a majority of adults in present-day Britain would be worse-off as a result of an egalitarian redistribution of all assets. This means that a majority have an interest in the social institutions being developed by the new orthodoxy. It also implies that they have an interest in the continued exclusion of the underclass and – if it resists – in its oppression. This situation is self-perpetuating, so long as interests are calculated in terms of competitive gain; hence the new orthodoxy is likely to continue to be able to construct a majority through the democratic process, so long as that process is used to further the material interests of the majority.

The reason why a majority would be worse-off if all the six assets (see chapter 4, pp. 60–1) were shared out equally (or the link between them and income advantages was abolished) is the overwhelming importance of jobs as assets. It is also because of the way in which households in Britain are polarized between job-rich and job-poor households. Among people of working age, those households with a man in full-time employment are most likely to contain a woman in full-time or part-time employment, and those with a man who is unemployed least likely to contain an employed woman. Job-rich households stand to lose more through the redistribution of employment than they stand to gain from other forms of redistribution.

Similarly, among the population over working age, the income advantages enjoyed by those with private, occupational and state earnings-related pensions are the most significant in differentiating between household incomes. Hence those with these job-related assets would have more to lose from a redistributive programme than to gain.

This creates a situation in which an underclass, excluded from open-market employment, has no common interests with the majority in the economic sphere. Even though large groups of men and women are exploited (in relation to wealth, control, skill, gender and race) among the employed, the income gap between job-rich and job-poor households is such that even exploited members of the majority sector have more to lose from sharing available employment with the underclass than to gain from the equalization of all other assets.

In order to demonstrate this arithmetically, I shall have to make some rather drastic simplifying assumptions, and to do some very rough-and-ready calculations. For example, I shall assume that the costs of sharing out jobs among a much larger workforce (training, equipping and accommodating the extra workers, and reorganizing the work process so as to absorb them in a new pattern of production) can be met out of the sum at present spent on benefits to the unemployed. In reality, the costs would probably be higher, especially in the short run. I shall also treat all differentials in earnings as attributable to holdings in the assets of skill and control, and hence calculate the consequences of equalization in relation to these two assets simply by taking mean earnings (initially treating men and women separately, since differentials between their earnings clearly do *not* reflect these factors alone).

To see how individuals are affected by redistribution of assets, let us first consider male employment. In 1985 there were almost exactly 12 million men in employment in the United Kingdom,[2] of whom about half a million were part-time[3] (another 2 million men were self-employed,[4] but they will be excluded from this calculation). There were 2.25 million unemployed male claimants,[5] and another 500,000 men engaged in 'work' or 'training' under Manpower Services Commission Special Employment Measures.[6] In calculating the size of the population among whom employment-based assets might be distributed, we can therefore use a figure of 11.5 million men as the number in full-time employment, and 2.75 million as the number excluded from open-market jobs.

In 1985, mean earnings for full-time male employees in the United Kingdom were £192.40 per week and median earnings £172.80.[7] If the same total of male earnings were divided between the 14.25 million candidates for full-time jobs the mean would fall to £155.27 per week and the median to £139.15. The latter would represent a reduction of £33.65 per week for the current median male worker, if employment was redistributed among all available males, but with the same range of earnings.

Assuming that differentials in pay represents holdings in the assets of control over production and skill, a redistribution of these assets (or an abolition of the advantages associated with them) among existing employees would imply a gain for the man on median earnings of £19.60 (the difference between median and mean earnings). But as we have just seen the redistribution of employment amongst all males of working age would imply the larger loss of £33.65 per week. So a substantial number of those earning less than median earnings would have more to lose from a redistribution of employment assets than to gain from a redistribution of control over production or skills. A majority of men would therefore oppose a redistributive programme involving these assets.

If wealth is included, the difference becomes more marginal, but the calculation is difficult to make. It is known that 93 per cent of marketable wealth in the United Kingdom is owned by the most wealthy 50 per cent of the population.[8] However, around half of this takes the form of dwellings, and another quarter consumer durables and other fixed assets. Amongst the forms of wealth which provide a money income, stocks and shares are actually distributed more evenly among the social classes and between the sexes than might be supposed: 29 per cent belong to members of classes C2, D and E, and 45 per cent to women.[9] Since only 8 per cent of household income comes from rent, dividends and interest (compared with 60 per cent from wages and salaries),[10] and since almost half of this is imputed rent for owner–occupied houses,[11] this implies that the redistributive effect of equalization of income from wealth would be very small. Even assuming that the whole value of the annual £22.73 billion going to the household sector in rent, dividends and interest were redistributed among the 43 million adult members of the population, this would give a weekly income to each adult of only £10.16 per week, not enough to offset the male majority interest against a redistributive programme.

Turning to women's employment, in 1985 there were 5.2 million full-time and 4.4 million part-time female employees, and 600,000 female self-employed, out of a total of 14.5 million women of working age in the United Kingdom.[12] It is impossible to assess how many of those not in employment would prefer to have a job, or what proportion would like to work full-time; benefit rules and availability tests result in only a small proportion of those seeking work being registered as unemployed. For the sake of simplicity I shall assume that half (2.3 million) of those outside the labour market would like full-time work, and the other half part-time.

In 1985, mean earnings for full-time female employees were £126.40 per week and median earnings £115.20.[13] For part-time women employees the corresponding figures were £51.10 and £46.60.[14] Doing the same calculation as for men, a redistribution of employment assets would imply mean earnings of £87.64 and median of £79.87 per week for full-time women, and mean earnings of £33.21 and median of £31.54 for part-timers. This would imply reductions of £35.33 and £15.06 respectively for current median full-time and part-time women workers from redistribution of employment with the same differentials.

Thus the extent to which the majority of employed women would stand to lose more from a redistribution of employment assets than to gain from a redistribution of control or skill assets is greater than for men. Full-time female employees would lose £35.54 from the former equalization and gain only £11.20 from the latter, and part-time employees would lose £15.06 and gain £4.50 per week. Even including notional wealth redistribution, they would have an interest in preserving the status quo.

However, the full implications of an egalitarian redistributive programme become clearest when we consider what would happen if male and female, full-time and part-time employment and earnings are considered together, i.e. equalization of the assets in employment, skills, control and maleness. If the total earnings of all employed people in the United Kingdom in 1985 had been divided between the 29.25 million people who were candidates for employment (excluding the self-employed but including male part-timers), each individual would have received £105.62 per week. Although this would have been a substantial gain for women part-time workers, it would have represented a loss not only for men but also for women full-time employees on current median earnings. More important, even if each partner of all the couples who were candidates for employment had received this sum, the majority of couples would be worse-off as a result. This would obviously be the case for the 27 per cent of couples in which both man and woman were in full-time work,[15] where the median income was £297.00. But it would also be true for most of the 34 per cent of couples in which the man was in full-time employment and the woman was in part-time;[16] their median income was £219.40, compared with £211.24 if all employment and gender-related assets were equalized.

This result comes about because far more married women whose husbands are in employment are themselves employed than those whose husbands are without employment. Whereas 61 per cent of the former have jobs, only 30 per cent of the latter do.[17] It is this polarization between households with two (or more) employees, and households with none, that explains why the job-rich majority of couples would lose from an equalization of employment, skill, control and maleness assets, and why – even though their wage rates are very low compared with men's, and their access to full-time employment is far inferior – the majority of women have more to lose as members of households from redistribution of these assets than they have to gain as individual members of a female coalition.

Finally, of course, this majority interest in the status quo becomes even more pronounced if we take the asset of whiteness into account, since the white majority would lose substantially from the equalization of incomes between white and black people. Although figures on earnings are not available, in 1985, 19 per cent of Afro-Caribbean and 18 per cent of Asian males of working age were out of employment, compared with 9.4 per cent of white males; and 27 per cent of Afro-Caribbean and 56.3 per cent of Asian females were out of employment or 'looking after home', compared with 28 per cent of white females.[18]

Calculation of the assets held by the retired sector is more difficult. We know that almost exactly half of the employed workforce have belonged to occupational pensions schemes since the early 1960s,[19] which implies that a substantial proportion now have occupational pensions. State earnings-related pensions are only just becoming a factor in the incomes of retired people, and are not yet significant. Over 50 per cent live in owner-occupied housing, and 45 per cent live in houses they own outright.[20] Figures from the Family Expenditure Survey suggest that a small majority of retired people have assets which confer income advantages over and above their state pensions, and would therefore stand to lose if these were redistributed among the whole retired population.

The survey suggested that in 1986 there were approximately 2 million retired people living in single-person households who were 'wholly or mainly dependent on state pensions', with an average income of £50.07 per week, 84 per cent of which came from social security benefit. There was almost a million other retired people, also living in one-person households, with average incomes of £115.35 per week, 21.5 per cent from investments, 31.5 from annuities, private or occupational pensions, and 36.4 per cent from social security benefits. Another just over 2 million retired people lived in two-person households who were 'mainly dependent on state pensions', and who had average incomes of £86.19, with 83.4 per cent of this coming from social security benefit. A final two and a half million lived in two-person households with average incomes of £189.73 per week, of which 16.7 per cent came from investments, 30 per cent from private or occupational pensions and 34.5 per cent from social security benefits.[21] Taking all these into account, it seems that a small majority have some income from property or from non-state pensions, and that employment-based pensions are the largest element that distinguishes this majority from the very substantial minority (around 45 per cent) who depend virtually entirely on state benefits. If this is so, then the majority would have more to lose from the redistribution of employment-based assets than to gain from the equalization of all income from assets.

In the future scenario of chapter 4, this pattern of interests which is already present in British society was taken a stage further, with an even higher concentration of full-time and part-time jobs, respectively for men and for women, in the same households, and an even larger sector of households with no member employed in the open labour market. In addition to this, the value of the basic state pension had been reduced, and a larger proportion of those who had retired received state earnings-related pensions or occupational pensions. This implied that the majority interest in excluding the underclass was strengthened, and that the appeal of egalitarian redistribution was further weakened.

So far in this section I have concentrated on showing that the political domination of a majority under the new orthodoxy's principles is based on the fact that its members would be worse-off if assets were equalized. This assumes that any redistribution of assets takes place within the population as a whole. However, of course, this need not be the case. Political opponents of the new orthodoxy might recognize that the interests of the majority lie in continuing to exclude the underclass from any share in economically advantageous assets, and hence choose to concentrate on redistributing income *within* the majority (market) sector, rather than between it and the underclass.

For example, the British Labour Party at present claims to represent the interests of the poor, and to regard unemployment as the greatest social evil perpetrated by the Thatcher government. But in so far as it argues for redistribution towards the poor, and especially for restoring full employment, it can be seen to be arguing for a programme which is against the interests of the job-rich majority. So it might do better (in electoral terms) by focusing on giving existing workers a greater share in control over production, and better access to well-paid skills, together with the income advantages associated with these. Indeed, this switch might be exactly what is implied in the recently-advocated notion of 'socialist individualism'.

My analysis so far has focused on the exclusion of the underclass from any share in the assets that confer income advantages in a modern advanced capitalist society. I have suggested that the new orthodoxy creates an economic system which divides the interests of the job-rich majority from the job-poor minority, and in the process divides exploited members of the majority from the underclass because they stand to lose by an egalitarian redistributive programme.

The politics of exclusion

At first sight, this would seem to be a telling argument against the new orthodoxy's claim to be a moral theory: that it gives the majority of citizens a common interest in excluding a minority from a share in the most important assets that confer advantages in terms of income. But the new orthodoxy attempts to justify this exclusion on a number of grounds, and in the process to justify the inequalities in terms of power which stem from this exclusion. Its political theory upholds the dominance structure of the future scenario, as its economic theory upholds the exploitation structure, and both are claimed to be in the interests of all.

In the first place, the new orthodoxy rejects the view that democratic governments should try to involve the whole community in the active joint pursuit of a good quality of life. In this it follows the very influential argument put forward by Joseph Schumpeter in his book *Capitalism, Socialism and Democracy*. Schumpeter argued against what he called the 'classical theory' of democracy, which was that 'the democratic method is that institutional arrangement for arriving at political decisions which realises the common good by making the people itself decide issues through the election of individuals who are to assemble in order to carry out its will.'[22]

He criticized the whole notion of a common will for the common good, and insisted that the most that could be said about individual voters was that they had certain preferences, like market preferences, and that they recognized and would follow their short-term interests. Since these competed with each other, they could not possibly form a common will, and democracy must instead be seen as a competition for leadership. His definition of the democratic method was 'that institutional arrangement for arriving at political decisions in which individuals acquire the power to decide by means of a competitive struggle for the people's vote'.[23] He made an explicit comparison between this form of political competition, and the economic competition of markets.[24]

The implication of this argument is that it is in the economic sphere, if anywhere, that common interests must be created, and that the political sphere is concerned with managing society in such a way as to earn the votes of the majority. Schumpeter thought that the interests created by socialist institutions were quite different from those created by capitalist ones, but that socialism was, under certain circumstances, consistent with democracy.[25] Even though the issues would be different, it would be the politician's business under either system to 'deal in votes'.[26]

The new orthodoxy regards socialism as an immoral system because it removes from individuals both freedom of choice and responsibility over goods important to their lives. It regards a socialist economic system as a manipulation of interests, brought about by coercive means, to perpetuate the power of politicians and bureaucrats. By contrast, it characterizes the political leadership associated with market capitalism as promoting both freedom and efficiency, giving individuals choice and prosperity. The aim of government is therefore to manage society in such a way that the largest possible number of people have an interest in preserving a market-based system, and avoiding a socialist one.

According to this view, there is nothing immoral in excluding from any share in political power all those with an interest in setting up institutions for egalitarian redistribution because such institutions are contrary to freedom, prosperity and morality. So it would be a legitimate aim of government to create economic interests in the exclusion from power of all those who are outside the market sector of the economy, just as it would be a legitimate aim to give as many people as possible an interest in the market.

This is what is implied in Mrs Thatcher's notion of a 'property-owning democracy'. Her government recognizes that there is no possibility, in the foreseeable future, of all households owning their own houses, or shares in companies or rights to private or occupational pensions. What the phrase implies is that her form of democracy consists in extending these property rights as widely as possible because they represent a stake in a market-based system. Success in this programme would be achieved when the elites competing for power are both (or all) trying to build coalitions of support from within the privileged majority, rather than appealing to the interests of members of the excluded minority. In this way, socialism would be defeated.

The United States' political system represents an example of such a democratic order. It is not that candidates from the major political parties never appeal to the poor for support; it is that they never do so in terms of egalitarian redistribution of the assets which give advantages in income and power. Because there is a permanent majority interest in excluding the poor minority, the latter take little part in elections, rarely bothering to vote.

Far from seeing this as a failure of democracy, the most influential American political theorists of the 1950s and early 1960s regarded it as a success, arguing that democracy was only safe so long as the poor remained outside the political process because their attitudes were authoritarian and simplistic – hence increased participation by poor people led to totalitarian government. Summarizing the research and argument of political sociologists of his era, S. M. Lipset wrote in 1959:

> non-voters differ from voters in having authoritarian attitudes, cynical ideas about democracy and political parties, intolerant sentiments on

deviant opinions and ethnic minorities, and in preferring strong leaders
in government ... a sudden increase in the size of the voting electorate
probably reflects tension and serious government malfunctioning and
also introduces as voters individuals whose social attitudes are
unhealthy from the point of view of the requirements of the democratic
system.[27]

In the later 1960s, the Democratic Party did attempt to involve excluded
minorities in the construction of a majority coalition, to encourage political
participation and to redistribute the advantages associated with one crucial
asset: whiteness. In the process, it also enlarged common interests in public-
sector goods among both majority and minority. This approach to government has since been attacked and largely discredited by the right.

The new orthodoxy does not argue for the deliberate exclusion of the underclass from the democratic process on the grounds of their psychological or
sociological unsuitability as voters. Rather, it emphasizes the importance of
widening interests in markets by breaking up public-sector monopolies, by
encouraging home and share ownership and by reducing dependence on the
local and national state services. Mrs Thatcher's reaction to the 1987 General
Election results was to concentrate the government's attention on the inner
cities: to reduce the power of local authorities, dismantle their housing and
educational empires and try to reduce interests in their provision of services.

Such a programme encourages the notion that the underclass are not
necessarily vicious or anti-social, but are incapable of fending for themselves,
of providing for (and in some cases even of knowing) their own good. The
new orthodoxy aims to make social services available only for this group, and
hence to ensure that - while it is protected from the worst consequences of its
lack of economic success - its interests in egalitarian redistribution are not
allowed to shape the social order or the political agenda.

The economics of exclusion

The new orthodoxy claims that its view of the scope of social services is quite
consistent with its overall conception of the common good. In the first place,
a market economy maximizes the material goods to be distributed among the
population as a whole. Secondly, it gives all an interest in trying to look after
themselves by being as useful as possible to others. Thirdly, since social
services go only to those who cannot provide for themselves through market
transactions, it concentrates assistance on those most in need.

Its criticism of social democracy is that on all these points it falls short of
yielding a good society. A large welfare state is a brake on efficiency and
prosperity. Instead of giving people incentives to be self-reliant, it encourages
them to rely on the state. And, above all, the benefits of the welfare state go
chiefly to people who do not most need its assistance - to those who could

afford to provide for themselves. Notoriously, the social services established under social democracy do not deal especially generously with poor or handicapped people, nor do the outcomes of their provision necessarily create societies with conspicuous material equality.[28]

In chapter 4 I argued that the new orthodoxy would find nothing morally repugnant in a future scenario in which about 20 per cent of the population were excluded from the market sector, and trapped in roles either as recipients of state income and services or as compulsory workers for the state. But I have not yet shown in any detail why such a scenario seems a likely one, in view of present trends in employment, earnings and policy.

Briefly stated, the argument is this.[29] Since industrial production can now be located anywhere in the world, because the structure of enterprises, the movement of capital and systems of communication now allow this, the relative costs of labour power between advanced and newly industrializing countries will mean that most production in the former will be capital-intensive. The result will be a relatively small industrial workforce, with high productivity as a result of high-technology methods of production, and high wages. But productivity in the service sector cannot (with the exception of services which can be provided much more efficiently by means of computerization or other microelectronic techniques) keep pace with productivity in industry. For example, in the vast majority of personal services which are provided on a paid basis, few technological gains in productivity have been made during this century, and few can be foreseen.

Historically, wages and salaries in the service sector have tended to rise in line with industrial wages, despite the fact that productivity lagged well behind. This meant that the relative cost of services has tended to rise, in comparison with manufactured goods.[30] One consequence has been that, in some sectors of the economy (such as transport, laundry and entertainment) consumers have substituted equipment (such as cars, washing machines and television sets) for services they previously paid for.

However, in recent years this tendency towards self-provisioning has been offset by a number of factors. First, enterprises have been able to bring down the costs of certain services by organizing their production in new ways, using labour-power more flexibly and taking advantage of the structure of households and of income taxation. For example, fast-food chains and supermarkets have organized shifts so as to have staff on duty at peak hours, and have employed large proportions of part-time workers to supplement regular staff. Costs have been reduced by paying low hourly wages to these staff, taking advantage of tax allowances for their small earnings and of the fact that – since most of them are married women or very young single people – they live in households in which there are several earners.

Secondly, private enterprises have been able to use similar flexible structuring of employment to compete with public-sector services. Market-minded local and national governments have offered such enterprises the opportunity to take over whole services, or parts of services, by using these methods to undercut the public sector, which has a far more traditional structure of employment, wages and training, and has the higher costs associated with holiday pay, redundancy payments, etc.

Thirdly, as the earnings of rich people have risen in relation to those of poor people, as income tax rates have been reduced, and as the value of benefits has been cut, the rich have increasingly employed poor people to do things for them that previously they did for each other or for themselves.[31] Examples of this include the increase in employment of nannies, domestic servants, gardeners, chauffeurs, handymen and so on. Although the wages paid for these occupations are often very low, they compare favourably with benefit rates, so long as those employed are part of households in which others are earning.

Yet there are clearly limits on the further expansion of all these sources of employment. Already it seems that the main expansion in retailing is in out-of-town shopping centres and hypermarkets, which simply relocate employment opportunities from city centres towards the periphery. Similarly, in the long run, privatization of state services will have finally restructured employment in this sector, and the scope for these changes will have been exhausted. But above all, the dynamic of expanding service employment has depended on very low wages, which are only viable if the worker is a member of a household containing several such earners, or one person earning a decent full-time wage. In Britain, the number of people in full-time work has been declining since 1965.

This means that government policy is caught in a dilemma, particularly in relation to households in which no one is in paid work. These households are particularly concentrated in areas of industrial decline and high male unemployment, and with poor access to new sources of service-based employment. This includes many inter-city areas, and outer-city estates, especially in the north of England, Wales, Scotland and Northern Ireland. The economies of such areas lack any stimulus or dynamism, and the majority exist on poverty-level state benefits. But even at this very low level of daily subsistence, people have some security, which they risk losing if they enter the fragmented, insecure world of part-time, short-term employment or self-employment, which is all that presents itself as an alternative.[32]

This alternative is made slightly more feasible in Britain by the existence of means-tested benefits which meet part of the housing costs of low-income households (housing benefit), and which supplement the earnings of households in which there is someone in substantial employment with low wages, and there are children (family credit). But despite the government's efforts to improve the incentives for low-income households by abolishing the poverty trap (the situation in which withdrawal of means-tested benefits and the simultaneous impact of income tax causing people to be worse-off as they earn more), all that has so far been achieved is the creation of a very broad band of incomes across which households make gains of 10p or less for each extra pound they earn.[33] An even greater disincentive is the complexity and delay associated with these benefits which – in combination with insecure and often short-term employment – often results in people who come off benefits being penalized, and running into debt.[34] Finally, high travelling costs from many poor areas to the nearest sources of employment often add to the expense and risk of taking a job.

The problem of incentives and employment opportunities for people living in depressed and impoverished areas has been one of the factors which has led the British government greatly to expand its special employment measures for long-term unemployed people, even though it was initially critical of their value. These measures are ostensibly designed to make people more fitted for the labour market, either by some form of training, or simply by getting them into the habit of doing regular work. As long-term unemployment has become a more and more significant component of the unemployment statistics, the government has relied increasingly on these schemes as a way of drawing people back into some form of economic activity, even if – as in the Community Programme – this consists of short-term, low-productivity, part-time, low-paid work, of marginal use to the community, and with little or no training content.

But these opportunities have been of limited appeal, partly because of the tasks involved and partly because of their low remuneration. The next step is for the government to make one of them – the two-year Youth Training Scheme – compulsory, in the sense that benefits are to be withheld from anyone who refuses a place on the scheme. It is easy to see how the same principle would eventually be applied to the various schemes for adult claimants, once these have been sufficiently expanded. Meanwhile, the benefit authorities are already being required to administer far stricter tests of the availability of claimants for all types of work (including low-paid work) as a way of restricting the payment of benefits.

Hence the argument that the new orthodoxy allows a much more benevolent approach to those in 'genuine need' turns out to be very misleading. As in the United States, with the adoption of 'workfare' (compulsory work as a condition of receiving benefits), the new approach leads to greater restriction and more compulsion, not to generosity. And although people may pass in and out of this sector during their working lives, low earners are very unlikely to be able to afford to provide themselves with private pensions or health care, and thus form the clientele of public services during sickness and retirement.

The oppression of the underclass

The crucial weakness in the new orthodoxy's claim to be a moral theory is this inability to provide a coherent account of the role of poor people in the good society. Although it purports to show that the state is concerned to provide for those in 'genuine need', it ends up by advocating a system of low benefits, policed by a stringent bureaucracy, with powers to require people to work for the state for a poverty-level subsistence. This is in marked contrast with the relative prosperity and freedom that is the hallmark of the market sector.

The new orthodoxy's account of the good society rests heavily on the idea that cooperation can be achieved through economic self-interest, yet it is unable to show how it is in the interests of members of the underclass to work, to save or to look after themselves. On the contrary, because of the nature of the state systems that deal with their needs, it is in their interests to remain passive, to stay outside the labour market, to consume all their income and to claim all the benefits and services available. In many instances this may involve avoiding caring for each other in households, since more generous provision (in cash and kind) may be available for individuals in need than for families – for example, benefits for individual adults are higher than for each of a couple, and financial provision for children in care is greater than the benefits paid for children living with their parents.

Because there is no structure of incentives for poor people to match the incentives for those in the market sector, the new orthodoxy comes instead to rely on threats and coercion to drive them into low-paid work.[35] It invents a social obligation to do this work for the good of society, or for the sake of improving fitness for the labour market, when there is no such obligation for the rest of society: their willingness to work is based on self-interest.

Finally, in creating a system of compulsory work for the state in exchange for benefits, the state gives its own agencies an incentive to use this form of labour in providing those services which are still public goods. Clearly, since the aim of government is to minimize expenditure on public goods (other than order and defence), the most attractive way to provide non-expert assistance for the clientele of the social services is to use the labour-power of those required to work in exchange for benefits.

In Britain there is already some evidence of the first steps in this direction. Within the Community Programme about a third of the 250,000 places are on schemes which concern health and social welfare (mainly for elderly people).[36] Although these are mostly organized through voluntary associations, and deal in practical tasks, they are coming to represent an important element in the network of social provision in areas like Liverpool, with high levels of unemployment and overstretched public services.

Once the state starts to use harassment and coercion as its means of inducing the poor to do as its systems require, then poor people come to have an interest in organized resistance to these methods. Whereas previously they lacked positive reasons for participating in economic and social systems, they come to have clear reasons for resisting compulsory participation and remaining outside the state's control. From being a neglected substratum of society, they turn into an oppressed underclass, whose domination by the majority, through the state's agencies, is a source of resentment and conflict.

The new orthodoxy's rationale for dealing with poor people quite differently from the majority is that they come to depend on the state because they are unable to compete successfully – to look after themselves in the market place. This implies that they are either less able than the rest or less self-disciplined. One possible rationale for compulsory work is to give them new skills and improve their ability to organize their lives in the ways required by the labour market.[37] But the reasons why people are poor are far more complicated than this. In particular, they reflect the local economy, access to new employment opportunities and the absence of family and community supports. Members of the underclass are concentrated in certain deprived areas or isolated from others around them.

The most striking example of exclusion concerns black and other ethnic minority people. They are discriminated against in membership groups such as political parties and trade unions, in terms of access to employment and to skills and in terms of housing opportunities. All these factors contribute to a disproportionate number of black people among the underclass, and to the identification by black people of white domination as the main factor in their exclusion from the market sector. For black people it is particularly clear that white people's control of the assets which give them power within the various institutions and processes of society allows them to exclude black people from a share in power, as well as excluding them from economic advantages.

In Britain, where black people have been able to gain some political power (in a few London boroughs), they have tried to use this to redistribute some of the assets which enable white domination. Although most of their policies have concentrated on white cultural hegemony, and to a lesser extent on the actions of the police, they have been denounced by central government and the press as dangerous and destructive. They have, in fact, served as a rationale for central government's attempt to reduce the powers of local authorities, especially in relation to education.

This example illustrates that, far from creating common interests in a good society, the new orthodoxy's policies create a conflict of interests between the majority and a significant class of those excluded from the crucial assets that give income and power advantages. The result is that the minority are barred from the conventional political process just as they are barred from employment, skill and wealth assets. Even if they organize to try to struggle for a share in power, they face a coalition of majority interests which will always act together against them.

In a very individualistic society, like the one that is promoted by the new orthodoxy, this leaves the underclass with strong incentives to use illegal means for achieving their ends. It is only by working while claiming that they can achieve the same incentives and rewards that people in the majority get in the labour market. It is only by stealing that they can accumulate property. It is only by violence that they can equalize the power differential between themselves and the individuals in the majority sector. In so far as a large proportion of members of the underclass take part in illegal activities like these, it becomes difficult for the policing agencies of the majority to catch more than a few of them. Therefore it is in the interests of the underclass as a class for as many individuals as possible to be as lawless as possible.

The only alternative for the underclass is to cooperate with each other forming a community of mutual support and assistance. Because they have very few resources, such cooperation is necessarily more like that of a simple community - reciprocity, sharing and some joint effort for communal facilities - than it is like the economic cooperation of market societies. But this alternative does not exclude the other; it is rational for the underclass *both* to cooperate in these ways in their communities *and* to maximize individual gain from illegal activity.

In practice, the authority structure of the majority does as much to discourage peaceful mutual assistance among the underclass as it does to control lawlessness. All its systems steer individuals away from voluntary community activity and into individualistic pursuits which give no advantages to members of this sector. For example, the Manpower Services Commission's work schemes already disrupt grassroots organizations, both by drawing individual unemployed people away from mutual assistance and into meaningless make-work; and by encouraging some community groups to turn themselves into MSC projects, and then prescribing aims, methods and structures which destroy the fabric of voluntary cooperation, mutual assistance and community purpose.[38]

Conclusions

The new orthodoxy constructs its theory of the good society out of individual interests in markets, which are supposed to encourage people to look after themselves and each other. It attacks any other notion of the common good as requiring excessive sacrifices of personal freedom and general prosperity. It sees democracy mainly as a means of ensuring that the market basis of society will be preserved, and therefore sees no harm to the common good in creating a majority interest in the exclusion from employment and power of a minority underclass.

The new orthodoxy's support among the majority rests on a recognition by those in the market sector but without holdings of wealth, without control over production, with less than average skills, and who are women, that they have less to gain from a share-out of these assets than they have to lose by a share-out of employment and employment-based income and power advantages. It also rests on a recognition by white people that they have more to lose by the abolition of the advantages associated with whiteness than to gain from redistribution of other assets. The new orthodoxy's majority support depends on exclusion of the poor and black minorities from the common good.

Because this means that the underclass has no interest in the majority system for economic cooperation, or in the democratic political system, it implies that the majority must compel poor and black people to act against their interests if they are to participate in society. This creates an active conflict between the two sectors, affecting every sphere of social life.

Already the moral principles of the new orthodoxy are shifting from a claim that the market-based economic system is consistent with care and compassion for those 'less fortunate' people in 'genuine need', to an insistence that those with no interest in economic participation must be compelled to work, to fulfil their obligations to the good society.[39] Instead of being included in the common good as dependants, the minority are to be seen as potential threats to the common good, unless they can be disciplined – if necessary punished – into compliance with the requirements of the majority.

This is an agenda for a kind of class war between the majority and the minority, in which it comes to be in the interests of the latter to resist, to harass and to revolt. The new orthodoxy's principles destroy the possibility of a common good which includes all citizens of an advanced capitalist society. In chapter 7, I shall consider the possibilities for an inclusive alternative form of citizenship.

Notes

1　Peter Taylor-Gooby, 'Conservative doubts behind the radical rhetoric', *The Listener*, 15 October 1987.
2　Central Statistical Office, *Annual Abstract of Statistics, 1988 Edition* (HMSO, 1988), table 6.1, p. 108.
3　Central Statistical Office, *Social Trends 17* (HMSO, 1987), table 4.8, p. 73.
4　Ibid., table 4.10, p. 74.
5　Ibid., table 4.9, p. 74.
6　Ibid., table 4.21, p. 79.
7　Ibid., table 5.2, p. 86.
8　Ibid., table A9, p. 17.
9　Ibid., table 5.21, p. 100.
10　Ibid., table 5.1, p. 85.
11　Central Statistical Office, *United Kingdom National Accounts, 1987 Edition* (HMSO, 1987), table 4.1, p. 37. See also Department of Employment, *Family Expenditure Survey, 1986* (HMSO, 1987), table 22, p. 64. This gives the proportion of total household income from investments as 4.2 per cent, and from imputed income from owner-occupation as 5.4 per cent. For households whose head was an employee, the proportions were 2 per cent and 5 per cent respectively.
12　*Annual Abstract of Statistics, 1988*, table 6.1, p. 108.
13　*Social Trends 17*, table 5.2, p. 86.
14　Department of Employment, *New Earnings Survey, 1984* (HMSO, 1984), Part B, B34, extrapolating from 1984 statistics.
15　Office of Population Censuses and Surveys, *General Household Survey, 1985* (HMSO, 1987), table 7.16, p. 115.
16　Ibid.
17　Ibid., table 7.17, p. 115.
18　*Social Trends 17*, table 4.4, p. 71.
19　Ibid., table 5.22, p. 100.

20 Ibid., table 8.7, p. 140.
21 *Family Expenditure Survey, 1986*, tables 1 and 22, pp. 1 and 64.
22 Joseph Schumpeter, *Capitalism, Socialism and Democracy* (1943) (Allen and Unwin, 1961), p. 250.
23 Ibid., p. 269.
24 Ibid., p. 271.
25 Ibid., ch. 23.
26 Ibid., p. 285.
27 Seymour M. Lipset, *Political Man*, (1959) (Mercury, 1964), p. 218. Other examples include B. R. Berelson, P. F. Lazarsfeld and W. N. McPhee, *Voting* (University of Chicago Press, 1954), who argued that limited participation and public apathy had a positive function for the democratic system by reducing the impact of conflict between extremes; R. A. Dahl, *Preface to Democratic Theory* (University of Chicago Press, 1956), who held that pluralist democracy required a consensus of norms among those active in political life, and that hence the exclusion of lower socioeconomic groups, most likely to be authoritarian in their attitudes, was functional; and G. Sartori, *Democratic Theory* (Wayne State University Press, 1962), who argued that once democratic institutions had been established, participation should be minimized and non-participation regarded as unproblematic.
28 Peter Taylor-Gooby, 'Conservative doubts behind the radical rhetoric'.
29 For a more detailed argument, see Bill Jordan, *Rethinking Welfare* (Blackwell, 1987), ch. 7.
30 J. D. Gershuny and I. D. Miles, *The New Service Economy: the Transformation of Employment in Industrial Societies* (Pinter, 1983).
31 Between 1982 and 1986, there was an increase of 400,000 in the number of people employed in 'other services' in the United Kingdom, see *Annual Abstract of Statistics, 1988*, table 6.2, p. 111.
32 Bill Jordan, 'Unemployment and the spirit of enterprise', *Social Science Review*, 3 (1988), pp. 102-5.
33 DHSS, *Reform of Social Security* (the Fowler Report, Cmnd 9517, HMSO, 1985), vol. 1, pp. 29-30. For a critique of the effects of the reforms, see Hermione Parker, 'Off target', *New Society*, vol. 75, no. 1206, 7 February 1986, p. 232.
34 Jordan, 'Unemployment and the spirit of enterprise', pp. 203-4.
35 See, for example, Lawrence M. Mead, *Beyond Entitlement: the Social Obligations of Citizenship* (Free Press, 1986).
36 Bill Jordan, *The Use of the Community Programme in Health and Social Care* (National Council for Voluntary Organizations, 1987).
37 Mead, *Beyond Entitlement*, pp. 24-5 and 44-5.
38 Mark Rankin, *Working in the Margin: Unemployment, Volunteering and Marginal Work* (Volunteer Centre, 1985).
39 In Britain, advocates of workfare include David Willets, Patrick Minford and John Burton.

7

The First Step towards an Alternative

My critique of the new orthodoxy has demonstrated the possibility of a fundamental conflict between two sectors of a society constructed on the new orthodoxy's account of individual interests and responsibilities. Under present
economic conditions, the majority has an interest in excluding and oppressing
a minority, by denying it access to assets giving key income and power
advantages. Conversely, the excluded minority has no interest in economic or
political participation, and will resist attempts to coerce it.

I have constructed an alternative account of interests and responsibilities in
relation to a common good, based on the common interests of all members of
society. A fair distribution of assets, or of the advantages accruing from assets,
would allow these interests to be recognizable, and hence encourage all
individuals and groups to participate in society's systems of cooperation. But
I have not yet shown how, under modern economic conditions, individuals'
and groups' competitive self-interest can be reconciled with the common good
in a society which is efficient, prosperous, democratic and harmonious. Nor
have I shown how it might be possible to move from an individualistic,
divided society to one which allowed a sense of membership and community.

This is a tall order. In the first place, it is clear that my version of the good
society must (in terms of its own principles) be constructed by a process
involving debate, participation, choice and ultimately consent. It therefore
has to be constructed democratically. But I have also argued that representative democracy is a system which is better suited to the expression of
competitive, self-interested preferences than common interests, and that
under present conditions a majority coalition has an interest (in these terms)
in excluding the claims of the underclass. The goal of a good society must be
that the political system allows the common good to be promoted, and social
institutions to be constantly adapted for the sake of a better quality of life.
This requires a more participatory form of democracy. But under present
conditions it is not in the interests of the majority to allow the underclass to
participate, still less to share power, and so this change is unlikely to emerge
through representative democratic processes.

Secondly, it is clear that the common good requires some form of redistribution of assets, or of the advantages they confer, so that all members of
society get a fair share. But in a democracy, if state power is to be successfully

used to create common interests in cooperation, a majority must be convinced that redistribution is fair for all.

In modern Western societies, distributive justice is a complex concept, including elements of entitlement (e.g. property rights), merit (e.g. rewards for skill or effort) and need (e.g. extra resources for those with special handicaps). Since any attempt at redistribution must start from the present allocation of assets, and the new orthodoxy's justifications of it, an alternative construction of a good society must deal with both interest-based defences of current distributions and philosophical arguments for them.

The new orthodoxy is robust in its justification of individuals' entitlements to property holdings, and of the rewards given by the market to entrepreneurial acumen and to skill. This leaves little room for redistributions based on need. Since self-responsibility requires people to try to be independent and self-sufficient, as individuals or in households, no provision for need should undermine the principle of independence. Needs-based income support and public services should be limited to those who can demonstrate that they have genuinely tried to be self-sufficient, and failed through no fault of their own.

The claim of the underclass to a fair share of assets on the grounds of their needs (as opposed to their entitlements or merits) is doubly problematic. On the one hand, it goes against the exclusive self-interest of the majority, and on the other, it fails to create common interests in participation and cooperation. If the poor qualify for a share of assets or their advantages purely by virtue of their neediness, it is hard to show how this encourages them to be responsible contributors to the common good.

A different approach would be to claim that members of the underclass are entitled to employment. The notion of a 'right to work' has the legitimacy of its long-term associations with socialism, and with the idea that redistribution will be achieved through a contribution to society, in terms of effort and skill. It also directly addresses the fact that job assets are the most important factors in determining advantage and disadvantage under modern economic conditions. It therefore seems obvious that entitlement to employment should be the moral basis of fairness in an alternative approach.

However, in this chapter I shall argue that there are serious difficulties in this approach. In terms of competitive self-interest, the sharing out of employment is difficult to justify unless it can contribute to economic growth and efficiency; in practice, it is difficult to see how it can do so. In terms of fairness, redistribution of employment towards the poor will only include the underclass in the common good if each poor household gets at least one decently paid full-time job, which gives income security and access to other forms of property, such as owner-occupied housing and a pension. This does not seem a feasible aim under present economic conditions.

A third approach would be to create a universal entitlement to income security for each individual as a member of society – a citizenship Basic Income. This would amount to reducing the income advantages associated with assets, through an integrated tax and benefit system, in order to allow members of the underclass incentives for participation and cooperation in the common good. At first sight this approach seems far less egalitarian than the first because it appears to leave asset holdings intact. But I shall argue that on closer examination it has radical implications for fairness, and is the most promising first step towards an alternative form of society.

I shall deal in turn with the opportunities and constraints imposed by democratic institutions, with ideas of fairness over redistribution, and with strategies for achieving fair shares in the common good.

Democracy and common interests

Representative democracy is not necessarily the ideal starting point for creating a social system with common interests between members. It may well be that Mr Gorbachev would have an easier point of departure for such a project in the Soviet Union, if such were to be the aims of *glasnost* and *perestroika*, than exists in modern Western societies. After all, it was not democracy but the Second World War and its aftermath that created the conditions (shared hardship together with massive state command over resources) that allowed the social democratic attempt at more egalitarian membership terms through redistribution of assets.

In chapter 6 I argued that representative democracy favours a competitive struggle between rival elites for the support of a majority of largely passive electors. In a market-based society, such as the one constructed by the new orthodoxy's principles, it allows the role of the voter to be very like that of economic consumer. Voters are encouraged to make choices in accordance with their immediate material interests, and to favour parties which will advance these interests, without regard to the fate of others.[1]

In conjunction with the new orthodoxy, representative democracy therefore promotes the pursuit of competitive advantage above cooperative forms of self-interest, and the creation of majority interests in exclusive goods over common interests in the common good. Instead of offsetting the inequities of the economic system, the political system reinforces these. Problems such as unemployment and poverty are eventually redefined as failures by the under-class to fulfil their citizenship obligations or as inadequacies and incompetences. This then justifies requiring them to act against their interests, under threat.

The discussion in chapter 5 implied a very different form of democracy, with a far more active, participatory citizenry shaping the goals and means of each system of cooperation, in every sphere. It implied that citizens should be drawn into these forms of active, cooperative behaviour by a common interest in contributing to, as well as benefiting from, the goods being produced. This suggested a society in which there was far greater participatory democracy in economic life, in local affairs, in the social services and in membership groups, as well as in the national political system.[2] This version of democracy can be recognized not merely in the republican tradition, but also among such later writers as de Tocqueville and John Stuart Mill, and in early socialists.

But there is no obvious way in which an advanced capitalist society might move from representative democracy towards participatory democracy, given present majority interests. Participatory democracy requires common interests. If interests are fundamentally divergent, then participation merely ensures that no decisions are made, nothing is done and open conflict is maximized. Participatory democracy can accommodate divergent interests only if there are greater interests in cooperation. As we have seen, the society promoted by the new orthodoxy creates a fundamental opposition between the interests of the majority and those of the minority. Hence, it is not in the interests of the majority to support any moves from representative to participatory democracy. Rather, it is in the majority interest to continue to exclude the minority from an influence in any sphere of society.

For this reason, there seems little point in urging greater participation as a *first step* towards a good society. While it is true that there can never be a good society without participation, because the common good must be created by common action, and requires a quality of life in which all contribute to the good of all, no move in this direction could come about so long as material interests dominate political systems, and the majority have an interest in excluding the minority from all forms of participation. Hence political parties which favour greater participation as the major means of moving from a corrupt to a good society - such as the British Liberal Party - seem to be putting the cart before the horse.

Redistribution and fairness

The project of redistributing assets (or their income advantages) so as to achieve common economic interests must therefore be undertaken before the project of sharing power through more participatory democracy. This faces obstacles of competitive self-interest and of philosophical argument. The strength of the new orthodoxy lies in its ability to combine an appeal to the self-interest of the majority with a justification of their advantages, by insisting that the market allocate assets and incomes in a way which is non-arbitrary, impersonal, 'natural', commensurate with efforts and skills, and hence fair.[3] Any attempt to interfere with its processes, or with voluntary transfers (gifts, bequests), is seen as an arbitrary restriction of choice. Imposing patterns (equal or unequal shares) is therefore unfair. In Robert Nozick's celebrated example, only unwarranted coercion can stop a combination of market forces and voluntary giving from providing the star footballer, Wilt Chamberlain, with a higher income than the egalitarian would prescribe.

The underclass is not a homogeneous group. It contains some people who are at a great disadvantage in the labour market because of illness, physical or mental handicap, injury, old age and so on, and those who provide unpaid care for them. It also contains people who are discriminated against in the labour market, especially black people, many of whom are doing work which is far less well paid than their qualifications warrant. And it also contains people with no obvious handicap, except their lack of skills, or their high travel-to-work or child-care costs, or the fact that they share a household with other unskilled people, for whom the labour market gives no adequate employment incentives.

The new orthodoxy is already willing to make limited redistributions of income and services, from taxation on the earnings of the majority, to the underclass. The justification it gives for these is that people who try to be independent and self-sufficient, but cannot be, need and deserve such assistance. However, this rationale only serves to consolidate exclusion, since need is only demonstrable through failure in labour-market competition, and income support is withdrawn as beneficiaries' earnings increase. It also justifies tests of 'genuineness', such as the offer of low-paid employment, or of unpaid 'training', as a condition for receiving benefits.

This suggests that no redistributive measures will include the underclass in the common good unless they allow all who are physically and mentally capable of doing so to contribute to economic activity. It indicates that the key to the success of the post-war social security system was not so much the benefits paid by virtue of needs, but the fact that these were linked to employment contributions, and a system of economic management which provided 'full employment'. This points directly towards a strategy of including the underclass by recognizing its members' entitlement to employment (a 'right to work') which would enable them simultaneously to play a part in society's productive effort and to gain a share in its assets.

This approach seems to have the double merit of directly addressing the most relevant aspect of underclass exclusion (lack of job assets), and of appealing to the socialist tradition of fairness, which is very widely endorsed in Western societies. Even when Mrs Thatcher's individualism was being endorsed by the electorate, public opinion polls suggested that a large majority saw mass unemployment as a social evil and full employment as desirable. Hence a strategy of employment creation is likely to command support as fair; indeed, the British Conservative government relies on this to justify its MSC training schemes and employment measures.

However, there are two major problems with this strategy. One is how to create more employment for the underclass without making the majority substantially worse-off (both in terms of lower earnings and in terms of higher costs of goods and services). The other is how to distribute new employment in such a way as to include the underclass in the common good, by giving them the same incentives and opportunities as the majority. Both these are very closely tied up with the restructuring of the labour market in advanced capitalist countries that has taken place in recent years.

In Britain, in the spring of 1988, the whole economy is growing at a rate of around 4.5 per cent a year, and manufacturing output at an annual rate of some 5.5 per cent. Yet overall employment is growing at only 1.1 per cent, and manufacturing employment is *declining* at 1.7 per cent annually. In other words, even when the economy is growing at the fastest rate for a century, industrial jobs are still decreasing, and the slow growth in employment is fuelled by service work, with its characteristic part-time, low-paid profile.

The United States has achieved a more fragile boom, on the back of enormous budget and trade deficits, but with a large expansion of employment. There, however, real incomes have fallen for a large sector of workers – the so-called 'jobs miracle' has been achieved by an enormous increase in the working poor, through a widening of employment in unskilled service occupations, and through cuts in public assistance.

In no advanced capitalist country has a sustained increase in secure, well-paid, full-time jobs been combined with economic growth. On the contrary, governments have seemingly been faced with a choice between three options. The first strategy is an outright pursuit of a 'free' (i.e. highly segmented) labour market, with increasingly divergent real wages, expansion of employment in the lowest-paid segment, workfare and cuts in benefits (as in the United States). The second is an attempt to sustain a unified labour market, protect real wages, retain minimum wages and continue to pay relatively generous unemployment benefits (as in many Western European countries, e.g. The Netherlands). The third is to try to encourage the expansion of low-paid employment, paying means-tested supplements to wages and reinforcing these with stricter benefits tests and 'training' schemes for the unemployed (as in Britain). The first and third strategies involve an increase in low-paid, part-time work to replace losses in better-paid, full-time jobs, and the second involves continuing high unemployment.

This suggests that the goal of full employment, in the sense that was implied in the post-war era, is no longer attainable. Full employment envisaged a society consisting of households with a male breadwinner and his 'dependants'. The breadwinner was to have a secure, full-time job, with enough pay to meet the basic needs of the household, including housing costs. With the changed structure of the labour market, in no advanced capitalist country are there as many such jobs as there are households containing a member of working age – and the number of such jobs continues to decline, while the number of households rises. This is why job assets are the key determinant of majority or underclass status, and it is why the creation of new employment seems very unlikely to include the underclass in the common good. Full-time, better-paid, secure jobs – as assets giving access to other assets, such as pensions, owner-occupation and share ownership – represent a kind of property, which will continue to be reserved mainly for themselves by organizations dominated by white, male interests.

Meanwhile, of course, households too have changed. Compared with the post-war era, there are fewer containing two adults and child dependants (now around 30 per cent of all households) and more with two adults, more with only one person, more with a single parent, and many with an elderly dependant. It is also no longer so clear that fairness can be achieved by creating as many decently paid jobs as there are households, because there is now a recognizable issue about fairness *between* household members. Why should men have access to better-paid, full-time jobs and women be confined to unpaid domestic roles? A 'full employment' strategy would not even address the issue of fairness as between paid and unpaid workers.

All this means that a traditional attempt to increase employment (for example, by increased government spending) would, under present and likely future conditions, make little or no impact on the problem of the underclass. A more radical approach is required.

Efficiency and flexibility

Another possible strategy for redistributing employment opportunities would be for job-holders (i.e. those with secure, decently paid, full-time employment) to forgo increases in earnings, for the sake of giving others the chance of a job. This strategy has been widely discussed in Western European labour movements, but not in Britain. It would amount to a very strict incomes policy, operated through consensual corporatist institutions of the state, to try to bring about results like those achieved in Sweden, where differentials in earnings are kept very low, public sector employment is high, unemployment benefits are generous, and unemployment has been held well below average for the advanced industrialized countries.

People who glibly mention Sweden as a model of a good society underestimate the enormous redistributive task that would have to be achieved to make an economy like Britain's remotely resemble that country's. The 'Swedish model' of economic management has been in place since 1932; there has been political continuity since then (with one break from 1976 to 1982, when the essential features of the strategy were maintained); and the extent of institutional controls, within the labour market and over earnings, would need a massive increase in intervention to be replicated in the British economy. To achieve the required fall in wage differentials, better-off employees would have to take large cuts in wages and salaries, and to provide the necessary increase in public sector employment and social security benefits would require far higher tax rates.

But even if members of the majority were willing to make these major sacrifices of their individual competitive interests for the sake of a corporatist, full-employment, earnings-sharing common good, there would be questions about whether the strategy could be sustained under modern economic conditions. Already in Sweden, for example, industrial employment has been declining since 1965, male economic participation and full-time employment have been declining since 1975, and public sector exceeds private sector employment. Industrial production has grown far more slowly than the average for the

OECD since 1975, as has productivity.⁴ Would better-off workers cooperate in reducing their earnings, and would all workers accept the huge dislocation that would follow the reduction of differentials (when wages rose in low-productivity jobs and fell in high-productivity ones), for the sake of a system which might well produce slower economic growth or even a fall in national income?

It seems more plausible to argue that a representative democracy is likely to adopt radically new systems, including new institutions and new values, if these offer the possibility of long-term gains in efficiency and in economic growth, from which the majority stand to gain. In Britain, the 'Thatcher revolution' was an example of such a process. Many trade unionists and former Labour supporters who were comfortably off under a social democratic system, and had benefited from the security if offered, risked all this for the sake of the possible gains associated with a free-market strategy. An alternative to the new orthodoxy would have a better chance of political success if it could claim long-term efficiency advantages. If redistributive measures could produce prospects for economic expansion over and above the growth that would otherwise have occurred in the next five years, then majority support for redistribution might be achieved.

This seems to be the way in which advanced capitalist democracies have accomplished major changes in their systems of income distribution – in effect, by showing that any apparent losses by the majority will be more than compensated by greater gains in national income, and hence in the shares of all. For an egalitarian programme this amounts to saying that the income gains of the poor will be paid for out of economic growth. It was the argument which largely sustained the social democratic system in Western Europe from the early 1950s to the mid-1970s. It was overthrown by the new orthodoxy when the latter was able to use economic theory and evidence to argue that, despite the stake that the majority by then had in that system, its short-term losses from the adoption of a more market-based order would be more than compensated by a long-term improvement in growth rates.

It is difficult at first sight to argue that productive efficiency would be boosted if those at present excluded from the labour market were given their share of employment. This is chiefly because the unemployed are mostly unskilled, younger or older workers, who could not be expected quickly to match the productivity of those in work, and because the others who are outside the labour market are those who would have the highest costs (associated with travelling to work or arranging care of relatives) for taking jobs.

What is widely recognized by market-minded economists is that future gains in efficiency depend upon flexibility in the use of labour-power in the productive process.⁵ In Japan, for example, a far greater flexibility, and consequently greater gains in productivity in manufacturing industry, have been achieved than in Western Europe or the United States. This is partly because trade unions have been less insistent on identifying their workers with particular skills and tasks, and partly because of the existence of a secondary (mainly non-unionized) sector of small firms, which are constantly forced to adapt their productive methods to the requirements of the large corporations, and hence to achieve the flexibility that would be difficult in larger and more formal productive structures.[6]

By contrast, in the United States it has mainly been in the service sector that new small firms have achieved the flexibility that allowed important productivity gains. In Western Europe, although some signs of both these kinds of efficiency-orientated changes have been visible, the scope for further flexibility seems rather limited. One important factor in this is that flexibility implies insecurity of earnings, employment or both.[7] Either earnings come to be related to such variable factors as profits, productivity or demand for products, with the danger of losses as well as gains in consequence; or jobs themselves become fragmented into part-time work, short-term contracts, self-employment, or some other formula which destroys the reliability of earnings and makes the worker's situation precarious.

So it could be the case that an argument from efficiency might aim to promote flexibility in the utilization of labour-power by giving workers a greater security of income in exchange for a greater willingness to accept insecurity of employment and variability of earnings. For example, it could be argued that the state should guarantee the incomes of working-age citizens in such a way as to allow a larger proportion of these to accept flexible terms of employment, rather than to insist upon present terms, including long-term contracts, regular weekly earnings, redundancy payments etc. This would, of course, fly in the face of trade-union negotiated agreements, and also the minimum wage legislation in many West European countries.

The notion of such an efficiency-orientated policy programme has important implications for a possible egalitarian alternative to the new orthodoxy. In the first place, since regular full-time jobs are the most important asset in the majority interest in the new orthodoxy's principles, it seems possible that efficiency considerations might lead to the erosion of the new orthodoxy itself. At present, the possession of a full-time job, or membership of a household in which one member has a full-time job, is the most important stake in the new orthodoxy's order. But if efficiency demands that a greater proportion of the population give up their claim to full-time jobs (in this traditional sense), then an efficiency-orientated programme will erode this stake in the new orthodoxy's principles. Hence there will be a dilemma for market-minded governments over the conflicting demands of efficiency and the new orthodoxy.

Secondly, it would be difficult to provide the income security necessary for current 'regular' workers to accept greater flexibility without giving the same benefits to existing part-time and short-term 'irregular' employees. In other words, policy measures aimed at giving income guarantees to those in secure employment to accept insecurity would tend also to extend those guarantees to people whose employment terms and earnings are at present precarious and variable.

Thirdly, the system for guaranteeing the incomes of those whose jobs and earnings would be made less secure for the sake of efficiency would also be likely to offer opportunities for many people, who at present do demanding full-time jobs, to reduce their hours of work. Instead of being forced to choose between full-time jobs or total retirement, more workers would be able to go part-time during their later working years. The system would also allow more people to take 'sabbatical' periods of part-time employment, for example, to take an increased responsibility for child care or for caring for a dependent relative. It would enable couples to share unpaid domestic work more equally. Hence, at the same time as enabling greater flexibility for the sake of productive efficiency, it would probably also allow greater flexibility for workers to choose to vary their hours and conditions of work.

Fourthly, if some present regular workers reduced their hours of work, this would enable extra workers from the hitherto excluded sector to be employed. It could also make it worth the while of previously excluded claimants to take part-time or temporary paid employment because the same arrangement which guaranteed the incomes of those in work would also apply to them, once they took a job. In this way some of the underclass could be absorbed into the workforce, and all would be given an interest in participating, if only in a part-time or short-term job.

Finally, if greater efficiency led to a rate of growth of output that was faster than the growth of productivity, then this factor would also result in an increase in employment for members of the underclass. In this way, it could be argued that the benefit to the previously excluded group was partly (or eventually even wholly) financed out of growth.

However, the major difficulty facing this kind of proposal is that it is opposed by trade unions representing the vast majority of the present regular workers who might be directly affected. This is because unions have traditionally regarded job security and collectively negotiated regular wages as being the basis of their members' interests, and because any erosion of these principles would seem to weaken the unions themselves. If the state underwrote the incomes of the workforce in the name of efficiency and flexibility, the reliance of workers on their wages – and on unions as negotiators for wages – would be reduced. Besides, earnings in insecure, part-time jobs and from self-employment have traditionally been low, compared with those of regular full-time employees, and so trade unions argue strongly that their members' interests lie in retaining a structure of regular full-time jobs, rather than allowing the further 'casualization' of employment.

Hence, any egalitarian programme for such an alternative to the new orthodoxy is faced with an awkward dilemma over the efficiency problem. On the one hand, it might use the issue of efficiency to expose a fundamental contradiction in the new orthodoxy: that its political support depended on a stake in exclusive employment assets, while efficiency criteria demanded that exclusive holdings in employment assets should be eroded. But, on the other hand, the traditional political base for any egalitarian programme has been the working class, and political success has depended on close alliance with organized labour. For example, it is difficult to imagine the British Labour Party adopting a programme which promoted the demand of efficiency and growth over the demands of the trade union movement.

The Basic Income principle: an alternative approach

The possible proposed solution to the efficiency problem allows us a glimpse of an egalitarian alternative to the new orthodoxy, though one which is surrounded by many obstacles. Furthermore, it is a possibility which is, in theory at least, consistent with a transition accomplished through representative democracy. It therefore offers a slender hope of a peaceful way in which a society based on the new orthodoxy's principles might be transformed into a better, and ultimately a good, society without a process of violent conflict.

The new orthodoxy declares that there is no way of giving the underclass self-interested motives in economic participation because they lack the skills to produce enough to earn a subsistence income. The best it can offer them is a means-tested supplement to their below-subsistence earnings (such as family credit or housing benefit) which makes up these to subsistence levels. But so long as this supplement is withdrawn while income tax is also being paid, the combined effects of these deductions from additional earnings produce an effective marginal tax rate which is very high (around 90 per cent in the current British system). Combined with the onset of expenses associated with travelling to work, child care and so on, this largely removes the incentives, and hence the self-interested motives, for employment.[8]

The new orthodoxy has been even less successful in overcoming the income insecurity associated with part-time and short-term work. Here the dilemma for the worker is that the only comprehensive measures for public assistance (such as income support in Britain) make very small allowance for part-time workers' earnings to be disregarded; above this level they are effectively confiscated. The rules also force workers to leave the programme once they exceed a set number of hours. Conversely, systems for supplementing employment earnings do not provide for those below a certain number of hours' work per week, and can only provide weekly additions to wages on the basis of average weekly earnings, which is not suitable for the variations associated with 'flexible' employment because it does not provide a secure basic income.

Above all, means-tested systems cannot provide motives for flexibility which appeal to workers at present in the market sector of the economy because they tie earnings to a poverty line. In effect, they relate the final incomes of those who qualify for benefits closely to the public assistance (income support, subsistence) level, and prevent them from rising significantly above this without penalty. They also penalize savings, since these are now taken into account in assessing people for supplements to their earnings in the British system. Hence they cannot be used as a basis for restructuring existing employment towards greater flexibility without damaging the interests of those at present in regular full-time jobs. This means that the scope for flexibility is largely confined to the 'component earnings' of married women and young people living with employed parents, since they can experience variations in earnings from the position of sharing a household with someone on an adequate regular income.

However, a different principle of income maintenance could overcome these problems. If every individual was guaranteed a Basic Income, sufficient for subsistence, by the state, then far greater incentives - both to those outside the present labour market to take paid work and to those at present in the market sector to share it - could be provided. The Basic Income principle would imply that each citizen was given an unconditional income, sufficient for basic needs, and allowed to build upon this from earnings. The Basic Income would not be withdrawn, but all other incomes would be taxed, so that at a certain point people would become net contributors to the system, and all adjustments to final incomes would be made through taxation.[9]

Clearly this principle could be used in various ways, depending on the policy objectives of the government which chose to introduce it. The Basic Income could be set at a level to maximize equality, to maximize its own relative level as a proportion of total taxable income or to maximize its absolute level. Robert van der Veen and Philippe Van Parijs have shown that each of these criteria gives different tax rates, different national incomes and different rates of Basic Income.[10] However, none of these egalitarian programmes would be likely to appeal to a majority in a society based on the new orthodoxy. Instead, a possible alternative might aim to maximize the national income consistent with a certain minimum level of Basic Income (probably related to current benefit rates). This 'growth orientated' criterion would allow the case for flexibility and efficiency to be combined with arguments from citizenship.

One great advantage of the Basic Income principle is that it treats everyone alike. It gives each able-bodied working-age adult the same Basic Income, irrespective of age, colour, sex, work or marital status. Hence it has obvious potential as a citizenship-based share of national income, in that it allows everyone to be treated in the same way. A political programme incorporating Basic Income could argue that this share constituted the income associated with membership of society, and the system ensured that each citizen got his or her due. (Clearly, disabled and handicapped people and old and frail people would have to receive higher Basic Incomes, in recognition of their higher living costs and of their disadvantages in the labour market. Ideally, those requiring personal assistance with day-to-day tasks could receive an allowance equivalent to the costs of the care they needed.)

Basic Income could only be represented as a citizenship share if it were acknowledged that employment is neither an obligation for all nor a privilege for those able to reserve this asset for themselves. In a society ordered around

Basic Income, all citizens would have incentives to take paid employment, even on a part-time basis, and none would be trapped into excessive work effort or excluded from any incentives to work. Each individual's quota of employment hours would therefore be (in principle at least) at his or her own discretion. Instead of men being forced to choose between full-time work or full-time claiming, and women being forced to find some balance between paid employment and unpaid household work (so that those with most obligations to others in the household have least access to employment), men and women would have opportunities and incentives to share both employment and unpaid work, not merely within the same household but also in such a way as to allow the excluded underclass to participate in economic life.

Market-minded critics of Basic Income argue that an adequate level of income security would cause too many people to reduce their labour market contribution, by withdrawing partly or wholly from paid work. They quote the American experiments in income maintenance (the SIME/DIME projects in Seattle and Denver) as evidence of reduced participation, especially among married women and young people.[11] However, this objection is largely misleading. In the Seattle and Denver experiments, the level of income guarantee was well above the benefits provided on existing public assistance programmes, so a degree of withdrawal by some groups – especially those who had no previous title to income maintenance in their own right, such as married women and young people living with their families – was to be anticipated. But more important (from the point of view of any egalitarian attempt to include the underclass in the common good) is the fact that the withdrawal from participation or reduction in working hours of some members of job-rich households would actually be beneficial for members of the underclass, while non-participation by any individuals or groups could be seen as a choice, rather than as enforced exclusion, as at present.

Critics from the organized labour movement argue that Basic Income offers a subsidy to employers who want to pay below-subsistence wages, and hence encourage low pay; it also allegedly encourages the 'casualization' of employment by allowing the flexible use of labour-power without reference to adequate living wages for the workforce. The first criticism is misplaced; by giving an *equal* Basic Income to all, the principle subsidizes *all* employers equally. It is means-tested supplements which encourage low pay by subsidizing only those with below-subsistence wages. Furthermore, the unconditional availability of benefits would strengthen the hand of unskilled employees, and probably lead to rather higher wages for unpleasant, dirty, low-paid jobs, which might not otherwise be done. The second criticism is more valid, given that the organized labour movement sees itself as defending its members' privileged access to, and defensive tenure of, employment assets in the form of regular full-time jobs. If trade unions are to aim to defend their members' income advantages (as they have traditionally done), then this objection must stand, and any egalitarian programme must expect to count them among its opponents.

Is Basic Income an egalitarian measure?

So far I have argued that Basic Income would represent a citizenship share of national income, and that it would allow a voluntary redistribution of employment assets from the job-rich towards the job-poor. If it were set according to the growth-orientated criterion, it would allow an argument from efficiency to be made to a majority in a representative democracy, exposing the contradiction between the new orthodoxy's appeal to the job-rich against the underclass, and its claims of a growth-maximizing economic order.[12]

Yet it could be argued that the Basic Income is no more than a mechanism for a smooth transition from the new orthodoxy's harsh form of market capitalism to a subtle and more deceptive form of exploitation and domination. After all, the Basic Income mechanism would not necessarily be redistributive in any major sense. It would not, unless it was specifically geared to do so, redistribute wealth, or do much to affect the income advantages associated with control over production or skill. It would probably in the long run lead to higher earnings for women (since it would effectively abolish the tax advantages of married women, which allow employers a premium on low-paid part-time employment). But it would do little to tackle the structural discrimination against black people. Above all, it would not in any obvious way address inequalities in power associated with the unequal distribution of assets, with the exception of gender-based inequalities of power which would be considerably reduced in the household sphere by the provision of an independent income for women. This would offset their economic dependence on men.

It is true that a Basic Income set according to the growth-orientated criterion would not necessarily, of itself, be a major contribution to quantitative equality of incomes, nor would it necessarily lead to a major shift of power within an advanced capitalist society. Indeed, if it set out to do either of these things, it would probably fail to win the support of a majority, given the interests against redistribution created by the new orthodoxy. Its advantage, given the present majority interest in excluding the underclass, lies in the possibility of reintegrating this oppressed sector, by allowing them once more to have an incentive for economic participation, albeit a rather limited one. In other words, the Basic Income creates a citizenship share in income, allowing all a self-interested motive for paid employment and hence creating a common interest in a fairer distribution of income, employment and leisure.

The real test of whether a Basic Income set according to these criteria would be a step towards a better society would be whether it would allow other changes, which would improve the quality of life and enable a more active, participatory form of citizenship and other common interests between sections of society to become established. If the Basic Income were nothing more than a technical mechanism for avoiding the coercion of the minority, and for creating a formal income share for all, then its significance would be very limited. In chapter 8 I shall explore the possible effects, in terms of increased participation and sharing in the active creation of the common good, of society structured around the Basic Income principle.

The main argument for this measure as a first step to a better society is that it addresses the master evil of the new orthodoxy – the exclusion and coercion of the underclass – in a direct way, which can be framed as a moral appeal to the majority, and which can allow common interests to be recreated, where previously there were only opposed interests and hence potential conflict. This is the line of argument which has been taken recently by leading converts to the idea of Basic Income – such as Ralf Dahrendorf and Samuel Brittan – who have emphasized the long-term dangers to social cohesion and economic efficiency of the new orthodoxy's principles.[13]

But the growth-orientated criterion for fixing the Basic Income might lead to a political and moral compromise. It has already been strongly argued, in The Netherlands and in Britain, that growth and efficiency criteria cannot provide a case for a 'full' basic income, sufficient to guarantee each citizen enough for subsistence.[14] This is because the great variety of living costs (and especially of housing costs) of the working-age population would require levels of Basic Income so high that the tax rates associated with them would severely affect work incentives, and hence reduce national income. The compromise proposal is a 'Partial Basic Income', which is not supposed to cover everyone's full living costs. In The Netherlands' proposed scheme, it would be supplemented – for those temporarily outside the labour market – by insurance benefits or means-tested assistance. In the British alternative, it would be supplemented by means-tested housing benefit for those whose other income was insufficient to cover their housing costs.

This does not imply that either proposal would make present claimants worse-off. In Hermione Parker's British costed proposal, the Basic Income is designed to be at least equal to supplementary benefit (income support) for single people, and hence more generous for couples. The costings of The Netherlands' scheme give a rather higher Partial Basic Income than Parker's, and provide the additional protection of insurance-based benefits and public assistance for those with no earnings.

However, both proposals would give poor people limited incentive. In Parker's, the fairly small numbers of those on housing benefit would lose this as their earnings rose from zero; hence, they would face effective marginal tax rates of around 70 per cent on their earnings. In The Netherlands' scheme, the same would be true for those on public assistance, and people who got insurance benefits would face an 'unemployment trap' rather than a 'poverty trap' because it would not be worth their while to work for a wage less than the amount of the benefit. In these respects, although Partial Basic Income proposals represent a considerable improvement on schemes which rely entirely on means-tested benefits, they still give poor people less incentive than better-off ones.

The important question must therefore be whether Partial Basic Incomes represent a first step towards a progressively more generous provision of Basic

Incomes, or whether such a scheme would get frozen at some such level (or even suffer cuts over time). To answer this question we need to consider the likely economic motives for introducing a scheme, and its probable effects.

If the aim was primarily to allow greater labour market flexibility, and hence efficiency and growth, a Partial Basic Income system would be of limited use. Because the Basic Income would be low, only a small proportion of the potential workforce would be affected. On the one hand, members of the previously excluded underclass would be given limited incentives to take work which would formerly have not been worth their while. On the other, some low-paid workers would receive a guarantee of income security sufficient to make more flexible conditions of employment worth the risk. But so long as the Partial Basic Income remained at a low-level (comparable with present benefit rates i.e. 13 per cent of median full-time male earnings per individual) the potential gains from flexibility would be very limited.

Supposing that the initial transition to a Partial Basic Income system had been successfully negotiated, it would seem likely that the potential benefits of flexibility would not be exhausted by the initial low level of provision. The same advantages, and greater incentives, could be extended to wage-earners higher up the scale of earnings and skills by increasing the Basic Income as a proportion of personal income. In this way, a broader section of workers could eventually be induced to accept the risks associated with those working conditions.

Eventually, the benefits in terms of efficiency and cost-saving would be exhausted. By this time there might well be some counter-pressure to reduce Basic Incomes, both from those facing increasing tax rates and from employers beginning to experience difficulty in recruiting low-paid workers willing to take dirty or unpleasant jobs. At a certain point, therefore, a coalition of interests – those of higher-paid employees and of employers facing labour-supply problems – would begin to oppose further increases in Basic Income.

However, by that stage there might well be a larger coalition of people with an interest in continuing to increase the proportion of Basic Income in personal income, and as a proportion of national income. A political struggle would then ensue between those interests favouring one of the egalitarian criteria for the level of Basic income and those favouring the growth-orientated criterion.

It is not my purpose in this chapter to consider the broader social implications of that political struggle; they will be discussed in chapter 8. My point in this section is that Basic Income is not necessarily an intrinsically egalitarian measure, but that the same arguments (in terms of efficiency and growth) which might lead to the adoption of a compromise system of Partial Basic Incomes might eventually lead to an expansion of the principle in the direction of a full Basic Income, and might give the egalitarian version of the principle or political momentum of its own.[15]

Conclusions

The Basic Income principle would create a citizenship share in national income, sufficient to give each person basic security. It would include the underclass in the same form of citizenship shared by all, and allow them the same freedom to determine their own level of participation, and the same economic incentives as the rest (subject to the proviso mentioned in relation to the compromise Partial Basic Income).

Of itself, this would only put an end to one form of exploitation and one form of domination: the 'super-exploitation' and 'super-domination' of the majority over the excluded minority. It would therefore leave unresolved the other inequalities of income and power in the society created by the new orthodoxy. I have argued in this chapter that the level of Basic Income might tend to rise in the short-run, but would encounter obstacles to further increases long before income equality was achieved.

However, it would also create new possibilities for voluntary cooperation outside the formal economy, and for a more participatory social and political life. In this way, it would allow an expanded form of citizenship, in which qualitative aspects of social relations became recognized as important, and common interests in these were constructed. It would also allow for new forms of partnership and cooperation in the domestic sphere.

In all these ways, the Basic Income might be the first step towards a new version of the good society. It might also allow a recognition of the possibility of wider communal cooperation, and an eventual reduction in the preponderance of the market as a system for producing social goods. This would reassert the importance of public goods, and focus attention back onto the quality of relations between individuals and groups in society.

It is important to recognize the limitations as well as the advantages of this first step. For example, since discrimination against black people is an important element in the creation of the underclass, any attempt to improve social relations would require anti-racist policies. New social institutions would have to address quite directly the origins of black exclusion in white dominance, and new ways of including black people in the common good.

The purpose of a Basic Income would be to recreate common interests and hence the possibility of public goods. Under the new orthodoxy, divided interests will always undermine public goods of all kinds because sharing with members of the underclass requires individuals to sacrifice their material interests. Once this is changed, other public goods emerge as being in everyone's interests.

But it is important that these are not created in ways which leave citizens as passive consumers. The alternative programme must, if it is to appeal to a new vision of a good society, show how public goods can actively involve people, and generate a better quality of life. This will be the subject of chapter 8.

Notes

1 For a summary and critique of representative democracy and the Schumpeterian theory, see C. B. MacPherson, *The Life and Times of Liberal Democracy* (Oxford University Press, 1977).

2 The theory of participatory democracy has been well set out by Carole Pateman, *Participation and Democratic Theory* (Cambridge University Press, 1970).

3 See, for example, F. A. Hayek, *The Constitution of Liberty* (Routledge and Kegan Paul, 1960).

4 Guy Standing, *Unemployment and Labour Market Flexibility: Sweden* (International Labour Office, 1988), chs 1 and 2.

5 Guy Standing, *Unemployment and Labour Market Flexibility: the United Kingdom* (International Labour Office, 1986), esp. ch. 7.

6 J. Atkinson and N. Meager, *Changing Working Patterns: How Companies Achieve Flexibility to Meet New Needs* (National Economic Development Organization, 1986).

7 Standing, *Unemployment and Labour Market Flexibility: the United Kingdom*, ch. 8.

8 Hermione Parker, 'Fowler's reform of social security: facts and figures', *Basic Income Research Group Bulletin*, 5 (Spring 1986), pp. 12-17.

9 Bill Jordan, *Rethinking Welfare* (Blackwell, 1987), ch. 9.

10 Robert J. van der Veen and Philippe Van Parijs, 'A Capitalist road to Communism', *Theory and Society*, 15 (1987), pp. 635-55.

11 Neil Gilbert, *Capitalism and the Welfare State: Dilemmas of Social Benevolence* (Yale University Press, 1983), pp. 36-8 and 98.

12 Recent converts who have urged just such a programme include Ralf Dahrendorf, *The Underclass and the Future of Britain*, Tenth Annual Lecture, St George's House, Windsor Castle, 27 April 1987, and Samuel Brittan, 'Capitalism and the underclass', *The Financial Times*, 1 October 1987.

13 Ibid.

14 For The Netherlands, see Netherlands Scientific Council for Government Policy, *Safeguarding Social Security* (WRR, The Hague, 1985); for Britain, see Hermione Parker, 'Costing basic incomes', *Basic Income Research Group Bulletin*, 3 (Spring 1985), pp. 4-13.

15 Ann Gray, 'Resisting Economic Conscription', *Capital and Class*, 34, Spring 1988, pp. 119-46.

8
Consumption, Community and Social Relations

The new orthodoxy can see no moral problem over consumption. Since people are entitled to what they earn, what they inherit and what they are given, they are also entitled to consume their income as they please. To gain an income, they must in some sense please or benefit others; but to consume it they need please no one but themselves. For the new orthodoxy, this is not selfishness, but the essential freedom around which its whole system is structured.

Consumption is the goal of self-interest. It represents not merely the satisfaction of needs, but also the achievement of projects. In this sense, consumption is not just a way of living, but a way of giving one's life meaning. We are what we consume, and our status is proclaimed by what we can afford to buy for consumption.

Almost all people's needs, preferences and projects can be supplied commercially because commerce depends on being able to satisfy its customers' wants, and even (in the case of the rich ones) their whims. The market will soon respond to signals of new needs and preferences, and provide an ever-widening variety of goods for people to enjoy. Indeed, through advertising, styles and fashions, it can stimulate consumption, creating new kinds of pleasures and even new projects.

Through markets, millions of customers shape production; through patterns of retailing, advertising and products themselves, producers shape consumption. But although markets can coordinate the process of exchange, they cannot coordinate consumption itself. Individuals are left to choose whether to enjoy the fruits of self-interest in a self-interested way or whether to share them with others.

The new orthodoxy is a theory about how individuals have common interests in producing the maximum volume of goods for consumption, but not about how individuals can share common interests in the process of consumption. People pay for what they consume as individual customers, even if what they consume is a mass event, and they are part of a large crowd or audience as at a football match or a concert. It points out that commerce provides efficient means of catering for mass tastes, but cannot suggest a commercial solution to problems like football hooliganism, which occur when crowds want to enjoy the same occasion in different ways.

According to the new orthodoxy, the moral sphere consists of all those goods which the market does not supply. There are a few things which the market does not supply to anyone, no matter how rich they are. For example, there is no market in children in the advanced capitalist countries (though it is probably feasible to buy one in a Third World country and bring it home). But, for many goods, there is a mixed situation. For example, activity, supervision and guidance for adolescents out of school hours is available - through boarding schools, holiday camps, evening and weekend courses - for those who can afford the considerable costs. But for parents who cannot, the new orthodoxy regards their adolescent offspring as their moral responsibility, and any problems they may cause as their moral failure.

As a result, the sphere of direct moral obligation is much larger for the poor than for the rich, and in deprived communities than in wealthy ones. Since markets provide goods which are both status-giving and labour-saving, it is in the interests of those with high earning power to maximize their earnings and use these to purchase services - such as care for their children - which the less well-off have to provide on an unpaid basis. Since it is possible to buy insulation from others, and security for persons and property, it is in the interests of the rich to live in areas of high-priced houses, to join exclusive clubs, to eat in exclusive restaurants and so on. Responsibilities for public order, the social and physical environment and community relations are thus put disproportionately on those who cannot afford to buy themselves forms of personal protection and insulation from others, and greatest responsibility is put on those who live in the poorest areas, who cannot even afford to buy privacy, and who live in closest proximity to each other.

In other words, for the new orthodoxy, the moral sphere is a residual one - what is left over after people have met their own individual needs and preferences, and discharged their commitments to each other, through commercial means. For the rich, what is left over is largely a matter of personal relationships and emotional complexities: the stuff of TV series like *Dallas* and *Dynasty*, and the private lives of Cabinet Ministers, but not something over which the new orthodoxy expresses much concern.

It is much more concerned with the far larger sphere of goods which the market cannot supply to the worse-off members of society. In chapter 9 I shall discuss the household, which is the main arena for non-commercial activity: the production and consumption of non-market goods. In this chapter, I shall be concerned with non-market consumption outside the household, in groups, associations and communities.

When Mrs Thatcher says that there is no such thing as society, only individuals and families, she is stating in a very condensed way the new orthodoxy's whole social philosophy. If every person lived their life as a market producer, a market consumer and a private moral being, there would be no social relationships. People would relate to each other only as fellow producers and consumers, and all these relationships - outside the purely private sphere - would be mediated by markets. There would only be economic relations.

The world that Mrs Thatcher describes is a kind of idealized suburbia, in which people's relationships have become almost entirely formal because they only share in a common life through participating in the same commercial system. They meet at the shops, the bank or the insurance office; they exchange politenesses over the fence as they tend their gardens with the very latest appliances.

But, in reality, this kind of existence is only available to the well-off, whose lifestyle allows them to segregate themselves from the rest of society, and to privatize their daily round: travelling by car between the office and the private housing estate, and using only private commercial services. For the rest, daily life involves negotiating a common use of certain resources and amenities, and recognizing that we have to share our enjoyment and our problems as part of the same social world with others who are in some ways unlike ourselves.

This, in turn, raises the issue of the role of the state in social relations. For the new orthodoxy, the state's role is confined to being a provider of the last resort for those who are unable to provide for themselves. Since the first option is always commercial consumption, and the second moral responsibility, the state's involvement is always implicitly a case of moral failure, or at least of failure in a moral task. The state concentrates not on social relations generally, but on individual moral responsibility. In so far as it is concerned with wider relations, it is as a disciplinary and moralizing force.

In this chapter I shall analyse the implications of the new orthodoxy's view of consumption and morality, and of the state. I shall argue that an alternative view of social relations, as concerned with shared aspects of life in a community, is inescapable. Finally, I shall propose an approach to the creation of common interests in harmonious social relations and a good quality of life which is derived from the republican tradition.

Associations and the market

In chapter 3 I argued that non-commercial cooperation could be recognized as self-interested under certain conditions, but that the market and the state had eroded traditional communities, and limited the number of social goods which people had self-interested motives to provide on a cooperative basis. This implies that voluntary associations are in some sense the residuum of archaic communities, and represent the forms of cooperation which are still in individuals' interests to pursue on a non-commercial basis under modern conditions.

According to the new orthodoxy, cooperation outside the commercial sphere is only possible when people are concerned for each other's good. This cannot happen unless they are bound together by relations of affection, trust, loyalty and commitment to common beliefs and values; or unless they have strongly altruistic motives, such as those associated with religious faith and duty. Only in a system of relationships and commitments of this kind can sharing and generalized reciprocity be maintained because these occasionally or frequently demand self-sacrifice. Altruism cannot be sustained without strong moral sanctions.

The new orthodoxy's account of non-commercial cooperation would suggest that people will only get together for common purposes under very limited conditions. On the one hand, they will form households, small units of people who live together, and maintain kinship bonds with relatives. On the other, they will form associations with like-minded people, who share their concerns over specific issues and problems, and who have similar beliefs and values about their solution. These wider associations would tend to take the forms of churches, charities and single-issue pressure groups.

On the face of it, the new orthodoxy appears to ignore (or fail to explain) a very large slice of the ordinary social life of every community. In reality, there are a great many more associations – informal groups, self-help groups, social clubs, recreational and sports clubs, community and neighbourhood associations – than its analysis would suggest. People seem to have non-commercial motives to cooperate in all sorts of voluntary groupings mainly for the sake of enjoying common activities or the pursuit of some valued skill together. In other words, there is plenty of evidence all around us that people can and do recognize a common interest in associating together, in a structured or an *ad hoc* way because it enhances their enjoyment of life and produces some material benefit for them.

If challenged to account for this, and to explain the new orthodoxy's apparent omission in relation to it, an advocate of its principles would probably reply that these phenomena had little real significance. Of course, people choose to get together to amuse and enjoy themselves, but this is really only a species of joint consumption. After all, the most common of all forms of association are gatherings in pubs, restaurants and in people's homes, where food and drink are consumed together. Many social clubs are just elaborate rituals for organizing drunken outings; many sports clubs are semi-energetic preludes to evenings spent at the bar; many community associations are no more than cheap places to meet and drink coffee. From the point of view of the hard-headed and market-minded, so-called voluntary associations are significant only in so far as they allow people ways of getting together as consumers of leisure products: to wear the clothes and employ the equipment appropriate to a particular joint activity. Far from being an alternative form of non-commercial cooperation, they are the expression of joint satisfaction of needs and wants, a chosen mode of market consumption.

The only true test of any association, in this view, is whether it can supply goods which the market cannot. For example, can voluntary groups and self-help associations meet the needs of young people, who cannot afford their own premises and equipment, who lack the social skills to entertain themselves and who require supervision and guidance? If they can, then they are supplying the community with something of real social value and significance.

But the new orthodoxy would argue that the commitment to provide such a service must be a moral one, and therefore must be explained in terms of its altruistic model of the non-commercial sphere. For adults to come forward as voluntary youth leaders, they must either be acting out of motives of altruistic concern for young people (for example, religious motives); or they must be part of a strong movement (such as the scout movement) with shared values and beliefs, which they share with each other, and with the young people in their charge.

The new orthodoxy would point out that voluntary associations tend to be rather short-lived and ephemeral, unless they evolve into commercial organizations or into charities. If a membership group provides substantial material benefits for its members, then it will probably change – gradually or quickly – into a fully fledged commercial company or at least into an organization committed to material gain. For example, in the nineteenth century there was a very extensive and elaborate system of voluntary mutual-aid organizations, focused on the more highly skilled and better-paid trades and more respectable working-class neighbourhoods. But, with time, friendly societies became commercial insurance companies, selling door-to-door for profit; cooperatives became chains of retail shops; building societies became commercial outlets for housing loans; savings banks became profit-orientated; and trade unions largely lost their function as organizers of benefits and pensions, and focused on negotiating over pay and conditions.[1] In other words, where there was real scope for self-interested cooperation, market forces were able to organize it on a more reliable and efficient basis, and to meet the same needs better than voluntary associations had done.

On the other hand, the best-known and longest-lived voluntary organizations are charities, bodies through which those activated by altruistic concern for a specific kind of suffering or disorder are able (either directly or indirectly by means of donations) to do something to help. The new orthodoxy would argue that there is no substitute for a moral concern for the needs of others, and that this alone – rather than some notional cooperative self-interest – can sustain the organized and systematic provision of voluntary effort. It would also point out that most charities are inspired by religious motives and many are focused around churches.

In this way, the new orthodoxy is able to reduce what I have claimed to be the non-commercial sector of social cooperation either to a form of market-based consumption or to a form of altruism. The implication of this reduction is that other forms of voluntary cooperation cannot be sustained: that harmonious social relations must either be market-based or morality-based (in the new orthodoxy's narrow sense of this term).

The basis of voluntary association

My answer to this criticism is to draw attention to the vulnerability of voluntary associations in modern advanced capitalist societies. Just as the few remaining archaic, communal, simple societies (remote tribes of the Amazonian rain forest, for example) are vulnerable to the encroachment of roads, clearances, missionaries, agriculture and settlement, so any development of groups and associations in modern society is perpetually at risk of being colonized or taken over, either by the commercial system or by the charitable, do-gooding ethos and methods of the middle classes.

Voluntary associations of many kinds come into existence and flourish briefly but, because of the predominantly commercial nature of the social system, they are under constant pressure to meet commercial criteria of success; if they show signs of succeeding, they are then under threat of being taken over by commercial enterprises. A new group, association or cooperative is unlikely to be able to borrow money unless it can produce a 'business plan' to show how it is eventually going to be profitable. If it demonstrates that it is meeting a need, then there will soon be a swarm of firms eager to sell a product or a service to meet the same need.

Alternatively, a voluntary association may try to avoid the whole market process and be resolutely non-commercial. But here it will find that most funding bodies will only give money to registered charities, and that to qualify as a charity it must serve some altruistic or educational purpose. Self-help organizations, or any association in which people (however deprived) cooperate to promote their own interests, are explicitly excluded from the tax advantages and most of the fund-raising opportunities of charitable status. For example, the rather enterprising claimants' union of which I was treasurer in the 1970s had to pay corporation tax on its income.

The result is that voluntary associations live a hand-to-mouth existence, and do indeed have a very high mortality rate. Yet, in spite of this, there has been a considerable growth in recent years of groups which are neither commercial nor charitable. In Britain, estimates from national surveys suggest that about 10 per cent of the population do some kind of 'voluntary work' on a fairly regular basis,[2] and local studies carried out in the late 1970s found that the number of voluntary organizations had risen by 8 per cent in two and a half years, growth being particularly marked among relatively informal organizations for mutual aid or neighbourhood care.[3]

These new, small, local, informal groups seem to be of three main kinds. The first arise mainly in deprived areas, as a local response to the lack of commercially-supplied facilities and the limitations of state services; they also include groups of unemployed people, single parents or other claimants from more prosperous areas.[4] They include, for example, credit unions which enable poor people to get credit in neighbourhoods where banks and building societies are reluctant to make loans; food cooperatives and non-profit collectives; tenants' associations, claimants' unions and neighbourhood groups. In some cases, these form a kind of federal structure on a large housing estate, providing a new basis of community organization in a previously disorganized and demoralized area. This has been most developed in Scotland and Northern Ireland. For example, the Craigmillar Festival Society, on an outer council estate in Edinburgh, started as a group to organize an annual music and drama festival and has become the means of coordinating a whole range of community groups and enterprises on the estate. In England, some of the most active and successful multi-group organizations have been in black communities, as in Harlesden People's Community Council and the recently developed cooperative enterprises on the Broadwater Farm Estate. In Liverpool, the Eldonian Association has focused on the housing needs of an inner-city community with considerable success.

The second growth area is in groups for recently retired people, including those who have taken early retirement. These groups, which involve people from a wide range of occupational backgrounds, recognize that many retired people are fit, active and in a position to develop potential creative energies which have often been stifled during their working lives.[5] The concept of a 'Third Age', not of withdrawal, disengagement and isolation, but of more active community involvement and more varied social relations, has captured the imagination of people in many areas, and a network of organizations, focusing on cultural, educational and outdoor activities, has developed.[6] Whereas the first kind of organization is often concerned with deprivation and social problems, the second is aimed at creating and sharing new common interests through association.

The third growth area is in groups which provide mutual support and care for people suffering from a particular disease or handicap, and for those who care for them on an unpaid basis.[7] These include large national organizations with local branches, and very small local *ad hoc* groups, sometimes recognizing a need for help from each other because there seems to be no official recognition of their condition and the problems it causes (such as Headstart, a group for people who have suffered head injuries in motor accidents). It has been calculated that there are about 1,500 national organizations and 25,000 regional branches concerned with illnesses, addictions, handicaps and disabilities, and more than 200 different associations for eczema alone. Characteristically, they both act as pressure groups on behalf of sufferers, carers or both, and provide advice and support, often of a very practical kind.

All these growth areas seem to illustrate that membership groups, giving mutual benefits, can create common interests which are neither commercial nor charitable, and which arise spontaneously even in a modern advanced society. However, even if these sustain their independence from both commerce and the charitable ethos, they may be at risk of losing their basis of association in another way. Many organizations have been tempted to accept funding from the Manpower Services Commission, in the form of part-time paid Community Programme workers, often in much larger numbers than they would choose, and with no training budget. Many small community groups have been swamped by the weight of numbers of untrained and unmotivated young workers, and by the bureaucratic organization that is necessary to fulfil MSC requirements.[8] In adapting themselves to being on an MSC project, they have destroyed the mutual aid basis of their own association; volunteers have become disaffected, and the group has collapsed. Alternatively, groups and cooperatives of unemployed people have been undermined by members being pressured into accepting work on MSC schemes. Finally, neighbourhood associations have been disrupted by the incursions of ill-planned and paternalistic MSC projects, which cut across their own organizations and tasks, and erode the mutual interests on which they are based.[9]

This is an example of how a state agency, concerned with reducing unemployment for its own sake, introduces a system of pseudo-production and pseudo-employment into a sphere which was previously organized around cooperative self-interest in membership groups. Members have to readjust their roles, to become workers and consumers rather than associates. This can undermine the whole basis of the association, and has done so in many cases.

Yet, in the absence of any other source of funding, community groups have to choose between being starved of resources or accepting MSC funding with its organizational strings. Already the MSC is the main source of finance for voluntary organizations in Britain, and has structured many well-established agencies (including many charities) to its requirements.

Association as a good

I am arguing here that notions of production and consumption, derived from the economic sphere, have obscured the important phenomenon of association, which was originally a political concept. The republican tradition saw association, creating common interests, as the whole basis of society, and society as necessarily political. For Aristotle, friendship was as much the stuff of politics as was power, and political association was concerned with both. The essence of citizenship was direct involvement in the process through which people associated together, and ruled over each other. A good political system gave them common interests in associating for the benefit of all, in a good quality of life.

Clearly, people continue to live their lives in advanced capitalist countries as if association was important. They exchange greetings, gossip, gather during tea breaks, meet in the park, form cultural groups and join together for sport and leisure. But these activities are either structured so as to be part of production (fitted into the gaps and interstices of the productive process) or else structured as a form of consumption. Association is not seen as an activity in itself, or as creating its own characteristic goods. Even though we value the skills of a raconteur or the wit of a conversationalist, even though we seek the company of those who are cheerful, who have empathy, who are reliable and helpful, we seldom gives names to, or place specific value on, what we create for each other by these informal processes of talking and sharing.

Still less do we have words to describe and appreciate what it is like to live in a good community, with mutual respect between different groups, and a lively dialogue about important issues. We can recognize tensions, prejudices, discrimination, oppression and exclusion, particularly when they lead to retaliation in the form of overt hostility, conflict and violence. But we seldom put a specific value on the ability to meet, both formally and informally, with people of different classes, colours, religions and cultural backgrounds from ourselves. People who devote their lives to groups and associations which promote community activities and community relations are usually seen as both admirably dedicated and insufferably boring, and few of us feel any guilt about failing to attend public meetings on important local issues, or about belonging to groups which are (for example) exclusively white, middle class and Protestant. In other words, we seldom regard the cultivation of community in which people have an active commitment to good relations and a good quality of life as a shared responsibility for all citizens. Instead, when tensions flare into conflict, or the crime rate rises, we blame politicians, church leaders or the police.

Unfortunately, the new orthodoxy is not alone in its neglect of the value of association in creating social goods. Socialist thinking largely adopted from liberal political economy its overwhelming emphasis on production and consumption. Although Marx was very much concerned with association in his early writings, and his vision of a communist society was one of voluntary association, this aspect of his thinking was not fully developed in his major works. Both socialism and social democracy have tried to substitute new forms of ownership, decision-making and management of production, and above all to provide certain goods for consumption through the state. In the event, however much new organizational forms have altered the consciousness of producers and consumers, they have scarcely addressed the issue of association as the basis of social relations. For example, in Eastern Europe, outside the Christian churches and few (often proscribed or harassed) intellectual and artistic groups, such associations as exist are almost exclusively official, formal and structured through the Communist Party; they do not reach a vast majority of apathetic, non-participatory, private individuals.

Under social democratic governments, welfare state services were developed in a way which largely mimicked the production and consumption of marketed services, and paid little attention to the quality of association in their communities. Those who planned, produced and delivered them seldom saw it as part of their responsibility to enter into a dialogue with their communities about needs, or to encourage consumers to participate in running their agencies. It has been interesting to notice, for instance, that when central government funding for local authorities in Britain has been cut, the latter have resisted by appealing for the protection of 'jobs and services'. This clearly portrays the nature of local government provision in terms of the interests of producers (employees in the services) and the consumers to whom (as individuals and households) they are 'delivered'. It entirely misses the notion of social relations as concerning the way in which communities associate together, and their quality of life. The common interests to which it appeals are very similar to the common interests between producers and consumers in market transactions, based on the wages of the former and the market value of services to the latter.

It is interesting to discover that British authors, anticipating the birth of post-war social services, saw the creation of new forms of association in society, and a new relationship between the state's agents and their clients, as essential; and that they described this change as political in the republican sense. For example, G. D. H. Cole in an essay published in 1945, wrote of the 'changing views of the province of State action and . . . the growth of the spirit and substance of democracy'. Social services should represent 'communal service, designed to widen and deepen the expression of the spirit of democratic co-operation'.[10] He described the ethos of the new agencies as both 'equalitarian' and 'democratic', and thought that it could be fostered by a common social science training for 'Assistance Board officers, Youth leaders, housing managers, hospital almoners, psychiatrists, probation officers, welfare supervisors, and a host of other professional groups'.[11] In the same volume, Una Cormack (writing of social casework) pointed out that:

> the principal object . . . of many of the war-time services has been to enable each individual to do his duty as a citizen, his social duty . . . this leads to the conclusion that case-work is an expression of the community's concern for those who cannot unaided meet their social obligations or play their full part in society; and the function of the case-worker is to give such help that the individual may derive the fullest possible benefit from the provision made by the community and be enabled to give the fullest possible contribution of which he is capable to the life of the community.[12]

Instead, what happened was that each new service developed its own bureaucratic and professional organization, and a characteristic hierarchy of command, demarcation of responsibility and pattern of accountability to an elected or appointed committee. Each agency and each worker within it became responsible for delivering particular services in accordance with perceived (sometimes measured) 'needs', through a process which excluded both citizens and consumers. Although this approach can be shown to have achieved considerable improvements in the living standards of particular social groups, it was always potentially vulnerable to a market-based critique of its efficiency and effectiveness, precisely because its organization and goals were in many ways comparable with those of commercial services. The new orthodoxy has been as much concerned with showing that profit-making enterprises could do the job done by state agencies at lower costs as with actually dismantling what are seen as unnecessary state interventions.

I am arguing that opponents of the new orthodoxy will always be contesting its principles on its own territory, so long as public services are seen mainly as administratively allocated goods, which are otherwise difficult to distinguish from their marketed counterparts, and so long as users of public services are seen as passive consumers, who do not even have the choices associated with the market. Public services should promote association, both as a good in itself, and as means of creating common interests in the public goods with which the state is concerned.

Association and Basic Income

The difficulty faced by the kind of argument that I am putting forward is where to locate voluntary association in the conventional account of society, which is framed in terms of production and consumption. In particular, since I am arguing for the creation and recognition of interests in association – and for association as based on cooperative self-interest – it is difficult to make such interests visible, let alone measurable, in a society which is organized around commercial interests, with state production and allocation as the only major countervailing force.

Obviously, people will be very unwilling to sacrifice their very material interests, in terms of income or power, in systems of production and consumption (either based on the market or the state), for the sake of far vaguer common interests in associations. Since the latter are clearly not efficient ways of producing goods for consumption, they will not become organizational units within commercial or public-service agencies. Representative democracy will not evolve towards participatory democracy because political elites will be unwilling to disperse and dissipate the concentrations of power which the representative system allows them.

The new orthodoxy is a plausible account of society because it is able to represent the whole of social life as consisting of production and consumption, with a small residual moral sector, mainly represented by households and altruistic, charitable organizations. So long as the interests created by money and power correspond with this division of society into major (material) and minor (moral) spheres, any reassertion of the claims of common interests in association, and the value of a political community of active citizens, seems doomed to failure.

Yet once again there is a glimmer of hope for an alternative project, represented by the Basic Income principle. The point about a Basic Income is that it is a citizenship share in the national product which is not paid in measure with people's contribution to the formal productive system. It therefore authorizes the release of everyone's time and energy from paid work in a new way and makes possible a new perception of, and use of, this 'free time'.

Up to now, time spent out of the formal economy has been classified as 'retirement', 'illness', 'unemployment', 'leisure' or 'household duties'. The first three have been framed as forms of involuntary withdrawal from the labour market, and incomes for them have been seen either as 'earned' through previous work, or as conditional on willingness to continue work as soon as this is practicable. Leisure has been seen mainly as an opportunity for consumption, and household duties as the expression of moral obligations to kin.

Yet, in practice, as we have seen, association, self-help and community activity have tended to flourish precisely where some form of income has been provided for people, without corresponding work obligations being enforced. Where there has been long-term unemployment, where women have got an income in their own right, where people have had a retirement income yet remained fit and healthy, association and voluntary action have sprung up, and a significant minority of people have participated. The evidence is that this association and activity is valued for its own sake, and that it is one of the most important sources of a remaining sen.⁻ of community in advanced capitalist societies.

This has occurred in spite of the overwhelming emphasis on production and consumption, and in spite of disruption and threat of attempts to turn part of it into a source of formal, state-organized paid work. It seems that, despite the obstacles, the discouragement and discincentives, people do recognize a value in association, and do create common interests through joining together. The very existence of 'free time', even though it is defined in such a way as to inhibit purposeful association, allows this to happen, and it occurs spontaneously.

The Basic Income principle would greatly strengthen and endorse this tendency. For the first time, a Basic Income would create a 'social wage' which corresponded to time and energy spent on association, in contrast with present income maintenance provision, all of which implies or enforces a form of exclusion, withdrawal, disengagement and isolation. The Basic Income principle would imply that there is a recognizable sphere in social life (which André Gorz has referred to as 'the sphere of autonomy'[13]), which is neither organized around formal production, nor around conventional consumption.

Part of the 'social wage' would clearly correspond to the activities which are based on the household; one of the main advantages of a Basic Income is that it provides an income that recognizes unpaid domestic and caring work. This will be discussed in chapter 9. But the Basic Income would certainly not increase the pressure towards the privatization of social life which is characteristic of the new orthodoxy. Instead, it would provide new opportunities for collective action, in which citizens would participate in their communities, and develop new social relations.

One objection to the Basic Income principle is that it seems to reward 'leisure' or even 'idleness', at the expense of industry, diligence and productivity.[14] Both the new orthodoxy and socialism claim to promote the common good by putting a premium on contributions to the output of formally produced goods. But experience of life in both advanced capitalist and existing socialist countries suggests that this devalues association, community and informal social relations to a dangerous extent, and creates interests in private consumption and in power which are a threat to the common good. By formalizing the social space for the associative element in human relations, the Basic Income principle allows the possibility of a republican notion of citizenship to re-assert itself.

Participation and local democracy

However, this slender opportunity could be greatly extended if local authorities were to give priority to promoting community groups and associations, and to encouraging participation in their own agencies and processes. Instead of being concerned almost exclusively with producing and delivering services, they might in addition (and, for some goods, instead) provide rooms, buildings, land, vehicles or other resources for people to act together in pursuit of their own mutual interests. This is an approach that has already been pioneered, to a limited extent, by some British local authorities, including (before its abolition) the Greater London Council.[15]

One reason why these authorities have already tried this approach is a recognition of the limitations of the service-delivery model of local government. Local authorities were increasingly caught between resource restrictions by central government, the demands of rival client groups and those of trade unions representing their own workforces. They were faced with the fact that many consumers did not regard the services as 'theirs', so that (if they were to resist pressures to cut back spending and to substitute commercial for public services) they had to encourage their electorates to feel a sense of involvement in and loyalty to local government agencies. Decentralization, consultation and community involvement, together with direct grants to self-help groups and cooperatives, were all attempts to find low-cost substitutes for services which were being criticized as remote, bureaucratic and paternalistic.

Criticisms of the new approach have focused on two main aspects. The first is the self-appointed and unrepresentative nature of the groups that have emerged through these initiatives. On the one hand, there is an unelected leadership which comes forward in previously disorganized or passive neighbourhoods; on the other, there are fringe groups, clustering around apparently marginal issues and minority interests. In this way, people who happen to put themselves forward achieve disproportionate influence in their communities, and eccentric or even deviant groups are able to gain resources out of measure with their distribution in the population at large. Well-publicized 'loony left' causes seem to be subsidized out of the compulsory contributions of respectable ratepayers.

But it should not be surprising that previously excluded or disadvantaged people are among the first to take opportunities of this form of participation and activity. Denied access to mainstream economic and political participation, for them this presents an alternative chance to organize and have some influence. In particular, black groups who are marginalized in the economy and have little political leverage have most to gain by using any assistance available to organize for self-help and solidarity, for forging an identity and publicizing issues of concern.

This links with the second major criticism: that greater participation and association, especially by poor and minority groups, far from increasing social harmony and cooperation, actually leads to an escalation of conflict between rival interest groups. With the formation of new associations and new forums for disputing local issues, a greater consciousness of differences between groups, and of competition for resources, is created, with no satisfactory process for resolving conflicts. Alternatively (as with the Community Development Projects in the late 1960s), a greater number of groups presses harder on the local authority for increased provision of resources or services for their neighbourhood, ethnic or religious group, and for a greater share of power.

Yet these consequences of earlier attempts to increase participation and community activity are hardly surprising. In the past, these have usually been fostered either as a lower-cost alternative to traditional service delivery or as a harmless safety valve for sections of the population (blacks, poor people) who were being offered no real share of income or power. In the former case, those who were for the first time involved and consulted by local politicians and officials saw all too clearly that they were being invited to take part in an exercise of rationing, of dividing up a smaller cake. It did not escape their attention that, while the local government budgets were growing, they were not asked their opinion on how to spend them. In the latter case, it was obvious that the real power still remained in the mainstream institutions and agencies, and hence that little would change unless they could be pressured to concede some of this power. Groups which found their strength through community activism quickly focused on this mainstream political process; for example, black people gained political office, and influence on policy, in some local authorities.

What this history illustrates is that participation in associations and groups cannot be an alternative to a share in the economic and political spheres and a way of fobbing off those who are excluded from the mainstream. Conflicts over resources will indeed appear, and be impossible to resolve, if people see that all they are being invited to participate in is their own deprivation. A society which excludes and oppresses a large minority of its population certainly cannot afford to encourage association and community activity. This is why, for instance, Margaret Thatcher's government is so determined to limit the powers of local government, and to tackle the problems of inner cities through central government agencies and private enterprise rather than through the kind of local council that wants to promote participation and citizen involvement.

Any policy for revaluing and enabling association and active citizenship would have to go hand-in-hand with measures to include all members of society in the benefits of economic growth, and to share power more widely. This is why a Basic Income programme seems a promising way out of the situation created by the new orthodoxy's approach to government. It would simultaneously enable a redistribution of employment in favour of previously excluded groups, and the greater involvement of all members of society in community activities.

At present, activists are most likely to come from the most deprived groups (who have no other legal way of meeting their needs) and (in larger numbers) from those with a secure income and spare time, mainly the recently retired. But the redistribution of free time which would be one of the main consequences of a Basic Income programme would allow a far broader section of the population to be active in local affairs, and hence a far better balanced participation. In this way, the official democratic process could become more of a participatory democracy, and could integrate into it what is at present the unofficial politics of direct action, confrontation, anger and frustration. Those taking part in the process of decision-making would be far more representative of the community as a whole.

In this way, the republican ideal of self-rule by citizens would be combined with a much higher value being placed on association, as a source of self-interested activity – for its own sake, as enjoyment and fulfilment of human potential, as well as for a share in what the political process delivers to its constituency.

Conclusions

The new orthodoxy's ideal citizens are private individuals, living in small households, in a suburban setting. Their needs are met by commercial suppliers. Their moral horizons stretch little further than their garden fence; they are concerned about each other, and wish their neighbours well, though not well enough to seek their well-being in any active way. They go to church to be reminded of their duties to look after themselves, and to be congratulated on their success in doing so. They subscribe discreetly to a charitable body which happens to have appealed to their sympathy.

For the new orthodoxy, association is part of what people consume during their leisure, from the proceeds of what they earn in the productive system. The purpose of association is pleasure, and all that is needed for its enjoyment can be supplied by market forces. Alternatively, if association is altruistically motivated, it is best organized through charitable voluntary bodies.

The republican tradition argues that association is a necessary part of the good society, and is the basis of, and the expression of, common interests in the common good. In a society which is organized around production and consumption of material goods, the associative basis of the common good becomes invisible, and retains only a shadowy existence, in the gaps between commercial activity and the processes of the state. It can only be revived, recognized and revalued by making a space for it, a sphere of its own, with its own income or 'social wage'. Within this sphere, people would associate for cooperative self-interest, mutual advantage.

In so far as the Basic Income allows all citizens the chance to participate as autonomous equals in such a social sphere, it would enable far more extensive and diverse forms of association than exist in advanced capitalist or existing socialist societies. The range and significance of these would be further increased by the enabling role of local authorities. Unless there was a strong trend towards an egalitarian redistribution within the economic sphere, greater participation might initially focus on struggles for competitive advantage between rival groups; but this would tend to draw all interests within society into a more participative democratic process.

The type of active citizenship that this society would require would not be particularly restful. Harmony and cooperation would not be achieved by passive private consumerism, as in the new orthodoxy's ideal. People would argue, dispute and negotiate; groups would debate priorities and methods, means and goals. Machiavelli pointed out that republican Rome was often rowdy and quarrelsome, and that its more prosperous citizens complained that it was disorderly because there were so many disputes and protests among the people; but it was only by strenuous and active guardianship over liberty that good government was sustained. In rather the same way, an active, vigilant, energetic form of citizenship seems an important part of any alternative to the new orthodoxy's version of the good society.

This seems a logical development as technological progress makes more material production possible with less labour. Eventually, as numbers employed in industrial production fall, and the relative costs of services continue to rise, a mechanism is needed through which more time and energy can gradually be allocated to non-commercial activity. To call this 'consumption' is to make it the mirror image of production, and to tie the right to enjoy it to the productive role. To call it 'leisure' is to demean it unnecessarily, to deny its true significance. Association is a far more active concept, and implies an important alternative use of time and energy, and the creation of significant social relations.

Post-war Britain was not like this. The energy it invested in creating a better society was reflected in the civil life of the community.[16] The spirit of the welfare state informed the way people behaved in public, and lived their lives together. It is this active commitment to public goods, as much as the social services themselves, that needs to be recreated by an alternative programme.

The Basic Income principle allows us to foresee the possibility of a gradual progression along the road from 'full employment' to a society based on free association, the kind of society that Marx envisaged as the final stage in the transformation to communism. The point of this change would not be that it would involve more and more private consumption, and particularly consumption of commercial services, as in the new orthodoxy. In its model, it seems that many people will spend half their time working in out-of-town leisure and shopping complexes, and the other half consuming their products.

Instead, an increasing proportion of time and energy would be spent in association that is neither production nor consumption, but the active creation of good social relations. Whereas the new orthodoxy treats the public sphere of social life as a somewhat unfortunate necessity (which the rich spend money to minimize), the republican tradition sees it as the expression of common interests in what people share as members of society. As less time and energy is spent on formal production, so more time could be spent on the common good.

Public goods are not alternatives to marketed goods, just supplied to individuals in a different way. They focus on the life we live together, and the interests we share in this being of good quality. Even when public goods are provided by central or local government, they affirm these common interests. A good society recognizes the importance of the public domain, and invests energy and pride in creating a civil order which visibly and tangibly reflects good social relations.

The new orthodoxy's public face is ugly. It reflects the high priority that individuals give to private goods, and their fearful, hostile and exploitative relations. The sordid appearance of the environment, the deterioration of amenities and services, the tense atmosphere and high rates of crime, all portray a society in which social relations are discounted, and public goods have fallen into decay.

Notes

1 G. D. H. Cole, 'Mutual aid movements in their relation to voluntary social service', in A. F. C. Bourdillon (ed.), *Voluntary Social Services: their Place in the Modern State* (Methuen, 1945), pp. 118-36.
2 S. Hatch, *Voluntary Work: a Report of a Survey* (Volunteer Centre, 1978).
3 S. Hatch, *Outside the State: Voluntary Organisations in Three English Towns* (Croom Helm, 1980).
4 David Donnison, 'The community-based approach', in M. Bulmer (ed.), *The Social Basis of Community* (Allen and Unwin, 1989).
5 R. Hadley and M. Scott, *Time to Give? Retired People as Volunteers* (Volunteer Centre, 1980).
6 Eric Midwinter, *The Wage of Retirement* (Centre for Policy on Ageing, 1985).
7 S. Hatch, *Mutual Aid in Social and Health Care* (Bedford Square Press, 1980).
8 Mark Rankin, *Working in the Margin: Unemployment, Volunteering and Marginal Work* (Volunteer Centre, 1987).
9 Bill Jordan, *The Use of the Community Programme for Health and Social Care* (NCVO, 1987). See also Mark Rankin. *A Question of Choice: the Expanded Community Programme and Restart* (Volunteer Centre, 1987).
10 G. D. H. Cole, 'A retrospect of the history of voluntary social service', in A. F. C. Bourdillon (ed.), *Voluntary Social Services: their Place in the Modern State* (Methuen, 1945), p. 29.
11 Ibid. Elizabeth MacAdam, writing in the same year, added factory inspectors and public health inspectors to this list of 'social servants', see *The Social Servant in the Making* (Allen and Unwin, 1945).

12 Una Cormack, 'Developments in case-work', in A. F. C. Bourdillon (ed.), *Voluntary Social Services: their Place in the Modern State* (Methuen, 1945), pp. 111-12.
13 André Gorz, *Farewell to the Working Class: an Essay in Post-Industrial Socialism* (1980) (Pluto, 1982).
14 See the criticisms of Robert Van der Veen and Philippe Van Parijs's article by Jerry Cohen, Jon Elster and Hillel Steiner in *Theory and Society*, 15 (1987), pp. 631-758.
15 David Blunkett, 'Towards a social policy: service "delivery" or community "participation"?', in Bill Jordan and Nigel Parton (eds), *The Political Dimensions of Social Work* (Blackwell, 1983).
16 Michael Ignatieff, 'The tide will turn: private affluence will lose all savour amidst public squalor', *Guardian*, 4 April 1988.

9
Family Life

The new orthodoxy glorifies the household as the primary expression of moral relations in modern society. Whereas it is competitive self-interest which makes an efficient economy and induces hard work, it is altruism, duty and concern for others which make a happy home. Within the bosom of the family, self-interested producers and consumers are transformed into self-sacrificing, caring, sharing partners, parents and relatives, and individual striving is set aside in favour of the pursuit of others' good.

On closer inspection, this does not seem a very adequate account of households in modern advanced capitalist societies. About a quarter of these consists of individuals living alone, another quarter of two people living together, and the rest of several people. Major responsibility for the unpaid work in the household is almost always taken by an adult woman, where one is present, and major responsibility for earning family income is usually taken by an adult man, where one is present. In other words, there is not an equal balance between participation in the economic and moral spheres, because men spend a disproportionate amount of their lives in (presumably self-interested) paid work, while women spend a disproportionate amount of their lives in (presumably altruistic) unpaid work. Earnings are shared between household members, but by no means equally – in most families with a male 'breadwinner', he consumes the largest share.[1]

Clearly, roles within households are gender-based to a far greater extent than can be explained by the demands of biology or reproduction. The new orthodoxy therefore appears to imply that women are (or should be) more altruistic than men – that it is somehow 'natural' for them to do most of the caring and sharing, and to leave to men the self-interested pursuit of efficiency and gain.

The feminist analysis points to male power as the explanation of this apparently voluntary subordination. Household cooperation takes place against a background of unequal holdings of assets, so that the family, like other social institutions, is structured as a form of exploitation and domination. But I have suggested that the overall pattern of interests in modern society works against change in this sphere because the majority of women have more to lose from sharing with the poor than to gain from challenging patriarchy.

This question about the nature of household cooperation, and the interests involved, is the first one that I shall tackle in this chapter. I shall argue that men's exploitation and domination of women could be eroded, and that this could contribute greatly to the creation of a better society, in which association in the public sphere of social life expanded at the expense of private, household-based consumption.

The second issue which I shall consider is how household provision of care for 'dependants' - children, sick, handicapped, frail and confused people - relates to provision of state services for health and social care. Under social democratic (and to an even greater extent under existing socialist) governments, the state seemed to take a far greater responsibility for these goods. But, on closer inspection, the social democratic state's part was limited and conditional. It was concerned with certain 'expert' services, like medical treatment, and with providing what was mainly an alternative to household care for those who did not have an informal (usually family) carer.

The new orthodoxy has reasserted the importance of the household as a moral sphere, and insisted that the state should only provide services where household members are unable to do so. This amounts to a two-pronged argument. In the first place, people who can afford health and social care should be encouraged to buy it, either through insurance schemes or directly. In the second, those who are capable of giving unpaid care should see it as their duty to do so, as part of their commitment to fellow members of their family. In this way, state care (or rather, that which is free at the point of delivery) is rationed to people who cannot afford commercial care and who lack an unpaid household carer.

In this chapter I shall argue for a different kind of relationship between state and informal care, which might follow from a change in household relations, and from a greater emphasis on association in the public sphere. The direction of the change would be towards a greater sharing between state agencies and informal carers, and a more communal, collective approach to informal care.

This leads on to the final issue to be addressed in this chapter, the overall relationship between the private and largely exclusive household groups and the loose-knit associations of the public sphere. Whereas the new orthodoxy's principles constantly increase the relative importance of the former, I shall argue for a revaluation of the claims of the public sphere in a good society.

Cooperation and households

On the face of it, the household would seem to be an ideal unit for voluntary cooperation, and the pursuit of the good of all by each. In most households, the adults have chosen to live together, and might therefore be expected to have committed themselves to common purposes and shared projects, including the rearing of children. The small size of the household unit allows members to monitor, adapt and renegotiate the burdens and benefits of their daily lives, and the close and intimate relationship between members allows the trust necessary for generalized reciprocity over a long time span.

But all this presupposes that the household makes itself, and that its members enter it as autonomous individuals, whose roles evolve through processes of chosen cooperation. But as households lack the resources to produce their own means of subsistence, household roles and the institution of the family have been shaped by the labour market and the state. Since the agrarian and industrial revolutions, a gender-based dual labour market has been characteristic of capitalist economies because most women live in households with men, and can therefore be treated as secondary earners. Women have played the role of an 'industrial reserve army', to be drawn into and excluded from the labour market according to demand, technology and organization of the productive process. Because of this structure of the labour market, responsibility for household economic self-sufficiency is seen as falling primarily on male members, which leaves female members primarily responsible for caring for dependants and doing unpaid tasks.

The state reinforces this household division of labour, for example by requiring the man to claim income support on behalf of his wife or cohabitee, and by assessing tax liability by counting a woman's earnings as supplementary to those of a man. But it also shapes the female household role by the way in which it provides and fails to provide social services, and by its legislation on the protection of dependants. The state sets standards of care, hygiene and safety, but only meets these through its own provision for a minority of people who require nurture or help. For the rest, it monitors household standards through services directed mainly at women.

This has meant that, in the absence of a conscious and costly effort to avoid this, women are perceived only secondarily as paid workers, and men only secondarily as unpaid household workers. In a society structured around production and consumption, men's projects, purposes and preferences are defined primarily in economic terms. They seek earnings, careers, status and power, for which they require autonomy, skill, energy, initiative, strength, rationality and ambition. Female projects, purposes and preferences are structured around the household, in terms of the needs of others. They are seen as needing to be loving, kind, helpful, feeling, giving, patient and self-sacrificing. Each gender is perceived as requiring the other's attributes only in a secondary way, incidentally rather than essentially.

As a result, there is a strong tendency for the interests of men to be defined in terms of competitive advantage, and the interests of women to be defined in terms of cooperative mutuality. The very obvious subordination of women, leading to their exploitation and domination by men in society at large, is the result of household roles which are complementary, which define the interests of the two genders by different criteria and which therefore obscure the economic and power differences between them. Women are treated as having chosen what the institution of the family ordains as their role. Psychological studies have even suggested that, from a quite early age, boys and girls develop different notions of fairness through the games they play: boys in terms of rights to gain or power through competition, girls in terms of needs to be included and cared for.[2]

There is nothing necessarily wrong with the notion of two spheres, the economic and the domestic, with different criteria of fairness and different systems of cooperation. What is wrong is that men and women do not enter the two systems on equal terms. Men enter both the labour market and the household with enormous advantages, in terms of income and power, over women. Men have better access to the labour market, better pay, training, promotion prospects and are more likely to be members of trade unions.[3] Conversely, in the household women are financially dependent on men, and this dependence is most extreme when their caring duties are heaviest; when they have young children or handicapped adults to care for, they are least likely to have an income of their own. The heavier the burden of domestic responsibility, the less likely it is to be shared.

Hence the household which consists of a male 'breadwinner' and a female 'housewife' with dependants cannot be regarded as a system of voluntary cooperation because the woman is in such a weak position to negotiate over the sharing of unpaid work. Female altruism is necessary because there is no basis for cooperation between equals for the sake of mutual self-interest. Membership is unequal because the woman lacks the autonomy and resources to insist on her own needs being met, or the opportunity to withdraw (either temporarily or permanently) from cooperation. It is as if in Axelrod's game one of the two players scored zero if she withdrew from a series of cooperative moves (in which she was already gaining a lower score than her partner), while he scored two points. Because she scores so low on self-interest, she must be supplied with motives which depend on duty.

On the other hand, where women do have paid jobs there is evidence that unpaid tasks are more equally shared, even though they still have primary responsibility for most of these. British research suggests that 67 per cent of wives with full-time jobs think that child-care tasks are equally shared between themselves and their husbands, and 44 per cent think that housework tasks are equally shared. This compares with 55 per cent and 23 per cent respectively for part-time women employees.[4] In other words, even though women do still have the major responsibility for unpaid work, better access to paid jobs helps them establish a greater sharing of tasks. Conversely, where women are entirely home-based, they get little help - even when their husbands are unemployed.[5]

It is unclear whether this fairer sharing stems from women's ability to contribute income to the household or from their having an independent source of their own income. The Basic Income principle would not, on its own, improve married women's access to part-time employment. In fact, in so far as it meant that their earnings would all be taxed, it would be something of a disincentive for women who have tax and National Insurance Contribution advantages on very low earnings in the present British system. But it would have two other effects which would be of advantage to women who wanted to enter the labour market. By treating men and women, married and single, in exactly the same way, it would remove the assumption that it is always women who are candidates for part-time jobs. Gender-based segmentation would be eroded as more men took part-time positions, and more women might thus get into full-time posts. And, following on from this, women's wage rates would tend to rise towards men's, as fewer low-paid jobs were reserved for women.

But above all, the right to an independent income for each married woman would strengthen her bargaining position in the household, and allow her to insist on greater fairness in sharing. With the tax and benefit system no longer reinforcing the man's role as breadwinner, and a more even sharing of paid work between the sexes, the way would be opened for a gradual change towards genuine cooperation between the partners in the household. Instead of requiring women's self-sacrifice as the price of economic dependence, family life could be based on relations of mutual self-interest between equals.

Women and caring

Even though married women's re-entry into the labour market during the past 20 years has been in a secondary and exploited role, it has signalled a gradual change in households towards greater equality. But demographic change threatens even this trend. As the proportion of the population over 85 years of age is the most rapidly growing one, and as a larger proportion of severely handicapped people of all ages live longer, the tasks of providing day-to-day assistance with ordinary living for these groups multiply. At the same time, lower birthrates in the inter-war period mean that numbers in the generation below that of today's very old people are relatively small. To compound the demographic arithmetic, state policy is moving away from institutional care for elderly and handicapped people towards care in the community.

In all these ways, a longstanding issue over the moral obligations of kinship is becoming a focus of urgent concern. Whereas couples have some control over when they have children, and some room for negotiation over how they combine bringing them up with providing a household income, the process of becoming someone who cares for an elderly or handicapped person is far more insidious and seldom planned. And whereas compulsory education represents a fairly clear and time-limited division of responsibilities between the family and the state, community care is both blurred in its definition of the respective obligations and open-ended in its time perspective. In practice, being someone who cares for a frail or confused elderly person can be a full-time role which lasts for a decade or more, and research suggests that a high proportion of those who take the role of carer (or have it thrust upon them) get no help at all from official sources.[6]

For all these reasons, the role of full-time carer represents a far harder challenge to the notion of moral obligation in families than do the roles associated with other household and caring tasks. It is often harder than a paid job, involving longer hours and heavier work (for instance, lifting a handi-capped person); statistics on physical injury and mental illness among carers testify to its danger and stressfulness. Yet it arises as an extension of such roles as spouse, daughter or daughter-in-law, and is seen as part of kinship. Carers often disown the name, saying things like 'I'm just being a wife.'[7]

But these onerous responsibilities are seldom shared, even when there are several apparent candidates, nor do they fall on one person at random. There seem to be implicit 'rules' of kindship, tacitly endorsed within family net-works, but seldom openly acknowledged or discussed.[8] In households which consist of two retired people, the role of carer seems usually to fall onto whichever spouse is relatively able-bodied; in this way, British research suggests that there are almost as many men as women acting as carers in such households.[9] But in any other kind of household, it is almost always assumed that a woman – mother, wife, daughter or daughter-in-law – will be the carer if one is needed. Often there is only one such candidate for the role, for example, if a handicapped child is born to a young couple living far from relatives.

But in other cases there may be an apparent choice of options, as when an old lady living alone is becoming increasingly disabled. Here it seems that there is usually a kind of tacit consensus within the kinship network on who will be the carer. Geographical proximity, previous close relationship and the lack of a full-time job are all attributes which line up a particular female rela-tive for the role, and she is usually prepared for it by a period of giving increasing practical assistance on an occasional basis. By contrast, male relatives are seen as having some kind of moral agency (for example, they are consulted about decisions over whether the family home should be sold), but not as being candidates for the practical role of carer.[10]

The obverse of this process is that for some elderly or disabled people in need of care there may be no candidates for the role of full-time carer. If all female kin are geographically distant, if there are no close emotional bonds or if all have heavy commitments to carers or other household members, then full-time family care is not an option. Additionally, there are many people who were admitted to institutional care in the era when this was routinely offered to certain families as an alternative to family care, and who therefore have lost their ties with any kinship network, and certain others whose links with family members have gradually withered through frequent admissions to mental hospital. A great many people in both these groups are now being returned to 'the community'.

As part of this haphazard process of selection, therefore, certain people, predominantly women, are acting as full-time unpaid carers for others who need constant assistance with such things as bathing, toileting, getting in and out of bed, dressing, eating and sometimes even breathing properly. Others may be supervising, occupying, restraining, accompanying and reasoning

with people who are physically fit but unable to be relied on not to hurt themselves or wander away from home. Research suggests that their motives for
taking on this role are a mixture of love and duty and that, although all carers
experience stress and tiredness, only some find it burdensome and resent it.
This seems to be related not so much to the physical labour involved as the
emotional quality of the relationship with the person they are caring for.[11] A
close and loving relationship can make even very heavy caring work a source
of satisfaction, but what is seen as ingratitude, indifference or hostility makes
the role a pure duty. In some dependency conditions (especially dementia)
what starts as a loving relationship can become a burdensome obligation.

   All this gives a bewildering picture of the role of carer, with a double focus.
On the one hand, there is plenty of evidence of the 'compulsory altruism'
which feminist critics have rightly identified as characteristic of women's
family role. Yet on the other there is apparent confirmation that very arduous
unpaid work can be voluntarily, even joyfully, undertaken where it is part of a
close, affectionate relationship, in which there has been generalized reciprocity
over long periods of time. Many mothers and daughters describe their relationships in these terms, and where these qualities are present, full-time
caring roles can be sustained for many years, to the apparent satisfaction of
both parties.

   How can we discover any principle which would introduce fairness into the
distribution of caring roles, and would make the burdens on those who care
more bearable? The new orthodoxy would answer that, to a great extent, the
idea of trying to do so is misplaced. Caring is a moral obligation of kinship,
and is perceived as such by those who do it, both those whose predominant
emotion is love and those who act mainly from duty. This is as it should be,
because caring is part of a set of relationships which are essentially moral in
character, and which we should encourage people to see as such. The state
should do nothing to discourage the sense of moral responsibility for kin, and
everything to increase it. Yet in practice, as I shall show in the next section, it
is difficult to see the state's role in these terms, either historically, or in recent
policies.

State services and family care

In the past, institutional forms of care (workhouses, asylums, hospitals) were
set up as an alternative to family care, and provided for people who had no
carer or who were rejected by kin. The main components in their population
were elderly people who had been living alone, and other isolated people, plus
orphan children, and some single-parent families (where the mother could be
used to provide some unpaid care within the institution).[12] Measures which
improved the lot of such people in the community tended to reduce their
numbers in institutional care; for example, in Britain, the introduction of old
age pensions in 1909 meant that more elderly people could survive outside

the workhouse, and that more families could afford to care for them in their households. The combination of improved income maintenance and domiciliary care for vulnerable groups has meant that, despite the enormous growth of populations in potential need of some form of residential care, the proportion in Britain actually receiving it has remained almost contant for the whole of this century.[13]

But new domiciliary and day care services, which have been developed as a way of helping disabled people stay out of residential and hospital care, have also been targetted on individuals living alone. Most recently, new kinds of care - small group homes, either staffed or supported - have understandably been focused on the needs of people coming out of long-stay wards of mental illness and mental handicap hospitals, as part of the process of deinstitutionalization. In all these new policy developments of the past 20 years, those who have received least services have been people receiving unpaid family care, even though they have often been more frail (physically or mentally) than the recipients of such services, and sometimes more frail than those still in institutions.[14]

This has prompted the observation that state care-giving services (whether residential or domiciliary) find it very difficult to *share* the tasks of caring for disabled people with families.[15] A literature on full-time carers has grown up, emphasizing how isolated and 'invisible' their role is, how little support they receive from the state and how policies and practices in health and social welfare services might better meet their needs.[16] New pressure groups for carers, new definitions of their needs and new voluntary organizations to support them have blossomed as the rising numbers in need of care and community care policies have converged to swell their numbers. Some agencies have experimented in new methods, designed to mesh paid care better with unpaid, and give carers better breaks (through respite and relief care), better practical assistance, more group support and more space for their own emotional and social life.

But the fundamental question remains: why should certain individuals have to shoulder all the burdens associated with family care, which others escape, and should not this whole notion of a morally obligatory role be abolished? The question becomes even more pressing when we take income factors into account. The rich have a great many options. The elderly person who needs care can, if he or she chooses, decide to live in a private residential or nursing home as soon as assistance of any kind is required. A son or daughter who feels a moral obligation can build a granny annexe and hire a nurse or companion, giving only as much unpaid care as they choose to give. At the other end of the scale, an old person who qualifies for means-tested income support can enter private (commercial residential care at the state's expense, but not receive financial assistance for domiciliary or day care; accordingly, numbers of old people in such homes have almost doubled since 1980. But someone who has an occupational pension and savings will only get an Attendance Allowance equivalent to a small proportion of the cost of the care they need; and a full-time carer will only get an Invalid Care Allowance if he or she gives up a full-time job to take on this role.

All this makes who gets paid and who gets unpaid care even more of a lottery. The irony is that for the rich and the poor there is something like a choice, with both carers and cared for having an option of residential care or family care, though the poor may get little in the way of support services if they opt for the latter. Yet the paid residential care-givers are increasingly small family firms (in many cases former guest-houses or hotels), so that the state is subsidizing commercially self-interested family caring as a substitute for altruistic family care-giving, if we accept the new orthodoxy's categories.[17] For middle income groups, paid residential care is harder to get, and unpaid care is likely to be costly in terms of lost labour market opportunities. The fact that women, because of lower earning power and secondary worker status, are almost always selected for the full-time carer's role, reinforces the unfairness in the gender division of unpaid duties.

The Basic Income principle could help sort out some of this confusion, so long as it was combined with an adequate allowance for disabled people, which corresponded to the actual costs of the care that the person needed.[18] If this were available, then there would be a real choice between paid residential care, paid day and domiciliary care and family care, which could be combined in the most favourable proportions, with an income attached to each, so that family members giving care were not penalized.

Because potential carers would all have Basic Incomes in their own right, and because those who needed care would have an income sufficient to buy it, there would be no moral pressure towards the full-time carer role, and no financial inducement (such as is represented by the Invalid Care Allowance). Instead, the role of carer could always be a chosen, and almost always a part-time, one. If, after negotiation, the person needing care wanted to spend most of his or her time with members of the household, there would be more opportunities for sharing the carer's role, since the Basic Income principle would put no disincentive or obstacles in the way of part-time paid employment by two or more family carers.

Women workers in demand

This approach to allowing real choice over how and by whom care is given may seem quite an expensive way of achieving some degree of fairness in this increasingly important field. But some such approach seems inevitable, given the likely economic consequences of demographic changes in countries such as Britain. On the one hand, the number of relatives available to care for elderly people who need care (in practice, this now means female relatives) is falling rapidly. It has been estimated that already each person over 75 has only 0.86 potential carers.[19] So there is a supply-side problem over unpaid carers.

But there is also a supply-side problem over paid carers. At present, married women are the main source of employees in these, as in other low-paid service, occupations. This is because they alone have incentives to take part-time work. Already some 60 per cent of married women with husbands in employment have jobs, and the proportion is much higher for those whose children are independent. But in future the demand of the commercial labour market (all those jobs in leisure complexes and out-of-town shopping centres) are going to compete with the demand of the public services for a dwindling supply of married women. Continuing falls in the birthrate will not help either; for example, it has been calculated that the National Health Service will need half the girls with the necessary examination qualifications to train as nurses by the mid-1990s.

Because of constraints on productivity improvements in caring, the relative costs of these and other paid services will continue to rise, while the shortage of married women for part-time work will enable them to bid up their wages. When this happens, paid caring will be an increasingly attractive role, and unpaid caring an increasingly unattractive one, for the available female population. At present, a government with new orthodoxy principles can rely on a supply of dutiful married women for unpaid caring, and a supply of exploitable married women for paid caring. In future, it may be able to rely on neither in sufficient numbers, and the costs of care will necessarily rise, appeals to altruism notwithstanding.

The search will then be on for the most cost-efficient form of paid care consistent with the needs of elderly people (assuming they will be consulted) and the aspirations of an increasingly confident and assertive group of married women. Whereas all the present trends are towards familializing care, in the sense that there are rapid increases both in unpaid family care and in paid care in small family businesses, the new trend may be towards collective care.[20]

This would probably not take the form of residential homes, which are very expensive and not popular with most consumers, but of new forms of care cooperatives. Research suggests that the most cost-effective way of caring for fairly disabled people, right up to the point where they really need to be looked after in hospital, is for households to buy in extra assistance, in the form of paid help at key times during the day or night (getting up, going to bed, mealtimes), and to allow the unpaid carer to take breaks or do a part-time job.[21]

But in a world in which a very high proportion of middle-aged married women were involved in either paid or unpaid caring or both, it would make little sense for all this to consist of a vast number of private commercial contracts between two or three individuals. (The situation would then be analogous to the present one in Britain, where it is in principle possible for two single parents to qualify for a £40-a-week Enterprise Allowance for paying to do each other's washing.)

Instead, it would make far more sense for groups of part-time paid and unpaid carers to form cooperatives, organizing their roles in a coordinated way. This would be greatly enabled by the Basic Income principle, which would allow them to use their personal Basic Incomes, and the costs-of-care allowances of those needing care, as a common fund, which could be administered in a far more flexible way than would be possible under individualized commercial contracts.

In this way, the very justifiable feminist criticism of inter-generational obligation as a trap for women, and of family care as isolating, frustrating and ultimately dangerously unhealthy for carer and cared-for alike, would be met. People whose chosen best option was exclusive, unpaid family care could not be financially penalized; but there would be many advantages for most people in a degree of collective, shared care, cooperatively organized.

What is more, this re-emergence of a more collective and cooperative mode of caring would mesh well with a more active and participatory community, and the notions of citizenship and association that I have been advancing in this book. Disabled people and elderly people, instead of being trapped in isolation, along with their carers, in exclusive household or private care, would have better access to the wider public sphere, and hence a better chance to be truly members of their community.

Households and work

This brings us back to the whole relationship between households and the labour market, and the divisions of labour between them. The issue of paid and unpaid caring, and the possible cooperative collectivization of both, raises other questions about how commercial and state services will in future mesh with work done in households, and how this in turn will influence wider social relations.

In recent years, the trend in services other than caring seems to have been mainly towards the substitution of unpaid for paid services. As the relative costs of the latter have risen, and those of manufactured goods have fallen, people have preferred to drive their own cars rather than use public transport, wash their own clothes rather than use a laundry and watch their own television rather than go to a cinema or theatre.[22] A further step in the same direction would be distance learning (the Open University) as a substitute for attending college.

Another set of economic influences which have added significance to household work has been a buoyant housing market, in which prices have often been rising more rapidly than the rate of general inflation, and the generous tax treatment of house-purchase loans and house-sale capital gains. All these in combination have made it very profitable for household members to improve their homes, and move upwards through the housing market, acquiring more valuable, comfortable and status-giving dwellings as they go. It has been calculated that inflation and tax advantages often effectively allow owner-occupiers to acquire a free asset, taken over a lifetime.[23]

When opportunities for higher earnings in the labour market are strictly limited (as they were in Britain in the 1970s) do-it-yourself home improvements can actually become a far better use of time and energy than extra hours of paid labour. Some authors have argued that this is reflected in the home improvement boom among owner-occupiers. But households with several earners are mostly likely to be do-it-yourself activists, since they are most likely to be able to afford to buy the house, the tools and materials.[24] By contrast, no-earner households in rented accommodation lack the incomes or the incentives for these forms of unpaid work. In this way, housing-tenure advantages and labour-market advantages reinforce each other, and together constitute the 'stake in society' which is in practice a stake in the new orthodoxy's system, and in exclusive private goods.

The effect of all these trends has been to focus the material advantages of unpaid work on the private household. While it may have contributed to a greater sharing of work and a breakdown of gender-based roles in advantaged households, it has also reinforced the self-interested exclusiveness of the suburban way of life. Apart from a limited amount of sharing of expensive equipment, the tendency towards home-based work by family groups impoverishes public life and communal activity, and increases investment in exclusive property at the expense of inclusive association.

In Britain since the early 1970s, enormous funds have flowed (mainly as a result of income tax relief) into owner-occupied housing, so that it is now (along with private pensions) the chief form of personal wealth.[25] It pays people to use houses as a store of wealth, to live in far larger houses than they need and to spend a disproportionate amount of time adorning them. Britain has a very large owner-occupier poulation, living in large houses by European standards, and it seems likely that they spend more time doing them up and maintaining them by their own labour than most Europeans. For this reason, it would seem to be a sensible policy aim of a Basic Income approach to promoting a good society to reduce the tax advantages associated with owner-occupation and especially those which allow people to move up the housing market so advantageously. If such tax concessions as were given were concentrated on first-time buyers, this would certainly be fairer than the present system.

In so far as a Basic Income system enabled unpaid work of all kinds, it would of course also allow people to improve, and pehaps even to take time off from the labour market to build, their own houses. But a fairer tax structure might encourage them to do this cooperatively rather than in the exclusive and competitive way that is characteristic of Britain in the grip of the new orthodoxy.

Conclusions

The new orthodoxy's glorification of the family turns out, on closer inspection, to be a recipe for the continued subordination of women, to reinforce their status as secondary, low-paid workers and unpaid care-givers. Its political strategy rests on giving such tax advantages to owner-occupier households that women will have more to lose from redistribution towards the poor as members of such job-rich and house-rich families than to gain from pressing their case for equality.

Private households depend on female altruism mainly because their terms of membership do not allow the possibility of true cooperation between equals. Because men and women enter them on such unequal terms, women are required to act out of duty, rather than because it is in their interests to do so; the burdens and benefits are not fairly shared between members. Strong bonds of affection, loyalty and trust may allow these fundamental inequalities to be overcome, either by constant negotiation, give and take, or because one person's (usually a woman's) caring feelings override her just cause for resentment, and she is able to transcend her disadvantages and spread goodwill all around her.

The new orthodoxy identifies the family as a source of bliss, and the very heart of the good society, both because it is where consumption takes place, and because of its positive moral connotations. In practice, the modern family is conspicuously a source of conflict and unhappiness, with one in three marriages ending in divorce, rising rates of violence – towards wives, towards children and towards old people – and a growing incidence of mental illness (especially among women). The new orthodoxy matches its praise for the happy family with an at least equal measure of blame for families whose members are juvenile delinquents, truants, low-achievers at school, heavy-drinkers, drug-users, homosexuals or plain unhappy. It even manages to blame the family for poverty and unemployment. On closer inspection, the new orthodoxy's prescription for family life seems less than harmonious and all that it can offer by way of a remedy for these ills is greater self-discipline and self-sacrifice.

The new orthodoxy's main hope for the future of the family – an increase in voluntary altruism by women, especially poor women – is doomed to failure. Ironically, this failure will mainly come about through market forces. Demand for married women as a source of cheap labour in part-time service jobs will collide with demand for married women as unpaid family carers for old people. The new orthodoxy's model for the economy will lose its dynamism as the flexibility from this reserve army of labour is lost, and women's wages rise, along with the costs of care.

At this point, future growth will depend on drawing in low-paid, part-time labour from the underclass, or forcing them to do caring work as a condition for receiving benefits (as was foreseen in the future scenario). The latter would be monstrously inefficient way of providing such services, and would not be at all acceptable to those who need care or to family carers. But the former is ruled out because the new orthodoxy's schemes for means-tested supplements to wages would not make such demanding jobs worth while for members of the underclass, even if they could be trained to do them.

Thus market forces will bring about the conditions in which the failures of the new orthodoxy will be experienced in terms of a slowing in the rate of economic growth, an increase in numbers of people requiring paid care and an escalation of tensions in families. This in turn will make an excellent case for a different kind of social organization, with a stronger cooperative, collectivist element. Citizens in a Basic Income society could organize caregiving in a more rational way, which brought the benefits of association to carers and those cared for.

The transition to such a society could also allow a shift away from household work focused on competitive gain ('getting on') towards greater communal cooperation. With fewer rewards for exclusiveness and private property, a greater premium would be placed on good citizenship.

Notes

1 Jan Pahl, 'Patterns of money management', *Journal of Social Policy*, 9 (1980), pp. 313–36. See also Julia Brannen and Gail Wilson (eds), *Give and Take in Families* (Unwin Hyman, 1987).
2 Carol Gilligan, *In a Different Voice* (Harvard University Press, 1982), pp. 1–10.
3 V. Beechey, *Unequal Work* (Verso, 1987).
4 Jean Martin and Ceridwen Roberts, *Women and Employment: a Lifetime Perspective* (Department of Employment and Office of Population Censuses and Surveys, 1984), tables 8.7 and 8.9, pp. 101–2.
5 R. E. Pahl, *Divisions of Labour* (Blackwell, 1984).
6 Michael Meacher, 'The results of a new survey into domestic assistance and respite care received by carers', Press Release, 9 October 1986. A total of 83 per cent said that they received no assistance whatsoever from any other person with the daily tasks of getting up, dressing, bathing, toileting and feeding the person who needed care. Only 26 per cent had a home help.
7 Clare Ungerson, *Policy is Personal: Sex, Gender and Informal Care* (Tavistock, 1987).
8 Janet Finch, 'Family obligations and the life course', in A. Bryman and B. Bytheway (eds), *Perspectives on the Life Cycle* (Macmillan, 1987); and 'Whose responsibility? Women and the future of family care', in I. Allen, M. Wicks, J. Finch and D. Leat (eds), *Informal Care Tomorrow* (Policy Studies Institute, 1987). See also Ungerson, *Policy is Personal*, chs 3 and 5.
9 The Equal Opportunities Commission, *Carers and Services* (1984) found that 41 per cent of carers for elderly people were men. Sara Arber, Nigel Gilbert and Maria Evandrou, 'Gender, household composition and receipt of domiciliary services by elderly disabled', *Journal of Social Policy* (forthcoming) estimate nearly 50 per cent, using the General Household Survey.
10 Unless he is an unmarried son living with parents, see Ungerson, *Policy is Personal*, ch. 3.

11 See, for example, Ann Richardson and Jane Ritchie, *Making the Break: Parents' Views about Adults with a Mental Handicap Living at Home* (King Edward's Hospital Fund, 1986), p. 35. They found that parents' feelings of being burdened were not related to their own age or health, but to difficult behaviour by sons or daughters.

12 G. Oxley, *Poor Relief in England and Wales, 1500–1834* (David and Charles, 1973).

13 R. M. Moroney, *The Family and the State: Considerations for Social Policy* (Longman, 1976), table 3.8, p. 42.

14 K. G. Wright, 'The application of cost-benefit analysis to the care of elderly people', University of York (unpublished).

15 Moroney, *The Family and the State*.

16 See, for instance, M. Henwood and M. Wicks, *The Forgotten Army: Family Care and Elderly People* (Family Policy Studies Centre, 1984); A. Briggs and J. Oliver, *Caring: Experience of Looking After Disabled Relatives* (Routledge and Kegan Paul, 1985).

17 John Vincent, *Petit-bourgeois Care* (University of Exeter, 1987).

18 Bill Jordan, *Rethinking Welfare* (Blackwell, 1987), ch. 12.

19 David Eversley, 'The demography of retirement – prospects for the Year 2030', in Michael Fogarty (ed.), *Retirement Policy: The Next Fifty Years* (Heinemann, 1982).

20 For a plea for collective care, for the sake of carers and cared for, with a continued respect for individual autonomy and choice, see Gillian Dalley, *Ideologies of Caring: Rethinking Community and Collectivism* (Macmillan, 1988), esp. ch. 5.

21 David Challis and Bleddyn Davies, 'Long-term care for the elderly: the community care scheme', Discussion Paper 386, Personal Social Services Research Unit, University of Kent, 1985.

22 J. Gershuny and I. Miles, *The New Service Economy: the Transformation of Employment in Industrial Societies* (Pinter, 1983).

23 Bernard Kilroy, *The Market for Civic Housing* (Institute of Environmental Health Officers, 1986).

24 Pahl, *Divisions of Labour*.

25 Central Statistical Office, *Social Trends, 1987* (HMSO, 1987).

10

Morality, Reason and Interest

So far I have argued for an understanding of social relations which makes visible and recognizable our shared concerns, as members of the same community, and hence our common interests. I have claimed that the idea of a social morality only makes sense in terms of such common interests, and that a good society involves cooperation between people whose quality of life depends on each other's actions.

But I have said little of how we learn about our common interests, or the scope for cooperation or the skills for creating common goods. All these remain disturbingly vague, the merest sketches of how a better society might get things done. So I seem to be asking the reader to take the possibility of better social relations on trust.

This contrasts with the new orthodoxy's precise analysis of how self-interest and self-responsibility lead, through individual choices, to its social order. For every individual decision, it is able to stipulate a market preference, or a personal commitment or a moral rule. The result is an apparently impressive structure, systematic and coherent.

My critique of the new orthodoxy has been aimed at demonstrating that choices which seem rational within the logic of this model give rise to social institutions which have serious unintended consequences. The most important of these concern conflicts of interest between large coalitions in society, leading to an eventual deterioration of relations, amounting to a state of war. Thus the new orthodoxy brings about a society which reflects exactly the problem which it claims to have resolved - the Leviathan trap, in which no individual can trust any other.

In this chapter I shall argue that individuals' interests can only be understood in terms of the social systems of which they are part. In the example of the stricken ferry, people cooperated, even though they were strangers and often had no common language, because their situation prompted them to recognize that their individual survival depended on each other's actions. In everyday life, common interests are not so obvious, but we can give each other reasons for cooperating. By reasoning with each other, we can organize ourselves into groups and associations, and conduct relations with other organizations. We can also develop traditions and vocabularies through which - even when there is little time to argue and discuss - we may appeal to shared concerns and common purposes. And even in the absence of words, we can signal to others our involvement in the issues over which we wish to make common cause, or lend our assistance in joint action and mutual aid. A CND badge invites others to join us in concern for peace; a donor card signals, even when we are already half dead, a desire to share in saving life.

According to the new orthodoxy, we are moved by preferences – which are coordinated through markets – and by sympathies – through which we commit ourselves to others' needs and make ourselves responsible towards them. Choice is an individual matter because we can only act from 'internal reasons': our own current desires, whether for pleasing ourselves or pleasing others.[1] Even taking a very optimistic view of our 'natural sympathies',[2] this leads to a dangerously privatized version of society. I have shown that it allows us to invest all our energy and intelligence in the pursuit of private, exclusive goods. It tells us that we are quite justified in seeing competitive self-interest as the guiding principle of our public lives, and in regarding our public duties as discharged if we break no laws and do our neighbours no active wrong. It leads us to share our lives with a few individuals who are similarly endowed by fortune, and to give their desires priority over the claims of all others' needs. And it induces us to identify ourselves with the use of political power in the defence of our material interests, and the oppression of those who threaten them.

In order to complete my case against the new orthodoxy, I must give an account of the kind of reasoning that can allow us to recognize the interests which the pursuit of competitive self-interest obscures. The new orthodoxy can claim on its side of the argument not only the long tradition of economic theory, and the achievements of modern commercial enterprise, but also the scientific and technological advances which prosperity has financed and encouraged. Science and progress are, it is argued, as much the products of rational individual choices (based on weighing evidence) as trade and industry. Philosophically, scientific method has its origins in the same elegant and coherent system of ideas as economic coordination. By contrast, political argument and social concern are imprecise, unreliable and messy.

I shall defend the contestability and messiness of dialogical reasoning partly by attacking the supposedly objective status of technical reason, and by criticizing the notion of private calculation as a basis for action. I shall argue that a dialogue between different cultures and traditions offers the only hope of escape from the traps of calculative reason.

Finally, I shall try to give an account of the role of individual judgement and choice in social relations, and of morality in the good society. Although my analysis has been conducted in terms of social morality, I shall suggest that the good citizen has to exercise such judgement, both in relation to the needs of strangers and in balancing his or her contribution to the common good.

Reasons and choices

The ability to reason makes the human condition uniquely problematic. In principle, we could ask ourselves to provide reasons for every action we take, and every option we turn down. Yet (as Hume pointed out) reason alone cannot explain our choices: we must be moved by the desire for something. Society must therefore in some sense be made up of individuals pursuing their desires, and using reason to achieve them. The new orthodoxy starts from this view of people as followers of calculated preferences (bargain-hunters).

This represents a considerable climb-down from earlier and more ambitious claims for the powers of individual reason. When the Enlightenment first promoted the rational individual to the front line of human progress, its foremost thinkers claimed that people would quickly learn the secrets of harmonious social life, as they were learning to unravel the secrets of nature. Rules of good conduct must be like natural laws, and it was just a matter of reason and experiment to discover them.[3] Once individual reason was seen not to possess these solutions, it became part of the problem.[4] As we saw in chapter 5, it was through a combination of the emotions and the interests (seen in economic terms) that potentially disruptive rationality was tied to a system of cooperation, through natural sympathy and the Invisible Hand.

It is easy to see the attractions for economic model-building of a theory of rational choice which so neatly overcomes the problems of decision-making and coordination that would otherwise beset any analysis of human action. It is also easy to see how the commercialization of social relations has made this account increasingly plausible. Since so much of everyday life is now structured by the price mechanism, so that choices are available costed in pounds and pence, we can indeed work out our 'interests' in these terms – if interests are defined as those of our pockets. In this way, markets have turned the Enlightenment project of a rational–moral reordering of Christendom into a series of rather simple calculations, in which individual reason is reduced to something long since surpassed by the capacities of a pocket calculator.

Yet despite the pervasiveness of markets and the plausibility of this account of bargain-hunting, human actions (and the language we use about them) obstinately escape this model. Living does not consist of solving a series of discrete, specific problems, or making choices between a finite range of options, each with its price-tag. Partly this is because, as Heidegger pointed out, we live in and through our actions, only pausing to deliberate when the 'ready-to-hand' fails us in some way or we are confronted with a new phenomenon. But it is also because of the inherent complexity, uncertainty, instability and uniqueness of the situations we encounter, and the need to engage in a dialogue with others to negotiate our relationships.

In all these, the skills we need are not those of calculative ordering of preferences, nor even those of technical problem-solving; they are skills of understanding, communicating, initiating, persuading and responding. These require a different kind of reasoning, one which is not internal and private, but shared with others, and open to question and challenge.

This kind of reasoning is therefore public, and concerns actions in which we are accountable to others. Even when we are close to home, we are often required to give such an account; to give a reason for acting in a certain way is usually to explain it in terms of the configuration of roles and relationships in which we are enmeshed. 'Why did you promise to visit your mother on Sunday, when we usually take the children to the beach?' is a question which demands a reason in terms of the claims of personal relations and how actions affect them. The wider our network of relationships, the more complex our choices become; in this sense, life in the public arena is both demanding and difficult, and we need considerable skills to steer our course through it.

While it is true that we need desires to move us to action, these can be changed or even created by 'external reasons', either by the arguments of others or by clarifying our own in response to theirs.[5] We can discover or be persuaded of a better way of achieving what we want, a different interpretation of the evidence or another and more important priority. Rational persuasion can make us change our plans, or we can change them ourselves, in the course of a discussion. In this sense, Kant was right that we could use reason to over-rule desire; but this process is a much more *ad hoc*, chaotic and contested one then he suggested. We do not live by rules which are universal, categorical and internally consistent, which our reason leads us to follow on all occasions, any more than we live by unmodifiable ordered preferences. We have to be prepared to debate our actions, and submit our rules of thumb to public scrutiny.

Market choices allow us some respite from this complexity and account-ability. In a competitive market, my individual choice has so little effect that I can disclaim responsibility; as a bargain-hunter I can remain anonymous, and leave impersonal economic forces to shape others' destinies. I do not have to give reasons for my preferences, which saves a lot of time. But it also allows me to ignore issues which might exercise my powers of reason, such as the arguments for and against buying South African products. Isolated individual calculation is possible precisely because I can discount the effects of my choices on others. By contrast, how I act as a member of my association, community or political party will have consequences for my fellow members, and could influence their actions.

This is why interests cannot be understood in terms of sympathies and preferences, but require analysis in terms of reasons. Because my actions do affect others, and theirs me, I must engage in a public dialogue about our lives together to discover what is possible, what is desirable and what the likely consequences of my actions are. Outcomes cannot be calculated in advance; I must know more about what they are planning and thinking, and try to influence their decisions. In other words, there is no way of knowing my own interests before I have this dialogue, because any choices I make in ignorance of their projects and purposes may have all sorts of unintended consequences.

Until I debate and negotiate with others, and coordinate my choices with theirs, I will not be able to follow my interests or act rationally.

So reasons and interests turn out to be linked in a far more complex way than the new orthodoxy suggests, and one which requires the recognition of common interests. In the explanation of human action, we are required to account for what happens in a public arena, where people cooperate or compete, support or oppose, act together or go their separate ways, but always recognize their influence on each other. And here we use a public language - of fairness, responsibility, sharing and helping - which appeals directly to the common good, and to reasons for cooperating in improving the quality of social relations.

Managing social problems

This argument seems to fly in the face of one of the most obvious phenomena of modern society. The growth of professions, experts in the management of human problems, suggests that the kind of reason to which social relations are susceptible is not political and contested but expert and technical. After all, the human relations professions - medicine, law, psychology, planning, architecture, housing management, social work - have been steadily expanding to the point where in the United States professionals make up between 15 and 20 per cent of the workforce. The mark of these professions is, so it is argued, that they possess a specialized skill in applying general theoretical principles to particular problems: the rigorous application of scientific knowledge and technique to individual human situations.[6] If this is so, how is it consistent with the idea of social relations as negotiated between reasoning participants?

The answers to this question are to be found within the literature of those same professions, as well as in the criticisms of those who have analysed them as outsiders. Faith in expert solutions to social problems has waned visibly in recent years, as increased professional input has yielded diminishing returns.[7] The literature of the professions themselves speaks of a 'crisis of confidence' in their effectiveness, and while it is usually only one profession at a time that comes under critical public scrutiny (currently social work in Britain), others are privately relieved that they are not in the spotlight. For example, British medicine has been able to retain its high prestige despite the fundamental questions about the ethics and effectiveness of 'treatment' raised by the Wendy Savage case (over childbirth) and about diagnosis in the Cleveland scandal (over child sexual abuse).

Discerning analyses of this crisis point to the limitations of the professions' model of technical rationality.[8] Experts are invited to intervene in human situations which are complex, uncertain, unstable and unique, with many interacting factors; yet their theory abstracts rather simple causal links, and prescribes solutions in terms of this simplified model. The aim is to select out particular features of the situation which are susceptible to technical manipulation, and to concentrate on these, to the exclusion of all other considerations. Yet this approach is often irrelevant, and can have unintended consequences. As one commentator put it:

> Managers are not confronted with problems that are independent of each other, but with dynamic situations of changing problems that interact with each other. I call such situations *messes*. Problems are abstractions extracted from messes by analysis; they are to messes as atoms are to tables and chairs . . . Managers do not solve problems: they manage messes.[9]

The way forward for the professions, I would argue, does not lie down the road of more esoteric theory or more instrumental problem-solving, but in more skilled dialogue with those who present problems, and a better overall appreciation of complex situations.[10] The same view is put forward by Donald Schön in his book *The Reflective Practitioner*. Generalizing across the professions, he proposes a method which owes much less to the paradigm of applied scientific technique, and more to that of art or craftsmanship. This approach recognizes the uniqueness of each situation, and tackles it by spontaneous and intuitive as well as measured responses. He insists that knowledge cannot always be specified, and that professional know-how is often tacit, implicit in action rather than explicit, and based on a feel for what is done rather than a theory about how to do it. Criteria for qualitative judgements cannot always be specified, nor can skills be defined in terms of techniques or procedures; often adjustments are made during a process, through 'thinking on one's feet' or improvization. In all this, Schön argues that the professional is not simply drawing on knowledge which is 'inside'. 'The reflective practitioner tries to discover the limits of his expertise through reflective conversation with the client'.[11] The client joins the practitioner in an open-ended inquiry into a complex situation, through which the professional becomes more accountable by means of a dialogue, aimed at reaching a shared understanding and solution.

Without this kind of dialogue, it is difficult to see how experts are going to counter the other major criticism of their practice. This is that they are better at the tasks their skills equip them for doing than at harnessing these skills to socially useful purposes. In consequence, they stand accused of creating new problems by the very remedies through which they seek to solve old ones[12] – for example, turning normal human processes, like birth and death, into medical events which require professional management. They also stand accused of using their expertise for their own exclusive advantage; the two accusations are linked because experts are seen as deskilling lay people, mystifying human experience and social relations, and creating dependence on their own knowledge, and control over spheres of people's lives.

To counter this, professionals must listen, negotiate, debate and persuade. They must enter into a dialogue about the purposes as well as the methods they pursue, and about values as well as technical solutions.[13] In other words, they must undermine their own claims to exclusive expertise, by allowing lay people to question their goals and means and surrendering their authority and power. It is not surprising that there is still little sign of rush to do this; yet it is hard to recognize any other way of ensuring that technical reason does not contribute to social irrationality, through its unintended byproducts.

This also illustrates a wider point about the relationship between social roles and interests. Social roles, such as those of professions and members of organizations, are shaped by the holder's relation to assets, such as skills or ownership of resources. Role-playing is therefore constrained by the interests associated with this role in the configuration of social relations which surround the distribution of assets. In this sense, professionals and those who hold organizational power are strongly influenced towards self-interested actions which are socially irrational, if we consider the wider view of society and social institutions. The crisis of legitimacy for those who claim to be experts in solving human problems arises, as we would expect, over their response to a conflict between the demands of their narrowly role-bound interests and their broader interests as members of society. Here, again, reason may allow them to interpret their interests as including common interests in the good of all.

The choice arises most clearly in relation to the fundamental division of interests in modern advanced capitalist societies. For British health service professionals, so long as the National Health Service exists in its present form, there is no such conflict. With the prospect of increased income from changes which allowed higher health spending through extended private insurance schemes, the situation would change. So far, the professionals have (to their credit) emphasized that the poor would be the losers in a two-tier, American-style system of health care; but so far it has not emerged how much they, as service-givers, might be the gainers from such a system. When the carrot of higher incomes is held out, then will be the real test of their commitment to the common good.

Knowledge and reason

There are obvious echoes of these ideas and arguments in new accounts of scientific discovery, and of knowledge itself, that have been developed in the past 25 years. Instead of seeing science as consisting of the patient construction of theory, via experiment, from facts, this new view presents major discoveries as discontinuities, involving *ad hoc* methods, and theories which contradicted known facts and experimental results.[14] .This in turn reveals existing knowledge as essentially conventional and theory-bound, and even observation and measurement as grounded in ideology and tradition. Reason therefore involves interpretation, and understanding is a matter of public communication and shared symbols, within an intellectual community.

The common theme of these ideas can be traced to Wittgenstein's famous account of games, which have their own rules and purposes, which bind those taking part, but which cannot be specified externally. 'What has to be accepted, the given, is, so to speak, *forms of life.*'[15] The individual's reason is expressed in language which is part of such forms of life. The meanings of words are conventional and language games cannot legitimate themselves or each other.

Science and knowledge therefore involve understanding which is situated in a language game which, like other games, involves submitting to its rules and accepting their authority: a normative framework of assumptions and purposes. Far from being objective and value-free, it involves interpretations which are conventional, including those about confirming or rejecting theories.[16] The scientist or researcher are not autonomous rational agents, but bound within a community and tradition which points the direction of their work, lays down standards of proof and evidence, and criteria for the relevance of their findings, already putting each observation within a context, connecting them with others, as part of a common culture. From such reporters there can be no 'unvarnished news'.[17]

On the face of it, these views would seem to demean both the rational individual and reason itself, but this is not so. First, although meanings are conventional and shared, acts of understanding and knowing require personal skill and judgement (in focusing on some features of a complex muddle) which alone give facts and events significance to us.[18] Hence all knowledge is personal, and not universal. It demands participation and commitment on the part of the individual, using reason and discrimination.

Secondly, although observations and inferences are grounded within traditions and cultures, these are not fixed and immutable. They need constantly to be adapted and developed, which can only happen through dialogue.[19] In this way, theories are amended or extended and ideas are clarified. The tradition is enriched, and individual reason is improved and sharpened.

Thirdly, new theories emerge to challenge old ones. In line with new accounts of discoveries and inventions, progress depends on the openness of the scientific community to novel perceptions and interpretations. As Feyerabend contends, 'No theory ever agrees with all the *facts* in its domain, yet it is not always the theory that is to blame. Facts are constituted by older ideologies, and a clash between facts and theories may be proof of progress.'[20] Hence 'the only principle that does not inhibit progress is: *anything goes*'.[21]

Fourthly, a dialogue between different traditions and cultures can lead to a deeper understanding of issues. Even if agreement is not reached, participation in debate can promote the progress of reason; recognition of the cultural and historical plurality of forms of life and conceptual schemes does not of itself require scepticism towards the idea of reason.[22] The limitations of our own intellectual community's tradition only became visible when confronted with the theories and interpretations of others. In this way, an approach which is trapped within its own criteria of truth and reason can be saved from fossilization, find new ways to overcome its weaknesses and move forward. Hence, as MacIntyre argues, reason should welcome exposure of its tradition to others, and the possibility that its theories may be defeated in the challenge.[23] Only by encountering other cultures, and incorporating some of their ideas and standards, can individuals and traditions develop a more refined and adaptable form of rational judgement.

Thus it is not only in social and political issues that the idea of isolated individual choice, based on calculative reason, stands discredited. In the sciences as well as the arts, the new theory of meaning, understanding and knowing requires reasoning to be located in dialogue and community, in debate and sharing, within a public language.

The organizational structure of intellectual and scientific communities is also instructive, as a model for how reason might best influence human affairs, and contribute to the good of society. They allow a balance between participation in teams and individual research (hence members of the community have both 'voice' and 'exit' opportunities). There are many ways in which ideas, research plans and findings can be exchanged, so that the future work of each team and individual can be informed by past and present studies. Some coordination is formal (as through grant-giving bodies), but most is informal, through exchange of papers, seminars, conferences and journals. Membership is extremely wide (international) and inclusive of many diverse groups, which are to some extent competitive in terms of status; but innovation depends on the chance to influence the direction of research and theory, through published findings and public debate. Yet each individual has the option of withdrawing (at least temporarily) from this process into his or her work. Feyerabend describes the ideal scientific community as an anarchy,[24] and it is easy to see, even in the sober outlines of organized academic life, a principle of self-government, under the authority of a tradition, within a 'game' or 'practice'.

Such communities are, like human society itself, future-orientated; they make their decisions through a kind of reasoning which anticipates the community's development and considers its common interests. Their members have the means to contribute to the identification and creation of the common good; they can influence the plans and purposes of the community by their participation in its work or by individual criticism. They contribute as rational equals in the community's choices, taking account of its future interests. Clearly the directions taken through this process will have much to do with trying to increase the community's share of material resources, and hence with this form of self-interest. But the way to counteract this tendency is not to insist on scientists being more 'scientific', or intellectuals more 'objective', it is to involve their communities better in the concerns of the wider community, to ensure that they contribute to the common interest in a better future society.

Reason which anticipates the future interests of a community or society is teleological rather than calculative. It does not derive interests from facts and figures, as in calculating economic interests. Indeed, no future-orientated decision can follow logically from factual premises. Rather, it is concerned with determining common purposes through shared commitments with fellow members, under the constraints of limited opportunities and resources. In this sense, it is like a much more complex and less spectacular version of the spontaneous cooperation among the victims in the ferry disaster. Social life, as Aristotle pointed out, is a voyage which we take with others, sharing the risks and responsibilities, as well as the benefits of our association with them. As in such a journey, our thinking about the route and the destination commits us to goals, and the means of achieving them to roles which require cooperation. This, as we shall see, has important moral implications.

Individual morality

Throughout this book I have been arguing for a social morality based on common interests in the quality of life and on shared purposes. But I have paid almost no attention to individual morality: to the choices which people make in relation to other individuals, including those in which they consciously sacrifice their own good to that of someone else.

This is because I have been arguing, against the new orthodoxy, that morality arises primarily from our commitments to members of our community, to associates, friends and kin. In a good society, these commitments become part of the lives of individuals through specific systems of cooperation, in which we assume roles and responsibilities to pursue agreed goals. We do not deduce our duties from categorical moral rules, but negotiate them with our fellow citizens. So moral responsibility cannot be understood in terms of private individual choice, but only in terms of our roles in networks of cooperation.

This explains why the words used for roles which involve responsibilities to others entain moral conclusions. Hume insisted that 'is' never implies 'ought', but A. N. Prior pointed out that 'He is a sea captain' implies 'He ought to do what a sea captain ought to do.'[25] A shared activity, such as a sea voyage, involves those who are experts in roles which give them special obligations to non-experts. To return to the example of the ferry disaster, after the *Herald of Free Enterprise* capsized, the assistant bos'n, Mr Mark Stanley, voluntarily accepted moral responsibility because it was his duty to shut the doors of the ship. He told the inquiry, in terms closely following A. N. Prior's example, that he was the assistant bos'n, so he should have shut the doors.[26] He refused to put blame on others, saying it was for them to acknowledge, but felt his own lapse made him morally as well as technically responsible. Mr Stanley was therefore courageously accepting the social view of morality; no one else involved has so far followed his example.

But our moral responsibilities are not always defined by our social roles. In

at least two respects, we are required to exercise personal judgement in deciding what we owe to others, over and above that which we use in negotiating our commitments under organized systems of cooperation. The first of these concerns the needs of strangers. Here we are not dealing with generalized reciprocity, such as helping neighbours or friends without reckoning the cost to ourselves. Rather we are dealing with a chance encounter, in which the needs of someone from outside my community and friendship network makes claims on my time and energy.

Suppose that I am driving along a country road, and see another motorist, with his head inside the bonnet of his car. As I am about to pull out to pass, he straightens up and signals for me to stop. He explains that his radiator is dry, and asks me to drive him back along the road to his house, a mile in the direction I have come from, to collect a can of water. To what is his appeal directed, and how can I use the kind of reasoning discussed in this chapter to decide whether to help? I would argue that he is inviting me imaginatively to extend my network of associations or to create a notional new association that includes both him and me. This might be something like the Association of Users of the B5219, or the Association of Mechanical Idiots or even the Association of People who Can't Afford a Decent Car. All these might be seen as *ad hoc* equivalents of the Automobile Association, in which all members are also potentially patrolmen, ready to offer each other emergency assistance because they know that they may find themselves in the same situation some day, and need the same kind of help.

The point about a request for help of this kind is that it appeals to something that strangers have in common, which outweighs the fact that they are not members of the same community or network. This may be what they have in common as motorists, or as people susceptible to bad luck, or simply as fallible people with equally fallible cars. The implicit assumption behind the request for help is that, if the roles were reversed, the needy person would do the same for the helper. But the helper is required to take the imaginative step of including the needy person in his or her notional community because the request for help need not be direct. For example, the wayside victim could not ask the Good Samaritan for assistance because he was unconscious; and those who passed by on the other side were ignoring his need, so refusing to treat him as one of their community.

Clearly, the capacity to perceive the needs of strangers as relevant and morally compelling is not just a matter of individual imagination and judgement. It is also closely related to the nature of social relations. Whether or not I stop to help a stranded or even an apparently injured motorist will depend on how I perceive myself as a citizen and the bonds I feel towards my fellow citizens. It will also depend on my own fears of being attacked and robbed if I stop. In this sense, the lack of trust that is characteristic of the Leviathan trap is cumulative, so that fear leads me to ignore the needs of those who may be fellow-victims of what I fear. Finally, what I can do to help others depends on my skills, and even on my means. However, it seems unlikely that the

Good Samaritan's ability to pay the bill at the inn was the most important factor in determining his intervention, as Mrs Thatcher appeared once to suggest.

But, in addition to all this, I must also make a judgement about whether the good I can do to the stranger is greater than any harm I may inflict on others as a result of responding to his request. If, for example, I am actually on the way to pick up someone who is disabled, or who is waiting outside in the rain or I am already late for an important appointment, then I may judge that I should explain to him that I must refuse his request. If he wants me to push his car, and I suffer from a bad back, then I owe it to others to whom I have commitments not to make myself useless by foolhardy helpfulness. But the more serious the stranger's plight, the more his claims will tend to outweigh those of my other responsibilities.

This judgement is not only used to decide between rival claims in particular situations, but also to maintain a balance between our various commitments. As members of society, we have to work out how we can best contribute to the common good – which associations to join, what roles and responsibilities to accept and when to limit our involvement. Since not all goods are compatible, and any individual has limited time and energy, we have to organize our lives in such a way as contribute most usefully, and avoid disappointing the expectations of those who depend on us. This means that being a good citizen is rather a learned skill; we would not expect a young person to be able to master the art of organizing (often strong and absorbing) commitments well enough to be entirely reliable, any more than we would expect an older one to be quite as energetic in enthusiasm for the cause.

Lastly, individuals can use their judgement to play the role of moral entrepreneur: to draw attention to new needs and to encourage others to act together in some new combination. If it is not an isolated stranger, but a whole group of people in society who are suffering and requiring help, then what is needed is concerted action to include them in the good of an associ-ation or of the whole community. Leadership and persuasive argument, as well as example, are necessary for the formation of new groups in response to changing social circumstances.

Conclusions

In this chapter, I have argued that the way in which we use reason to discover our interests is very different from the new orthodoxy's account of rational choice as individual calculation. Because we share our world with others, as part of a community, we can know our interests only by debating with those others about the future direction our society should take. We cannot know what is best for ourselves or for others by isolated deliberation because our interests are linked with theirs, and we share responsibility for our future.

This understanding of reason and interests accords with new accounts of skills in social problem management, of science and of knowledge. All these emphasize that these activities are 'practices' which depend on shared meanings, within communities governed by agreed conventions. Both philosophically and practically, they involve an active process of focusing and debate to extract clarity and purpose from complexity and muddle.

The kind of individual skill and judgement (including moral sensitivity) that this approach to social relations requires is far more demanding than the calculative and technical rationality that is represented by the new orthodoxy. It rehabilitates reason in human affairs, and requires individuals to take far more responsibility for themselves, as equal and autonomous beings, in their communities. Instead of relying on impersonal economic forces and emotions to create cooperation, it demands negotiation, tact, perceptiveness and powers of persuasion.

The new orthodoxy purports to provide a model of society which solves the problems of competition and mutual mistrust. In practice, its unintended consequences include a deterioration of social relations, to the point where no common interests between individuals are recognizable and hostility and mistrust are universal. As this process progresses, the system is forced to rely more and more on power to enforce cooperation and punish opportunism, irresponsibility and aggression. Society devotes an increasing proportion of its energies and resources to methods of social control, and the need for more drastic measures of coercion grows with mutual fear and antagonism. Eventually, the whole system depends - in Hobbesian fashion - on threats of state violence because all possibility of negotiated agreements and cooperative solutions, in which the common interests of all are served, has disappeared in mutual recrimination.

This brings us back to the problem of power in social relations. We first encountered the problem with the formation of states as a response to intercommunal aggression. In the final chapter I shall consider whether this still poses an insuperable barrier to human cooperation.

Notes

1 Martin Hollis, *The Cunning of Reason* (Cambridge University Press, 1987). Hollis argues against the view taken by Bernard Williams in his paper 'Internal and external reasons', in R. Harrison (ed.), *Rational Action* (Cambridge University Press, 1979) that any reason which actually moves someone to act must be internal to his 'subjective motivational set'. Williams calls his internalist position, 'sub-Humean', and Hollis calls his externalist position 'sub-Kantian'.

2 Such as that of Howard Margolis, in *Selfishness, Altruism and Rationality* (Cambridge University Press, 1982). Margolis regards the desire to balance others' interests with our own as largely unconscious; we have a quasi-instinctive sense of 'fair shares'. But, on his account, my decision to help others through any particular action would be fully rational, even if I took no steps to investigate their needs or consult them about their wishes. And, so it seems, any others will do.

3   Both Decartes and Locke, for example, believed that a mathematical method of reasoning could be used to adduce ethical truths. Decartes wrote, 'If someone were to explain correctly what are the simple ideas in the human imagination out of which all human thoughts are compounded, and if his explanation were generally received, I would dare to hope for a universal language, very easy to learn, to speak and to write. The greatest advantage of such a language would be the assistance it would give to men's judgement, representing matters so clearly that it would be almost impossible to go wrong . . . I think it is possible to invent such a language and to discover the science on which it depends' (Descartes to Mersenne, 20 November 1629, in R. Descartes, *Philosophical Letters*, ed. A. Kenny, Oxford University Press, 1970, p. 6). Locke thought that ethical science was demonstrable like mathematics: 'I doubt not but from self-evident propositions, by necessary consequences, as incontestable as those in mathematics, the measures of right and wrong might be made out' (*An Essay Concerning Human Understanding* (1690), ed. Peter Nidditch (Clarendon Press, 1975), bk IV, ch. 3, s. 18).

4   See Thomas A. Spragens jr, *The Irony of Liberal Reason* (University of Chicago Press, 1981), chs 1 and 2.

5   Hollis, *The Cunning of Reason*, ch. 6.

6   See, for example, N. Glazer, 'The Schools of the minor professions', *Minerva*, 3 (1974), pp. 346-64.

7   A review of the declining effectiveness of interventions through social services is provided by Roger Hadley and Stephen Hatch, *Social Welfare and the Failure of the State: Centralised Social Services and Participatory Alternatives* (Allen and Unwin, 1981). Among the most savage outside critics of medicine and other human relations professions is Ivan Illich; see, for example, his *Medical Nemesis* (Calder and Boyers, 1976).

8   See, for example, Donald A. Schön, *The Reflective Practitioner: How Professionals Think in Action* (Temple Smith, 1983).

9   Russell Ackoff, 'The future of operational research is past', *Journal of Operational Research Society*, 30 (1979), pp. 93-104.

10 Bill Jordan, 'Counselling, advocacy and negotiation', *British Journal of Social Work*, 17 (1987), pp. 135-46. See also Hugh England, *Social Work as Art: Making Sense of Good Practice* (Allen and Unwin, 1986); and John Paley, 'Social work and the sociology of knowledge', *British Journal of Social Work*, 17 (1987), pp. 169-86.

11 Schön, *The Reflective Practitioner*, p. 296.

12 For the concept of 'iatrogenesis' see Ivan Illich, *Medical Nemesis*.

13 Bill Jordan, 'Is the client a fellow citizen?', *Social Work Today*, 6 (1975), pp. 471-5.

14 See, for example, Thomas Kuhn, *The Structure of Scientific Revolutions* (Chicago University Press, 1962); Imre Latakos, *Criticism and the Growth of Knowledge* (Cambridge University Press, 1970); and Paul Feyerabend, *Against Method: Outline of an Anarchistic Theory of Knowledge* (Verso, 1975).

15 Ludwig Wittgenstein, *Philosophical Investigations* (Blackwell, 1953), II, 226.

16 Peter Winch, *The Idea of a Social Science and its Relation to Philosophy* (Routledge and Kegan Paul, 1964); and Charles Taylor, 'Interpretation and the sciences of man', *Review of Metaphysics*, 25 (1971), pp. 3-51.

17 W. V. O. Quine, 'Two dogmas of empiricism', in W. V. O. Quine (ed.), *From a Logical Point of View* (Harvard University Press, 1953).

18 Michael Polanyi and Harry Prosch, *Meaning* (University of Chicago Press, 1975), p. 44.
19 H.-G. Gadamer, *Truth and Reason* (1960) (Seabury Press, 1975); Georgia Warnke, *Gadamer: Hermeneutics, Tradition and Reason* (Polity Press, 1987).
20 Feyerabend, *Against Method*, p. 55.
21 Ibid., p. 23.
22 Warnke, *Gadamer*, p. 171.
23 Alasdair MacIntyre, 'Relativism, power and philosophy', *Proceedings and Addresses of the American Philosophical Association*, 1985.
24 Feyerabend, *Against Method*, p. 1.
25 A. N. Prior, 'The Autonomy of Ethics', in A. N. Prior, *Papers in Logic and Ethics*, ed. P. T. Geach and A. J. P. Kenny (Duckworth, 1976), pp. 88-96.
26 *Guardian*, 25 July 1987.

11

Conclusion: the Good of Mankind

This book has been about the good society; I have assumed throughout that a society consists of a nation state. Yet my argument leads to the questioning of this assumption. If the idea of a good society only makes sense in terms of people's common interests in the quality of their life together, then this notion of society is too restrictive. Since the nations of the world are increasingly interdependent, and individuals mix more and more with citizens of other states, the interests we share in a good life cross national boundaries. Indeed, as the Chernobyl nuclear accident reminded us, even in peacetime our very survival depends on the actions of people in other countries.

In chapter 3 I argued that the use of power in and between societies stemmed from competition for territory between groups. This implies that the state is a regrettable necessity, imposed on us by the threat of inter-communal war. But I also argued, in chapters 4 and 5, that the state could be a redistributive agency, sharing resources and power to create an egalitarian form of citizenship. This allows membership of a society to involve self-rule, mutual responsibility and cooperation in the pursuit of common interests.

So the problem that this final chapter addresses is this: there is such a thing as the good of mankind, but there is no such thing as world citizenship. We are all affected by such international phenomena as the depletion of natural resources, environmental pollution, terrorism and AIDS. We are moved by the plight of people in other countries, afflicted by famine or natural disasters. Above all, we are all threatened by the risk of nuclear war. Yet there are no international institutions which can effectively treat us as members of the world community, by giving us a form of universal citizenship that would promote the common good of mankind.

Instead, there are competing nation states, which use power to pursue their ends, as if the interests of their citizens were always potentially in conflict with those of others. The rules of this power game have been known since the birth of 'civilization', and were spelt out by the Athenians to their rivals, the Melians, just before they slew all their menfolk, enslaved their women and children, and colonized their city:

> For ourselves, we shall not trouble you with specious pretences – either
> of how we have a right to our empire because we overthrew the Mede,

or are now attacking you because of wrong you have done us – and make a long speech which would not be believed . . . Of the gods we believe, and of men we know, that by a necessary law of their nature they rule wherever they can. And it is not as if we were the first to make this law, or to act upon it when made: we found it existing before us, and shall leave it to exist forever after us; all we do is make use of it, knowing that you and everybody else, having the same power as we have, would do the same as we do.[1]

I have argued that it is not a 'necessary law of nature' that human beings use power against each other; indeed, that for the majority of time that there have been human communities on earth, power was not a feature of relations within or between groups. However, this does not contradict the Athenians' prediction that it would exist forever after them. There is little in the international scene to suggest that power relations are diminishing or will cease, except perhaps the prospect of total nuclear annihilation of the human species.

In the first part of this chapter, I shall address the issue of international relations and the good of mankind. I shall argue that, in the absence of international institutions to restrain the use of power, or any prospect of an equalization of power between states, the only slight hope of change lies in the development of systematic neutrality and better communications. Paradoxically, the threat of nuclear war has made common interests in peace more obvious, and may have increased the possibility of developing such a system of international relations.

In the second part of the chapter, I shall turn to the issues of uneven development and inequality between members of different states. If we accept that sharing within states rests on a notion of membership, this makes sharing among states in some ways more difficult. But the economic basis of citizenship shares proposed in chapter 7 (Basic Income) is consistent with a continued rapid industrialization – for better or worse – of less-developed countries. This leaves the vexed question of how issues of citizenship are to be resolved during the process of industrialization as matters for political dispute within these developing countries.

Finally, I shall consider the question of the good of mankind from the perspective of human rights and in relation to moral theory. Although the republican tradition upholds a concept of membership of the state which is egalitarian and participatory, it is also associated with a rather narrow nationalism. The wider view of the good of mankind requires us to expand our moral horizons, and to engage with entirely different traditions and cultures.

Power and international relations

International relations have, ever since recorded history began, been a search for aggrandizement and dominance, motivated either by greed or fear. Our

present system – created by the gradual extension of European nations'
relations throughout the world – is one of 'powers', and characterized by
power politics. Power is tested by warfare and, in Bismarck's notorious
expression, great questions are not settled by resolutions and majority votes,
but 'by blood and iron'.[2]

The international order has consisted of one or two predominant powers
(nation states that could take on a coalition of all the rest on land, at sea, or
both), a small and apparently diminishing number of great powers (usually
states which might be prepared to risk a war with any other single state, and
which have interests throughout the world) and a varying number of lesser
powers (some of which seek dominance in a region, as recently South Africa,
Argentina and Israel have appeared to do).[3]

The orthodox view of international relations is that, whether or not Hobbes
was right about the state of nature being a state of war between each individual
person and all others, he was certainly right when he said that the permanent
posture of nation states towards each other is one of readiness for war.[4]
Because no effective international system of government is possible where the
actors are sovereign states, each is caught in the Leviathan trap, unable to take
the first step towards cooperation and trust. Hence their interests are necessarily in permanent conflict, and their relations characterized by violence,
dominance and submission.[5] War and threats of war have been the instruments of policy in ancient and modern systems.[6]

Yet there is no satisfactory theory to explain or justify this situation. As in
Hobbes's account of the state of nature, power is defined as the end and the
means of all social action, and is also the explanatory variable; states seek
power by means of power, and succeed in so far as they mobilize power.[7] As
an explanation of war this is at best incomplete, and it explains nothing else.
The only theory of peace to which it gives rise, the balance of power hypothesis, is incoherent, because in a changing situation states have no motive to
preserve the balance except a consensus for the preservation of peace, which is
impossible under the assumptions of power theory.[8] The only alternative,
therefore, is peace imposed by a predominant power, which again is impossible, since it must *ex hypothesi* seek ever greater predominance.

Yet power theory is a self-fulfilling prophecy. If states all perceive their own
and each other's interests in terms of a power struggle, then it becomes
impossible to break the cycle of suspicion, opportunism and threat.[9] For
example, in the Middle East, the mutual hostility between Israel and the Arab
States has become a vicious circle, and power rivalry is self-perpetuating and
cumulative. Any attempt to set new goals is seen as prejudicing long-term
security, and compromises are taken as weakness or appeasement.

Once this happens, it is only by changes in the system itself, that come
about independently of the actors' motives and intentions, that a break in the
power struggle can occur, and the possibility of a shift to a different form of
international relations can arise. Some theorists argue that this is now possible
because of an unexpected and paradoxical consequence of the superpower

nuclear arms race. On the one hand, neither of the predominant powers can use its overwhelming nuclear threat because of mutual assured destruction. On the other, the threat of total destruction means that for the first time, all nations have a strong interest in peace between the predominant powers. Finally, the dangers of total war, and the alignment of states in two power blocs, have led to the emergence of non-aligned states, with a new theory and practice of relations with each other and the aligned states. The goal of non-alignment is the preservation of peace, through the active prevention of war, a policy of non-interference in others' internal affairs and refusal to resort to force or the threat of force.[10]

This would have little importance if it were simply a consequence of the nuclear arms race. For example, if bilateral nuclear disarmament were negotiated, it would lead to a return to power politics. This is precisely what is feared by those who think that disarmament would make the West European countries more vulnerable to a land attack by the USSR. But – despite the emphasis on power politics by President Reagan and Mrs Thatcher – the importance of these negotiations is the possibility that the predominant powers may enter a relationship of limited trust and cooperation.

The first step in this process is the recognition of the zero-sum fallacy in questions of disarmament: that both sides can gain from reduced arms spending. This makes possible conditions of peace (rather than non-war) in which states compete without arms races, adjustment to change is achieved by negotiation and communication.[11] The final objective is a system of international relations which does not depend on the threat of force, but which all members have an interest in maintaining through cooperation.

The first departure from power politics in the post-war world came in the spontaneous emergence of non-alignment, with a collection of smaller states acting non-discriminatorily in relation to the superpowers and their allies, treating both sides on the same basis, and trying to mediate between them.[12] The basis of this model of relations was negotiation and non-interference in the internal affairs of sovereign states. This raised the possibility of a gradual evolution of a system for maintaining peace, in which eventually the superpowers accepted the communications approach, and abandoned subversion and discrimination.

The only hope for this lies in a situation being reached where the new approach is sufficiently widespread for threats and subversion to become counter-productive – where what the superpowers lose by way of favour with all the lesser states through these activities is more than they gain from power policies. This possibility is clearly remote, mainly because of the advantage that the superpowers can still gain by exacerbating regional conflicts. Until this changes, international power struggles will still act as a major obstacle to the reduction of force inside societies, and contribute to the perpetuation of internal violence.

National inequalities

If we share interests in a better world with the rest of mankind, should not this be recognized by some form of universal membership of world society? And should not this in turn involve us in sharing our resources more equally? So far I have given no reasons why the people of the world should be divided into a particular number of membership groups presided over by states, and why the income levels they enjoy should be so starkly contrasting. I have argued for an inclusive notion of the common good, which excludes no individual from a basic share in welfare; yet the idea of citizenship is clearly exclusive. The notion of the common good which I have advanced (and which is represented by the Basic Income principle) is of a maximum equal share of basic welfare resources for each citizen consistent with the continued increase in prosperity of society as a whole. This version of citizenship could limit the scope for movement between states, and increase the problems already experienced, by refugees in particular.

This is a very large subject, and not one to which I shall be able to do justice in this short section. My main answer to these questions is that no one system of sharing basic resources is consistent with the growth and development of economies at all the existing stages of agricultural or industrial transformation. For example, in many countries the most relevant asset for income distribution is land, and the most important question concerning shares between members of society is therefore about its ownership. In rapidly industrializing countries, issues about housing, education and the urban environment are paramount, along with ones about public and private ownership of productive resources. It is only in the advanced countries that a significant Basic Income would be consistent with growth, and hence with the interests of the whole society.[13]

For this reason, there could be no mechanism for systematic sharing, according to principles of fairness, between the members of the world community. Instead, nations which are at different stages of development are required to seek ways of distributing the assets which most influence life chances between their citizens, so as to reconcile justice with the growth of prosperity. But there is an important issue over whether the kinds of sharing adopted by richer countries impede the development of poorer ones, and therefore damage the interests of people in far greater need.

Here the debate in the advanced capitalist countries over the transformation of world industrial production, and the new international division of labour, is whether the interests of workers in the rich countries are opposed to those in newly industrializing ones. Trade unionists and socialists have often argued that these changes have 'exported jobs' to the developing countries of South-East Asia, the Middle East, South and Central America and Southern Europe. Their complaint is that international corporations have been *too* efficient as instruments of transnational capital migration, allowing resources to be shifted rapidly between countries, in search of short-term profits.[14]

Whereas corporatist economic management was, for a 25 year period after the Second World War, able to harness capital to national economic interests, it has now found ways of eluding every attempt to tie it to state targets and purposes.

Accordingly, socialist policies have often (with trade union support) tried to restore 'national economic sovereignty', by restricting capital movements; tariff protection of domestic industries has also been canvassed. The aim is to protect employment, and prevent international companies from gaining the advantages associated with production abroad. Quite apart from the failure of these policies to yield significant results, and their effect in increasing costs to home consumers, they present the interests of their own industrial workers as competing with those in the newly industrializing countries. I have argued for an approach to the sharing of assets which does not rely on this form of competition for jobs. Instead, a Basic Income system would maximize the efficiency advantages available through the new international division of labour, and allow capital from the rich countries to play its part in the development of the poorer ones. There is a good deal of evidence that this process has already allowed some of these to 'catch up' in terms of *per capita* incomes with the advanced countries.

This, of course, begs the question of whether international capital is simply the instrument of exploitation and dominance in these countries, and whether investment from the rich states actually harms the members of the poor ones. I do not see a way of answering this question which would help us to solve the problems of sharing resources on a global scale, since any form of international sharing would have to take account of world economic and national political institutions. The optimistic point of view is that transnational enterprises, having escaped from the fetters of national policies, are now able and willing to strike bargains with governments of every political persuasion, and to find ways of adapting to any political institutions, cooperating with local enterprises in, for example, Eastern Europe or China, where this has proved advantageous. In other words, global capitalism is eclectic and pragmatic, and does not necessarily impose any particular pattern on the states in which it chooses to expand production.

This places the onus for creating terms of membership which are fair and inclusive back onto the political process in each nation state. Clearly, this is a heavy burden to bear because the actual distribution of assets in the less-developed countries usually reflects a history of conquest and colonization. There is often a very difficult balance to maintain between notions of entitlement based on historical occupation of territory (which often contain strong undertones of racial or religious exclusiveness), and more diffuse notions of membership being acquired through participation in the economy or society, or through forced migration. The potential clash between these justifications of asset distributions was vividly illustrated by events during 1987 in Fiji, where the entitlement claims of ethnic Melanesians clashed with the migratory participation claims of the Indian population.

There is no magical way to resolve these fundamental disputes about membership shares, especially when they involve groups which have organized for conflict with strong historical grounds for mistrust and hostility, as in South Africa, the Lebanon or Northern Ireland. But nor is it obvious that membership of a necessarily vague international order would resolve them. While we do indeed all share an interest in peace and justice, our opportunities for helpful intervention in these conflicts are very limited.

Morality and human rights

This leads into the question of how individuals and groups in one country can best express their concern and support for the victims of injustice or misfortune in another. What I said in the last section could be taken as an argument for moral isolationism; this is not what I am advocating. If there is no obvious formal way of sharing individual resources fairly, and few opportunities of intervening helpfully in others' conflicts, there are possibilities of direct assistance and influence.

Many people in countries which have suffered oppression, and especially members of persecuted minorities, can make little sense of the concept of citizenship. They understandably regard it as an ideal associated with liberal democracy, and hence as inapplicable to their situation. Hence appeals to standards of freedom, equality and fairness are often made in terms of 'human rights', and refer to charters of international organizations such as the United Nations or the European Community. In other words, they appeal to precisely such a membership of the international community of mankind as I seem to have been discrediting in the previous sections.

My point is not that the idea of human rights is itself flawed or fruitless; it is that it rests on a certain kind of moral argument, whose characteristics should be recognized. The idea of universal, fundamental human rights appeals to the notion of certain common needs and vulnerabilities which are shared by all human beings, and invites us to respect others as like ourselves. Since the seventeenth century there have been writers who referred to 'natural rights', although if there were such rights in nature, they had certainly not been recognized before that time.[15]

What we normally mean by a right is a claim that we have against someone else, or a licence to do something, based on rules. Hence rights are the products of human associations; we create rights by the terms on which we associate. I have a right to the benefits of membership of a club (if I have paid my dues); I have a right to unemployment benefit (if I have paid National Insurance Contributions); and I have a right, as a British citizen, to trial by jury if I am charged with an offence before a British court. But if I am washed up on a desert island, these rights are of little use to me because I have lost touch with the associations whose rules they reflect. And no matter how much I may search the island, I will not discover any natural rights, or any human rights, to replace them.

So when we appeal to people's human rights, what we often mean is that these people lack the kind of rights (in their particular country or situation) that we would like them to have. We mean that the state in which they live is denying them the freedom or the resources to do the things that we think that they should be allowed to do. And often we make this appeal even though (as in the case of Russian psychiatric patients or South African prisoners), they have been treated correctly according to the laws of their own countries; and even though we have psychiatric patients and prisoners of our own, many of whom would claim that their human rights were not respected, and some of whom might claim that they were not even being legally detained.

This means that appeals to human rights (and charters of human rights) are not so much concerned with people's actual rights, as with ideal extensions of their rights. There is nothing wrong with this; we can imaginatively extend to the victim of injustice in a tyranny the benefits of a system of justice in an egalitarian democracy. We can imaginatively allow dissidents, eccentrics, minorities, vulnerable individuals and high-principled protesters the freedoms of the most tolerant community. But what we are doing by this move is to make a moral appeal, to those who make the rules that apply to their situation, to change those rules, so as to grant new rights or to make exceptions in favour of particular individuals.

This makes such appeals more like the moral reasoning that we apply to strangers whom we encounter in unexpected situations of distress, and less like the moral reasoning we apply in negotiations with people who are part of our own reciprocity group, or membership group or community. We are arguing for an extension of the common good to include them, on the basis of a greater sharing and inclusiveness than actually exists. This is important, indeed essential; but human rights are as contestable as any other moral claim. So long as they remain part of unenforceable charters, they involve arguing each individual case as the exception to the rule. The moral argument has been successful when the rule is changed; in other words, when citizenship is modified to include the freedom or resource claim in question.

Moral reasoning of this kind plays a very important part in the development of social morality, and in the gradual inclusion of outsiders in the common good. Small, simple communities shared and cared for their own members, but would often maltreat or kill isolates from other groups who strayed into their territory. Close-knit societies are often intolerant and rejecting towards those who do not embrace their beliefs and customs. In the ancient world, Christianity was one of the forces which reduced exclusiveness. Jesus frequently invited his hearers to extend their moral horizons from the family, kin and tribe to include groups and races who were regarded as outcasts.

During the social democratic era, states seemed to take over the role of moral entrepreneurs, providing increased public goods to which all citizens contributed. But their moral leadership waned over new issues, many of which were international. The example of Bob Geldolf's entrepreneurial role in famine relief shows that individuals and voluntary groups have a very important part to play in mobilizing public goodwill towards those who suffer in other countries, and creating new institutions for offering assistance.

Conclusions

Social morality is not a set of constant principles and institutions, which stand for all time. It involves a perpetual adaptation to change, in which people create their lives together, and discover new ways of getting things done. Issues emerge which require fresh ideas and methods. Today's harmonious and cooperative society is tomorrow's corrupt and conflictual one, unless institutions are modified and updated.

For example, the British prison service was at times, in the nineteenth and early twentieth centuries, the most humane and progressive in the world. First evangelicals, and then new liberal idealists, threw all their energy and commitment into making them systems of compassion and reform, in which the staff could engage the inmates' willingness to trust and cooperate.[16] Today, Britain's prisons are a disgrace,[17] and reflect the scant regard that British society now has for those who violate its principles of individual responsibility.

No one country or culture has a monopoly over social morality. Ideas about the common good evolve through meetings among political, religious and intellectual traditions, which borrow and adopt from each other. Openness to the good in other societies saves a culture from ossifying, and its social systems from being captured by obsolescent wisdoms.

The new orthodoxy has become an international movement, which threatens to engulf much of the world. Although it is an official version of the good society, and usually handed down by government elites, it has influenced the way ordinary people live their lives. Fortunately, there are still many other influences which persist, even when the new orthodoxy has modified so many social institutions. Amidst the cultivation of private goods, concern for the common good survives.

It is ironical that the liberal tradition, which claims as its basis the sanctity of the individual, should degenerate into a powerful system for sustaining selfishness and punishing misfortune. As many authors have pointed out, this is not the first time that individualism has proved to be a cul-de-sac, or that liberal rationality has led to tyranny.[18] Yet it is a tradition whose longevity bears witness to its robust resilience and adaptability. It badly needs the influence of more collectivist philosophies, more communitarian vision, and more social perception of the common good.

I have argued for ideas and institutions which reassert the claims of common over private interests, and public participation over private duty. It is easier to move in these directions from where we are now than it will be from where the new orthodoxy would like to take us by the end of the century. Individualism, materialism and exclusiveness have already impoverished the public sphere, and present policies will continue to destroy the fabric of social solidarity. It is far easier to undermine common interests in a good quality of life than to recreate them.

Society must somehow be constructed out of a combination of individual self-interested preferences and reasoned decisions which recognize common interests in the common good. The attempt to construct a social order out of preferences, balanced only by individual altruism, gets trapped in its own unintended consequences. Like any other system of relations, it will produce paradoxical and unplanned features, which were not chosen by any individual, but which evolved through interaction between social institutions.

The emergence of power as the basis of relations between and within societies is a striking example of this process of evolution leading to unchosen features of a system, which cannot be managed, or used for the benefit of all, through the self-interested preferences or altruistic choices of individuals. It has to be understood and handled in terms of everyone's interests in fairness and cooperation, as members of society, and ultimately of the human race.

The new orthodoxy has provided a radical means of escape from some of the traps which were the perverse consequences of social democratic institutions - stagflation, overloaded government, the fiscal crisis of the state - but it is now, in its turn, in grave danger of being trapped by its own logic.

In this book, I have given examples of how social relations can come to be characterized by conflicts which, if they are anlaysed solely in terms of interests and duties (in the new orthodoxy's sense), cannot be resolved. Members of the underclass cannot *prefer*, in the individualist analysis of choice, to be industrious, self-disciplined and law-abiding; they have an interest in being opportunistic, dishonest and lawless. Conversely, individuals within the majority, no matter how well meaning, cannot choose to include the underclass in the common good, because they can only perceive its members' behaviour as a threat to their interests and a failure of social duty. So, instead of using political power to create common interests in a good society, they will vote to use power to coerce, punish and exclude the under class. Conflict will escalate, and social relations - the quality of life for all - will deteriorate further.

The new orthodoxy's philosophy is not the only way to become entrapped in such destructive conflicts. There are many melancholy examples, all over the world, of other communities locked in internecine strife, entered upon by other routes. Coercion, exclusiveness and intolerance are not the prerogatives of any particular political or religious system, nor is any one immune from their influence. How these intractable conflicts resemble each other is in the failure of the parties to recognize any common interests in harmony and cooperation. It is far easier to create a Leviathan trap, by narrow adherence to the dogma of an orthodoxy, than it is to get out of it, once the Hobbesian door shuts behind us.

Notes

1   Thucydides, *The Peloponnesian War*, trans. Richard Crawley (Modern Library, 1951), V, 90. See A. B. Schmookler, *The Parable of the Tribes* (University of California Press, 1984), II, ch. 2.

2   A. J. P. Taylor, *Bismarck: the Man and the Statesman* (Hamilton, 1955).

3   Martin Wight, *Power Politics* (Leicester University Press and Royal Institute of International Affairs, 1978), chs 1-5.

4   'Yet in all times kings, and persons of sovereign authority, because of their independency, are in continual jealousies, and in the state and posture of gladiators; having their weapons pointing; and their eyes fixed on one another; that is forts, garrisons and guns, upon the frontiers of their kingdom; and continual spies upon their neighbours; which is a posture of war' (Hobbes, *Leviathan* (1651), (Collins, 1963), ch. XIII.

5   Wight, *Power Politics*; and H. J. Morgenthau, *Politics among Nations: the Struggle for Power and Peace* (Knopf, 1972).

6   Michael Mann, 'State and society, 1130-1815: an analysis of English state finances', in M. Zeitlin (ed.), *Political Power and Social Theory* (Jai Press, 1980), p. 196. See also Wight, *Power Politics*, chs 1 and 2.

7   J. W. Burton, *International Relations: a General Theory* (Cambridge University Press, 1967), pp. 46-54.

8   Ibid., pp. 56-9.

9   Ibid., p. 21.

10 Ibid., chs 12ff, and especially ch. 20.

11 Ibid., p. 246.

12 J. W. Burton (ed.), *Nonalignment* (Deutsch, 1966).

13 A European Basic Income seems a feasible idea, but this would have to cope with the inequalities of income between (say) Denmark and Greece, and with markedly different levels of industrialization.

14 See, for example, Stuart Holland, *The Socialist Challenge* (Quartet, 1975); and the Labour Party's Election Manifesto of 1983.

15 Alasdair MacIntyre, *After Virtue* (Duckworth, 1981), pp. 64-7.

16 W. J. Forsythe, *The Reform of Prisoners, 1820-1900* (Croom Helm, 1987); and *The Reform of English Prisoners, 1895-1939* (forthcoming).

17 Her Majesty's Inspectorate of Prisons, *Annual Report* (HMSO, 1988) stated that the conditions endured by some prisoners bordered on the intolerable.

18 See, for example, Thomas Spragens jr, *The Irony of Liberal Reason* (University of Chicago Press, 1981), and Michael Sandel, *Liberalism and the Limits of Justice* (Cambridge University Press, 1982).

Index

accumulation 42, 45-6, 49-51, 55, 76, 90

Ackoff, Russell 172

Acton, H. B. 37

adolescents 127, 129-30

AIDS 9, 174

altruism 1-3, 5, 7, 10, 13, 17, 21, 24, 27, 30-1, 33-7, 39, 41, 44, 48, 70, 73-4, 79-80, 83, 128-31, 136, 144-53, 156, 168-70, 183
  compulsory 14, 35, 150

Arab states 176

Arber, Sara 157

Argentina 176

Aristotle 17, 69-70, 72, 83, 86, 88, 133, 168

Asquith, H. H. 78

assets 18, 34, 42, 47-50, 52, 56, 58-62, 65, 67, 78, 81, 83, 86, 90-7, 104-5, 108-10, 112-14, 116, 120-1, 144, 154, 165, 178-9

association 16-17, 48-52, 55, 69-73, 78, 82-5, 127-42, 145, 157, 159, 162, 168-70, 180-1

Athenians 52, 174-5

Atkinson, J. 65, 125

Australia 14

Austria 14

Axelrod, Robert 17, 39-45, 53, 84, 147

bargains 1-3, 5-6, 10, 27, 36, 48-9, 161-2, 179

Barry, Brian 20

Basic Income 7, 19, 109-10, 118-24, 136-41, 147-8, 152-5, 157, 175, 178-9, 184

Becker, Gary 20

Beechey, V. 157

Berelson, B. R. 107

Beveridge, Sir William 78, 86, 88

Bismarck, Otto von 176

blacks 4-5, 15, 57, 61, 81-2, 90, 95, 104-5, 112, 121, 124, 132, 138-9

Blunkett, David 143

Bosanquet, Bernard 77-8

Bowles, Samuel 54, 66

Brittan, Samuel 122, 125

Broadwater Farm Estate 132

Burton, John 107

Burton, J. W. 184

care
  allowance for 119, 152, 154
  child 7, 30, 48, 58, 103, 112, 117-18, 127, 145-9
  family 2, 5, 7, 19, 58, 90, 103, 117, 144-57
  reciprocal 43, 149, 181
  residential 5, 148-53
  unpaid 112, 132, 137, 144-57

Carneiro, R. 54

Castles, Francis 20

Challis, David 158

charity 3, 35, 49, 83, 129-30, 133, 140

Chayanov, A. V. 53

Chernobyl 174

child abuse 9, 15, 156, 163

China 9, 179

Christianity 19, 43, 69, 83, 134, 181

churches 9, 36, 129-30, 134, 140

citizenship 7, 17-18, 50, 56, 63-5, 67-89, 109, 119-20, 124, 133-42, 168-9, 174, 178-80

claimants 4-6, 32-3, 50, 60, 81-2, 91, 102, 117, 122
  unions 131

Clarke, John 88

Cochrane, Allan 88